MINDSET MATTERS

A TEENAGER'S GUIDE TO MENTAL WELLNESS

HEIDY WANG

Library of Congress Control Number: *2026908240*

Published by Hemingway Publishers

Cover design by Hemingway Publishers

ISBN: Printed in the United States

Dedication

I thank God for being my constant source of hope and strength. He has guided me through every challenge and given me the opportunity to rebuild my life. Sixteen years ago, I felt invisible and uncertain of my future. Today, by His grace, I have grown into a communicator, educator, public administrator, investigator, author, and much more.

This book reflects my faith and my calling to serve others with compassion and conviction.

To my spiritual parents, especially my spiritual father, this book is dedicated to you in gratitude and love. You stood beside me during my darkest season and helped guide me toward healing. I will always cherish and appreciate your support.

To my parents, thank you for your unwavering love and sacrifices. You gave up your own comforts and dreams to create a better future for me. Your belief in me carried me through difficult days and helped shape the person I am today.

This book is a piece of my heart. May it bring strength, hope, and encouragement to the next generation.

Acknowledgments

For Our Father

My deepest gratitude goes first to God, my unwavering strength and guiding light. During seasons of stress, uncertainty, and darkness, Your boundless love sustained me. When I felt lost, You illuminated my path. When I felt weak, You strengthened my spirit.

Thank You for granting me faith when I felt empty, for placing people in my life at the exact moments I needed them, and for giving me a second chance at life. Without Your grace and inspiration, I would not be here today.

In Jesus' name, Amen.

For My Supervisors and Team

I extend my heartfelt appreciation to my colleagues at the New York City Children's Center, Brooklyn Campus.

To Executive Director Mr. Mark Bibby and Campus Community Service Director Mr. Michael Omezi, thank you for your trust, leadership, and unwavering support. Your encouragement has strengthened my professional growth and inspired me to write this book.

To the entire NYCCC team, thank you for your collaboration, compassion, and dedication to the children and families we serve. You uplift me daily. Together, we are making a meaningful and lasting difference, and I am honored to work alongside you.

About the Author

I'm Heidy Wang, and I am honored to walk alongside you on this journey.

When I moved to the United States, I faced nearly ten years of mental health challenges marked by stress, uncertainty, and emotional hardship. Through faith, resilience, and the support of those around me, I persevered.

Today, I serve as an interpreter, translator, and teacher at the New York State Office of Mental Health, New York City Children's Center. In this role, I dedicate my energy and real-world experience to bridging communication gaps and supporting vulnerable youth and families. I am currently pursuing my second master's degree in Interpreting and Translation at Hunter College, The City University of New York, expanding my ability to serve diverse communities.

My passion is helping others rediscover hope and strength within themselves. Outside of my professional work, I enjoy journaling, exploring New York City, and listening to music.

Do not give up on yourself. I hope this guide empowers you to overcome challenges and build a life filled with resilience, faith, and purpose.

Our Father

He gives strength to the weary and increases the power of the weak. Even youths grow tired and weary, and young men stumble and fall; but those who hope in the Lord will renew their strength. They will soar on wings like eagles; they will run and not grow weary, they will walk and not be faint.

Isaiah 40:29–31 (NIV)

These words remind us that exhaustion—whether physical, emotional, or spiritual—is not a failure but a human condition. God is with you, no matter how messy or heavy your heart feels. Even when you feel unseen or unheard, He understands your struggles and promises to help you overcome every difficulty you face. Sometimes, it may take longer for Him to respond to your answer, and waiting can feel discouraging and lonely, but He will always be there for you! His timing is never accidental, even when it feels confusing.

My dear friend, don't be afraid to talk to a parent, teacher, or counselor—they could be part of God's way of sending you help. Often, God works through people, placing them in our lives at the exact moment we need support most. Take it one day at a time and keep your faith strong. Just as you might feel unwell, which can make it hard to focus on your studies or work, you may need to see a doctor or seek help at a professional medical facility. Asking for help is not a weakness; it is a step toward healing. However, many people don't think mental health matters as much as physical health. That's not true. Your mental health is just as important as your physical health.

Mental health includes your emotional, psychological, and social well-being, just like physical health. It shapes how you think, feel, act, and cope with everyday stress. If we rate overall health on a scale of 100, physical health might represent 50%, with mental wellness making up the other 50%. These two aspects are closely interconnected and inseparable. For example, it's common to catch the flu, and a doctor might recommend rest and medication for a few days. Similarly, your mental health can experience its own 'flu.' This doesn't mean you are broken; it simply means you need care. Individuals diagnosed with mental health issues should seek professional help and psychotherapy. While recovery may take longer, avoiding treatment can lead to unmanageable conditions, causing life to feel overwhelming and unbearable, potentially resulting in severe consequences or even fatality.

When you start feeling better, hold on to that progress. Celebrate small victories, even on difficult days. Keep fighting negative thoughts—magical things can happen if you maintain your hard work, and healing often grows quietly before it becomes visible, and it may ultimately help make your dreams come true. Be patient, stay courageous, and trust the process. Growth is rarely quick, but it is always meaningful. This will guide you toward the heights you aspire to reach. Nobody is perfect; it's only a matter of time. Give yourself grace along the way.

Remember, your peers may be facing mental struggles and prefer to keep them private. You are never as alone as you feel. Others have overcome their challenges, and you can too. You are a unique individual, so ***stay focused***. Your journey does not have to look like anyone else's. ***Trust yourself***. You have the potential to achieve things beyond your wildest imagination. Never lose hope!

Trust in yourself; only you can control your life.
Don't lose your life or your time easily!

Mental Health Awareness Month: Supporting Teens' Mental Health

Mental Health Awareness Month, established by Mental Health America in 1949, takes place every year in May. It was established to educate the public about mental illness, promote understanding of research and treatment options, challenge the stigma surrounding mental health, and celebrate recovery. Since its beginning, this month has served as a reminder that mental health is just as important as physical health and deserves equal attention, care, and compassion.

Mental Health Awareness Month encourages individuals to understand the impact of mental illness, access available resources, and promote mental health advocacy. Increasing awareness and education are essential for breaking down the stigma surrounding mental illness. Stigma often prevents people, especially teens, from speaking openly about their struggles or seeking help. The month provides a focused opportunity to initiate dialogue, foster open discussions that dispel myths, reduce stigma, and motivate those struggling to seek help and build support systems. These conversations can be life-changing for someone who feels isolated or misunderstood.

This month also educates teenagers about the challenges of living with mental health conditions, emphasizing that despite these difficulties, they can lead meaningful and fulfilling lives. It sends a powerful message that a diagnosis does not define a person's future. For teens, this month is very important, as half of all mental health issues begin at age 14. Many warning signs appear early, but they are often overlooked or dismissed as "just a phase."

Early intervention can make a significant difference. During this month, schools, communities, and families are encouraged to create safe spaces where young people can openly discuss mental health, access resources like counseling or support groups, and learn coping strategies for issues such as anxiety, depression, or stress. By fostering a culture of acceptance and understanding, Mental Health Awareness Month empowers individuals of all ages to prioritize mental wellness, advocate for systemic change, and support one another in building resilient, inclusive communities.

A memorial poster with a young teenage girl

One day last summer, I saw a memorial poster on our office door featuring a young girl's picture. It instantly caught my attention and stopped me in my tracks. She was a beautiful girl with dark skin, wearing a high school graduation cap and gown, with a radiant smile on her face. The poster had a navy blue border with a clear white center as its background. She had just turned 18 years old, but unfortunately, her life ended that day. The contrast between her youthful smile and the finality of the poster was heartbreaking. A colleague told me she was a patient in our department. She had lived with her mother, and after her mother's passing, she lived with her older sister. She had already endured significant loss at such a young age. A very smart and talented girl, only if she had not ended her life, she would have had a bright future.

I felt deep sadness because of her demise at such a young age. It left a heaviness in my heart that lingered long after. I thought she might have faced a moment of overwhelming despair that led her to make such a rash and unwise decision—a moment that she felt endless to her, but was tragically permanent. Sadly, she never knew how many wonderful moments she would miss. Her imagination often inspires me, and a voice keeps urging me to help innocent young adults overcome their struggles. That loss became a turning point for me. I've taken that voice to heart, turning my pain into purpose. And now, the torch must be passed. It's your turn to help those innocent young people. Every caring adult has a role to play. So, I decided to write this book to guide the younger generation with my personal story and heartfelt advice. It will also provide mental and emotional support, encouraging teenagers to face challenges rather than contemplate ending their lives at such a young age. No young person should feel that death is the only way to escape their life.

This teenager's mental health guide includes the latest research data for teens, parents, and healthcare professionals. It bridges science, lived experience, and compassion. It is a temporary resource offering solutions to help teens gain control over their mental health struggles. However, no single resource can replace professional care; education can be a powerful first step. By fostering mindfulness about mental health, encouraging self-care, and addressing common questions, it emphasizes that seeking professional treatment is the best way to help adolescents get their lives back on track.

Table of Contents

Alone

I am alone; it's very quiet around me.

I've been afraid for quite some time.

There's a voice that often speaks in my mind.

From the beginning of this companionship,

I felt good about this new friend speaking to me when I needed support.

After a while,

This new secret friend seems to get tired of talking to me.

She becomes mean and forces me to do bad things.

She gets very mad when I don't obey her.

I want her to leave my head, but she won't let me go.

Anyhow, it gets worse and worse.

What can I do? I feel so helpless.

My classmates and friends don't understand me.

I need help!!

I am so alone.

CHAPTER 1
Your Mental Health Matters!

MENTAL WELLNESS (HEALTH)

Mental health relates to our emotional, psychological, and social wellness. It is present in every part of our daily lives, even when we don't consciously think about it. It shapes our thoughts, feelings, and actions as we navigate life's challenges. It impacts how we manage stress, communicate with others, and make life choices. In other words, mental health is about whether you can achieve a balanced way to manage how you think, feel, and act. Balance does not mean feeling happy all the time; it means learning how to cope and recover.

Let's consider another example: People always say, "We have to keep our bodies healthy and in shape." In this context, the phrase doesn't only indicate physical health and wellness; it means promoting whole-body health with a connection between mind and body. True wellness cannot exist without addressing both.

This connection becomes clearer when we reflect on what mental health truly involves. Mental health is not just the absence of illness; it is the presence of emotional strength, resilience, and self-awareness.

As discussed earlier, mental health comprises emotional wellness, psychological health, and social wellness, which together contribute to a person's overall mental well-being.

EMOTIONAL WELLNESS (HEALTH)

Emotional wellness is the ability to understand, accept, and manage your emotions, especially during times of stress or significant life changes. It allows individuals to respond thoughtfully rather than react impulsively.

It is very important to be able to cope with stress, adapt to emotions and feelings in life's positive and negative sides, and maintain a sense of balance, which supports both mental and physical health outcomes, such as reduced stress-related illnesses.

For example, Sarah, a high school student, feels very nervous before her New York State Regents' test. She notices her anxiety and accepts that it's normal to feel nervous. Instead, she takes deep breaths, talks to a friend for support, and studies in small, manageable chunks. By doing this, Sarah stays calm, performs well on her exams, and feels confident afterward.

Poor emotional health involves struggling to recognize, accept, or manage emotions, leading to ineffective coping during challenges.

Here is another example of a high school student named John, whose behavior is the opposite of the previously described behavior: John, a high school student, feels anxious about an upcoming exam. He doesn't acknowledge his anxiety, showing a lack of awareness, and tells himself he shouldn't feel this way, rejecting his emotions. Instead of addressing his feelings, he avoids studying, dismisses his friends' offers to help, and stays up all night worrying. On exam day, he's exhausted, unfocused, performs poorly, and feels even worse.

Psychological Health

Psychological health is the sum of mental, emotional, social, and spiritual dimensions, and it represents how we think, feel, relate, and exist in our daily lives. Moreover, our thoughts, perceptions, emotions, motivations, interpersonal relationships, and behaviors are a product of our experiences and the skills we have developed to meet life's challenges.

Psychologically healthy people possess several core characteristics:

- **They know their real strengths and weaknesses.**
    1. They are not easily affected by emotions such as fear, love, anger, jealousy, guilt, or anxiety.
    2. They understand their identity, have a realistic view of their abilities, and value themselves even though they recognize their imperfections.

- **They make people feel safe and accepted, treat everyone with respect, and demonstrate empathy.**
    1. They build strong, lasting relationships, treat others fairly, and avoid being taken advantage of by anyone. They can also see that some people have greater needs, and they are willing to take responsibility to help others.
    2. They show love, care about others' needs, make time to assist others, and value individual differences.

- **They treat themselves with kindness.**
    1. They understand their own weaknesses and are careful and fully aware of their problems in life, and try to find the best solutions. They will set limitations and things they cannot control.
    2. They avoid being selfish, vain, or too hard on themselves.

- **They keep anxiety and tension under control.**
    1. They understand what causes their stress and anxiety and try to avoid negative thinking, anger, excuses, or blaming others.

2. They use tools and support to learn ways to manage stressful situations in their lives.

- **They're ready for life's demands and responsibilities.**
    1. When they identify problems, they deal with them right away, take accountability, and prepare for the future.
    2. They create practical goals, rely on their own thinking, and make independent choices. Accepting that change is inevitable, they embrace new opportunities.

- **They manage their emotions in healthy ways.**

    They identify and resist impulses to react with anger, recklessness, self-interest, revenge, or self-doubt. Rather than stepping over others to advance, they lend a hand to help those around them.

- **They stay optimistic about life.**

    They start each day expecting good things to happen. They face the future with excitement instead of fear. Enjoying life and carving out time for themselves are key parts of their routine.

- **They accept people no matter their race, beliefs, or identity.**

    They feel comfortable with people of different genders, religions, races, ethnicities, ages, or political views. They stay open-minded and don't push their beliefs or values on others.

- **They cherish the environment and treat it with respect.**

    They love the environment, are fully aware of their place in the universe, and responsibly work to protect their surroundings.

<u>Spiritual Health</u>

Spiritual health is about finding meaning and worth in life, feeling at peace in the heart, and being connected to others. It helps you understand your purpose, cope with challenges, and feel inner peace even when life is hard. We can explore it in different ways, such as practicing a religion, which can guide you toward spiritual health when you're at peace with life and can find hope and comfort, even during tough times.

<u>For example</u>, some people may feel spiritually connected by sitting quietly in nature, listening to the wind, watching the trees, or feeling the warmth of the sun, which makes them feel calm and a sense of unity with the world, without being religious (through meditation). Some people may feel spiritually connected by praying in a church, which is a part of their religious practice. Both paths are valid and can bring comfort, hope, and a sense of connection to something greater than oneself.

SOCIAL WELLNESS (HEALTH)

Social health means getting along well with others, both one-on-one and in groups. It involves forming relationships that are supportive, respectful, and meaningful. Socially healthy people enjoy connecting with family, friends, and partners in positive ways. They can listen, share their thoughts, form strong bonds, act responsibly, and find their place in society. Good social skills help reduce stress, improve mood, and give a sense of belonging.

For example, if you're a high school student, you have a couple of good friends at school you can hang out with. You feel comfortable chatting with them about your favorite video games or sharing what's going on in your life. When you're stressed about a big test, you talk to your parents and teachers, who give you advice on how to study. You also respect others' boundaries, like not pushing a friend to share something they're not ready to talk about. When they are in a bad mood, you are there to support them. These small actions strengthen trust and create lasting friendships.

This means you're building positive, healthy social relationships. It also shows that you can navigate conflicts, handle peer pressure, and contribute positively to your community. It also means you're leaning on family for support, adapting to new situations, and acting in kind, respectful ways. Developing these skills early helps you manage stress, feel confident in social settings, and create a network of people who support your mental and emotional well-being. These connections and skills help you feel good about yourself and handle life's ups and downs.

Family Support, Social Support, and Community

There are three significant external factors that are crucial for teens' mental well-being: family support, social support, and community involvement. These create a network of love, guidance, and belonging during a critical time of growth for teenagers. Strong support systems help teens feel safe, understood, and capable of navigating life's challenges.

1. Family Support

Families provide emotional security and stability, helping teens build confidence and cope with challenges like stress or peer pressure. A supportive family serves as a safe foundation, where teens can express themselves, learn from mistakes, and develop resilience. Supportive families guide teens in developing critical thinking and social skills to tackle challenges, share feelings appropriately, handle stress, and build confidence and purpose. Teens raised in caring, nurturing environments are more likely to grow into balanced, successful adults. Positive family involvement during adolescence can reduce risky behaviors, improve school performance, and strengthen emotional health. As adults, ongoing family support strongly predicts better health and happiness.

Teens growing up in environments where there's violence, mistrust, anger, neglect, substance abuse, major parental conflict, or any form of abuse (sexual, physical, or emotional) often struggle to adjust to life and face a higher risk of mental health issues. Exposure to these conditions can create feelings of fear, isolation, and insecurity, which may continue into adulthood.

2. Social Support

The National Institute of Mental Health (NIMH) states that social support from family, friends, and community resources is vital for teens dealing with mental health challenges. Social support provides a sense of belonging, reduces feelings of isolation, and encourages teens to seek help when needed. These supportive connections help teens feel safe sharing their emotions and seeking professional help without worrying about judgment.

For instance, a teen with anxiety might be more willing to talk to a school counselor if their friends openly discuss issues on their minds. In addition, peers play a key role in helping us discover our identity and life goals. Through friendships, teens learn communication skills, empathy, and how to negotiate conflicts in healthy ways. We often share our thoughts with them to check if our ideas make sense or seem fair. Studies show that college students with strong social support enjoy better overall well-being, have lower suicide rates, and experience greater life satisfaction. Even casual peer interactions, like checking in with a friend or participating in group activities, can strengthen emotional resilience.

3. Community Support

Community support refers to the resources, relationships, and networks provided by people and organizations outside of a teen's immediate family and close friends, such as school staff, neighbors, local organizations, faith-based groups, or mental health services. It includes both emotional and practical support.

Below are key reasons why it's very important that community support matters to teenagers.

1. Teenagers can go through times when they feel misunderstood or alone, especially if they face challenges like bullying or family issues. During these moments, teens may feel isolated, anxious, or even hopeless. Community support provides a safe space where they feel accepted and valued, reducing feelings of isolation that can lead to anxiety or depression.

2. Community support includes access to professionals like counselors or social workers who can help teens address mental health challenges early. Early intervention is crucial because waiting too long can make issues harder to manage. This is very important since many teens may not have family members who recognize or can address these issues.

3. Community support helps teens learn ways to cope with tough situations such as fights with friends, school pressure, or past trauma. Structured programs and mentors can teach problem-solving, coping strategies, and healthy communication skills. Programs such as youth mentoring or community workshops teach skills like solving problems and managing emotions, which build strength and resilience.

4. Community support normalizes conversations about mental health, making it easier for teens to seek help without fear of judgment. When mental health is openly discussed, it reduces stigma and

encourages teens to ask for help early. Community programs often promote awareness and provide safe spaces for teens to share their experiences.

5. Not all teens have supportive families or friends, especially in dysfunctional households or isolating environments. For these teens, community resources may be the primary source of guidance, stability, and encouragement. Community support fills this gap, offering trusted adults or programs that provide guidance and care, which can be lifesaving for teens at risk.

6. Community support helps teens build social skills, confidence, and a sense of purpose, which in turn improve their mental health as they grow into adults. Close community connections also lower the chances of issues like drug use or suicide.

<u>Dysfunctional Families</u>

Teens growing up in environments where there's violence, mistrust, anger, neglect, substance abuse, major parental conflict, or any form of abuse (sexual, physical, or emotional) often struggle to adjust to life and face a higher risk of mental health issues. In these families, the absence of love, safety, and trust can cause lasting psychological harm to children. However, not all teens from dysfunctional families struggle with mental health, and not all teens from supportive families are perfectly adjusted. The difference often comes down to their support network, community, self-confidence, and unique personality.

COMMON QUESTIONS ABOUT TEENS' MENTAL HEALTH

<u>Why Am I Dealing with These Mental Health Challenges?</u>

Mental health issues can feel confusing, but they're more common than you might think—about 1 in 5 teens experiences them. You are not alone, and experiencing challenges is not a sign of weakness. They can come from a mix of factors, and it's not your fault. They often result from a combination of factors.

- **Genetics**: If your family member has had mental health struggles, like anxiety or depression, you might be more likely to experience them too. It's like inheriting eye color—it's just part of your biology.

- **Life_Experiences**: Teenagers may face tough moments, such as bullying, family problems, the loss of someone important, or even stress from school, which can impact how they feel. For example, 19% of teens reported being bullied at school, which can affect mental health.

- **Brain_Chemistry**: Your brain uses chemicals to manage emotions. Sometimes, these chemicals get out of balance, which can lead to feeling anxious, sad, or overwhelmed.

- **Environment and Stress**: Challenges like social media pressure, (11% of teens report problematic use), academic demands, or major family concerns.)

Reaching out is the first step.

It's important to know that there is nothing wrong with you if you are going through a difficult time. Feeling overwhelmed or struggling emotionally is a normal part of life, especially during adolescence. We all experience moments when we feel less mentally healthy, and it's perfectly normal. In fact, according to the National Survey of Children's Health, 82.6% of U.S. adolescents aged 12–17 who were identified as needing mental health treatment or counseling in the past 12 months received some form of professional mental health care. Seeking help is a sign of strength, not weakness.

The Good News:

Many mental health challenges can be improved or managed with the right help and strategies. Recovery is possible, and support can make a real difference in your life. It is essential to seek support when needed. Mental health conditions are treatable; for example, talking to a trusted adult, counselor, or therapist can help you understand what's going on. Many teenagers have fully recovered or learned to manage their symptoms with support, such as therapy, lifestyle changes, and medication.

How Do I Know If I Need Help for My Mental Health?

If you're experiencing emotional or mental challenges, start by talking to a trusted adult, such as a parent, teacher, or school counselor. They can guide you on the next steps, such as seeing a therapist. They can listen, guide you, and connect you with the right support, such as a therapist or counselor.

It's great to see that you're noticing how you feel—about 20.3% of teens have a diagnosed mental health condition, and many wonder if their feelings are "normal" or need extra support.

Here are some signs that something might be wrong with your mental or emotional health:

- **People Notice You're Acting Different**: If your family, friends, or teachers say you seem quieter, withdrawn, or not like your usual self, it could mean something's going on. For example, if you're normally chatty but now avoid talking, they might notice and point it out.

- **Feeling upset for a Long Time**: If you feel sad, worried, or angry almost every day for weeks or months, and it's making school, friendships, or daily life harder, that's a warning sign. If you can't focus on homework or don't want to hang out with friends because you're very upset for a while, it's worth paying attention to.

- **Changes in Your Daily Habits**: If you're sleeping a lot more (or barely sleeping), eating too much (or not eating enough), or stopping activities you used to love, like playing sports or drawing, it might be a sign. For example, if you used to love gaming but now don't care about it, that's a clue.

- **Feeling Overwhelmed and Unable to Handle Stress**: If things like schoolwork, bullying, or other pressures feel too heavy, and usual ways to feel better (like talking to a friend or chilling out) aren't working, it's a sign you might need extra help. For instance, if you're stressed about grades and can't relax no matter what, that's important to notice.

- **Thinking About Hurting Yourself or Others**: If you have thoughts about harming yourself or not wanting to be alive, that's a very serious sign. It's crucial to tell someone you trust, like a parent or counselor, and get help right away. For example, even if these thoughts come and go, they're important to share with someone who can support you.

Does having challenges with mental health mean I am weak, broken, or does it indicate anything bad about me?

Absolutely not. Many of the world's top athletes, gifted actors, artists, musicians, and business leaders have faced mental health challenges and still achieved great success. Struggling with mental health does not define your worth or potential.

Here are examples of well-known individuals from various fields—athletes, actors, artists, musicians, business people, and world leaders—who have openly discussed their mental health challenges and how they overcame or managed them.

1.   Actor: Dwayne "The Rock" Johnson

Dwayne Johnson was a wrestler and is now a famous movie star. He went through a tough time with depression when he was younger. He faced problems with his football career and family issues, which made him feel lost and very sad.

His actions for handling his issues:

- **Talking to Others:** Johnson shared his feelings with close friends and family, which really helped him. He said on social media, "It's so important to talk about how you feel," and encouraged others to do the same.

- **Staying Active: Getting Professional Help:** At first, he didn't see a therapist, but later he worked with mental health experts to understand his feelings and learn ways to cope.

- **Speaking Out:** Johnson started talking publicly about mental health, especially for men, to make it okay to ask for help. This also kept him focused on his own health.

Outcome: Johnson turned his struggles into strength, building a huge career and inspiring others to get help without feeling hopeless.

2.   <u>Musician: Lady Gaga</u>

Lady Gaga, a famous singer, has been open about her struggles with depression, anxiety, and post-traumatic stress disorder (PTSD) caused by tough experiences from her childhood and the stress of being famous. She felt very overwhelmed and alone, which made it hard to create music and enjoy her personal life.

Her actions for handling her issues:

- **Talking to a Therapist:** Gaga worked with therapists who used a method called cognitive-behavioral therapy (CBT) to help her change negative thoughts. She said therapy let her "release" feelings she had kept inside.

- **Taking Medicine:** She used medication to help control her symptoms, which made her feel more stable.

- **Starting a Foundation:** Gaga created the Born This Way Foundation to support young people's mental health. This work gave her a sense of purpose and helped her feel less alone by connecting with others.

- **Using Music to Heal:** Writing songs and performing allowed her to express her feelings. Her music helped her cope and connect with her fans.

Outcome: Gaga's efforts helped her manage her mental health, keep making music, and become a strong voice for mental wellness, inspiring others to seek help.

3. <u>Business Leader: Elon Musk</u>

Elon Musk, the CEO of Tesla and SpaceX, has talked about dealing with a lot of stress, anxiety, and possibly depression from the huge pressure of running several companies. He worked extremely long hours, up to 120 hours a week, which left him feeling overwhelmed and hurt his mental and physical health.

His actions for handling his issues:

- **Better Schedule:** Musk changed his routine to make sure he got more sleep and some downtime. He said getting at least six hours of sleep helped him think clearly and feel better.
- **Talking to Loved Ones:** He leaned on close friends and family for support, sharing his problems with them to get new perspectives.
- **Calming Techniques:** He tried meditation and breathing exercises to reduce stress, which helped him stay calm during tough moments.
- **Finding Purpose:** Focusing on his goals, like improving technology and exploring space, gave him a reason to keep going and lifted his spirits.

Outcome: With lifestyle adjustments and help from others, Musk has managed his stress more effectively and continued running his companies, while acknowledging that mental health remains an ongoing focus.

4. <u>Athlete: Michael Phelps (Swimmer)</u>

Michael Phelps, the Olympic champion with 28 medals, faced tough times with depression and thoughts of not wanting to live. After the 2012 Olympics, he felt so low that he stayed alone in his bedroom for days, as he shared in a CNN interview.

His actions for handling his issues:

- **Talking to a Therapist:** Phelps worked with a therapist, which changed everything for him. Therapy helped him understand his feelings and find ways to cope.
- **Sharing Thoughts with Loved Ones**: He opened up to close friends and family about his struggles, which made him feel less alone. He said in the CNN interview that life got easier once he started talking.
- **Helping Others**: He began supporting mental health causes, working with groups like the Boys & Girls Clubs of America to inspire others to get help. This gave him a sense of purpose.
- **Staying Active and Calm**: He added exercise, like swimming, and calming techniques, like mindfulness, to his routine to reduce stress.

Outcome: Phelps' efforts helped him manage his depression, return to swimming, and become a strong voice for mental health, showing others that asking for help is a sign of strength.

5.   Writer: J.K. Rowling

J.K. Rowling, who wrote the *Harry Potter* books, went through a tough time with severe depression in her 20s. As a single mom living in poverty, she felt hopeless and even thought about ending her life, describing it as a "dark time" in interviews.

How she managed her illness:

- **Talking to a Therapist:** Rowling used cognitive-behavioral therapy (CBT), which helped her change negative thoughts and find ways to cope.

- **Writing to Heal:** Writing the *Harry Potter* series gave her a way to express her feelings. The Dementors in her stories came from her depression, showing how it felt like a heavy darkness.

- **Leaning on Friends:** She turned to close friends for support, which made her feel less alone.

- **Finding Purpose:** Taking care of her daughter and focusing on her writing gave her a reason to keep going and added structure to her life.

Outcome: Rowling beat her depression, released her incredibly successful *Harry Potter* series, and now openly talks about her experience to inspire others to seek help. She also backs mental health initiatives.

How to take care of your mental health?

Taking care of your mental health is about making time for activities that keep you healthy and happy, both physically and mentally. It helps you handle stress, stay healthier, and feel more energized.

Here are some easy self-care tips to help you feel better for your mental health:

Stay Active: Try to walk for 30 minutes each day to lift your mood and stay healthy. Regular physical activity can boost your mood.

Eat Well and Drink Water: Choose healthy foods and eat regular meals. Drinking enough water keeps you energized and focused.

Get Enough Sleep: Make sure you get enough sleep to recharge your mind. Avoid using phone or computer screens before bed, as their blue light can keep you awake.

Relax: Make time for fun, low-stress hobbies like listening to music, reading, or being in nature. Doing things you love can help you relax.

Plan Your Day: Decide what's most important to do now and what can wait. Keep a journal to list daily tasks, set realistic limits, and avoid taking on more than you can handle. At the end of the day, celebrate what you've accomplished.

Think Positive: Notice negative thoughts and try to replace them with helpful, positive ones.

Stay in Touch: Talk to friends or family who can listen and support you when you need it.

Feel free to talk to trusted adults, teachers, school counselors, or mental health experts if you're having a tough time.

If you've been feeling very upset for 2 weeks or more, talk to a professional for help. Look out for signs like:

- Trouble sleeping

- Eating more or less than usual, or unexpected weight changes

- Feeling very tired to get out of bed in the morning

- Hard time focusing

- Not enjoying things you used to love

- Struggling to do your normal tasks

- Feeling cranky, frustrated, or restless

Remember! Asking for help when you're not feeling your best is a sign of strength, not weakness.

SEEKING MENTAL HEALTH SUPPORT

Ways to Get Help for Your Mental Health

- **Professional Help Matters:**

  Mental health struggles require expert support, just as physical health problems require specialized medical care. Ignoring mental health is like ignoring a broken bone; it can get worse without proper attention. Both deserve serious attention.

- **Therapy and Counseling**

  What is therapy or counseling? It's a safe place where you can share your emotions, thoughts, and worries with a trained expert who offers support and guidance. Therapy is not just for crisis; it's also for learning skills to manage stress, improve relationships, and build resilience.

- **Finding a Mental Health Expert:**

  Ask your parents, school counselor, or doctor for suggestions. They can guide you to the next step, such as a therapist or counselor whom you might need. You can also check local clinics, online directories, or mental health hotlines. Remember, finding the right professional can take time, and that's okay.

Crafting An Action Plan For Your Mental Health

Taking care of your mental health is a journey that can help you continue throughout your life. It's like keeping your body healthy by eating well and exercising—your mind needs regular care too. A mental health action plan is a simple, personalized plan that can help guide you to feel better, manage stress, and stay strong, even during challenging times.

<u>**What should be included in your mental health plan?**</u>

- **Set Clear Goals for Your Mental Health**

Create a plan for what you'd like to work on or accomplish for your mental health. A plan, similar to a proposal, will provide a clear goal, such as feeling calmer, improving sleep, or rediscovering joy in hobbies. Make your goals clear and achievable so you can see how you're doing over time. It also helps you focus on positive changes, boosts your motivation, and makes mental health care feel manageable.

- **Reach Out for Support When You Need It**

Reaching out for help is a brave step, not a weakness. Support can come from trusted adults (like parents, teachers, or counselors), friends, or mental health professionals, especially if you're feeling sad, anxious, or overwhelmed for more than two weeks. Support from others reduces isolation and provides guidance. Professional help, such as therapy, effectively treats issues like anxiety or depression.

Peer support groups or youth mentoring programs can also be part of your support network, providing shared understanding and guidance from teens who have gone through similar experiences.

- **Make Self-Care a Daily Habit**

Self-care means doing activities that keep your mind and body healthy, like exercising, sleeping well, eating right, and relaxing. These habits help you manage stress, feel more energized, and stay resilient, even during tough times like bullying or family concerns. Self-care can also include creative expressions, like journaling, drawing, or making music, which allows you to process emotions. Spending time in nature, practicing mindfulness, and limiting screen time are additional ways to protect mental health. Making self-care a routine helps prevent burnout and builds emotional resilience.

- **Track Your Progress and Stay Flexible**

A mental health action plan serves as a guide. This guide helps you check how your plan is working, celebrate progress, and adjust it as needed to fit your life. Staying flexible keeps the plan helpful over time. Monitoring your progress boosts self-awareness and motivation, while staying adaptable ensures the plan remains realistic.

CHAPTER 2
Major Categories Of Mental Disorders

What is a Mental Health Disorder?

A mental health disorder is a condition that impacts a person's thoughts, feelings, and behaviors. These disorders impact brain function, resulting in a range of symptoms and daily life challenges.

Mental health disorders affect a person's behaviors, thoughts, and emotions, which can impact their happiness and health, and also cause changes in areas, such as trouble focusing, avoiding others, or excessive worrying.

A mental health disorder is a condition that affects how a person thinks, feels, and acts, changing how the brain works and causing various symptoms and daily struggles. These disorders can bring upsetting thoughts, emotions, and moods that harm a person's happiness and well-being, and also lead to behaviors like trouble focusing, staying away from others, or feeling anxious all the time. Mental health disorders can range from mild, short-term issues to chronic conditions that require ongoing care. They may affect sleep, appetite, energy, motivation, relationships, and performance at school or work. Early recognition and treatment are key to managing symptoms effectively.

For example, John, a teenager, feels sad all the time, stops enjoying activities he loves, and struggles to do well in school. He might also withdraw from friends, avoid extracurricular activities, or have trouble sleeping, which can worsen his overall well-being.

Action: After noticing his struggles, he decides to seek help, such as talking to a counselor or getting support from family, so he can manage his symptoms, feel better, and succeed.

<u>Another example</u> is Jay. A 16-year-old Jay starts hearing voices that others can't hear, making him feel scared and confused (affecting his thoughts and feelings). He becomes convinced his classmates are plotting against him, despite no evidence, which leads to distressing thoughts. These symptoms, caused by changes in brain function, make it hard for him to concentrate at school, and he begins skipping classes and avoiding friends (behavioral changes like trouble focusing and social withdrawal).

Actions: Noticing his struggles, Jay's family encourages him to see a doctor, who diagnoses schizophrenia and starts him on medication and therapy. With support, Jay learns to manage his symptoms, reconnects with friends, and pursues his love for art. These examples show that teens with mental health disorders can still lead happy and fulfilling lives with the right care and support.

Additional Note: Mental health disorders are not a reflection of personal weakness or character flaws. They are medical conditions that require understanding, support, and treatment just like any other health condition. Teens and their families should be encouraged to seek help promptly and not wait for symptoms to "go away on their own."

Mental Fitness = Physical Fitness

Just as we exercise to stay physically healthy, we need to care for our minds to keep our mental health strong. Mental fitness helps you handle stress, solve problems, make better decisions, and maintain positive relationships.

Just as physical fitness protects the body from illness, mental fitness protects the mind. By practicing small daily actions—such as writing down three things you're grateful for—these habits build resilience over time.

Here are some suggestions to help you stay strong both mentally and physically.

Daily Practice—Like regular exercise builds a healthy body, daily habits will keep our mental health strong. We need easy everyday routines to keep our minds strong.

Examples of daily practices include spending five minutes meditating, setting intentions for the day, taking short walks to clear your mind, or writing down three things you are grateful for. These small actions build resilience over time.

Creating Routines—Taking care of mental health is like building healthy habits. Just as we set routines for physical health, like working out at the gym or jogging, we can create habits that boost mental well-being, such as practicing mindfulness or writing in a journal. Routines could also include setting a regular bedtime to improve sleep, scheduling "screen-free" times to reduce stress, or having a consistent study or homework plan to reduce anxiety about deadlines.

Mental Fitness Routines—Keeping our minds healthy is a lot like staying physically fit—we need to use and challenge our brains in different ways. Trying new hobbies, being creative, or doing brain games can help keep our minds sharp and active. Other activities that strengthen mental fitness include reading, learning a new language, solving puzzles, volunteering, or practicing musical instruments. The goal is to challenge the brain, learn new skills, and keep curiosity alive.

Stay strong through challenges—Just like working out makes our bodies stronger, using our minds helps build emotional strength. Facing challenges and learning from them helps us handle life's ups and downs. For instance, if you struggle with a difficult school project or a friendship problem, facing it instead of avoiding it can teach problem-solving, patience, and confidence—skills that improve your mental endurance.

Balance and Variety—Just as we exercise various muscle groups to maintain physical health and prevent injury, we must nurture different dimensions of our mental well-being—such as emotional health, social connections, and clear thinking—to keep our minds strong.

Improving Step by Step—Just like getting fit takes regular work over time, improving your mental health happens little by little. Doing small, everyday tasks can slowly lead to big, positive changes.

Seeking support—Just like gym coaches help us stay physically fit, talking to therapists, counselors, or support groups can make a big difference in facing mental health challenges and feeling better.

Support can also come from family members, mentors, or friends who listen without judgment. Guidance from others can teach new coping strategies, help manage stress, and provide encouragement during tough times. Never hesitate to ask for help; it's a strength, not a weakness.

CATEGORIES OF MENTAL HEALTH DISORDERS

A mental health disorder is also called a mental illness, and it is a condition that changes how you think, feel, and act. It can affect your emotions and make it hard to manage them in your life. You might feel nervous, sad, or empty, have overwhelming thoughts, or struggle with eating or sleeping. These challenges can interfere with school performance, relationships, self-esteem, and daily responsibilities, especially during the teenage years when emotional and brain development are still in progress.

There are more than 200 mental health disorders, such as depression, anxiety, schizophrenia, and so on... You might experience mood swings, have changes in eating habits, see or hear things that aren't real, or lose interest in things you enjoy. Treatments like talking therapy and medications can help you manage these symptoms.

The most common mental health disorders among teenagers include:

- Depression: Feeling sad, hopeless, or tired for a long time, with trouble sleeping or enjoying things.

- Anxiety Disorders: Feeling scared or worrying too much and finding it hard to stop, sometimes with a fast heartbeat or other physical symptoms.

- Bipolar Disorder: Extreme mood swings, from high-energy "manic" periods to deep depressive lows.

- Attention-Deficit/Hyperactivity Disorder (ADHD): Trouble paying attention, keeping things in order, which can impact school and friendships.

- Eating Disorders (e.g., Anorexia, Bulimia): Worrying too much about body image or food, leading to extreme dieting, overeating, or throwing up.

- Schizophrenia: Hallucinations (seeing/hearing things that aren't real) or delusions (false beliefs), often affecting daily functioning.

- Post-Traumatic Stress Disorder (PTSD): Anxiety, flashbacks, or nightmares triggered by a traumatic experience.

Important Reminder: Having a mental health disorder does not define who you are. With early support, proper treatment, and understanding from others, many teens learn to manage their symptoms and live healthy, meaningful lives.

DEPRESSION

According to the U.S. Census Bureau's 2023 estimates, there are about 25.2 million teenagers aged 12–19 in the U.S. Approximately 20% of them, or roughly 4.84 million teens (which makes 19.2% to be exact)—about 1 in 5—experience depression.

Depression is a serious mental health condition that goes beyond feeling sad for a short time. It's like a heavy cloud that affects how you feel, think, and handle daily life, such as school, friendships, or family time. For teens, it can make everything feel overwhelming or meaningless.

Unlike temporary sadness, depression does not simply "go away on its own." It can quietly affect motivation, self-esteem, and energy levels, making everyday tasks feel exhausting or pointless. Many teens describe depression as feeling numb, disconnected, or stuck rather than just sad.

For teens, depression symptoms include:

- Feeling sad, angry, or empty most of the time.

- Not enjoying things they used to love, like gaming, sports, or hanging out.

- Being tired all the time, even after sleep.

- Trouble concentrating on homework or conversations.

- Eating too much or too little, or experiencing headaches or stomachaches.

- Feeling worthless or hopeless, like nothing will improve.

- Thoughts of hurting themselves or not wanting to live. (If you feel this, tell someone you trust immediately.)

For parents, you might notice your teen:

- Is moody or withdraws from family and friends for weeks.

- Loses interest in school, hobbies, or activities.

- Sleeps too much or too little.

- Talks about feeling hopeless or mentions death. (Act quickly if you hear this.)

<u>How Can You Get Help?</u>

Depression can improve with support. Here's how:

For Teens:

- Speak Up: Tell a parent, teacher, or counselor how you feel. It's brave to ask for help.

- See a Professional: A doctor or therapist can suggest talk therapy or, if needed, medication.

- Stay Healthy: Try to eat well, get enough sleep, and move a little (like walking).

Get Help Now: If you're thinking about hurting yourself, call or text 988 (Suicide & Crisis Lifeline) or talk to someone right away.

It's important to remember that asking for help does not mean you are weak or broken. Many teens who seek help learn coping skills that make them stronger, more confident, and better prepared to handle future challenges.

For Parents:

- Listen Calmly: If your teen shares their feelings, listen without judging.

- Seek Professional Help: Consult a doctor or therapist for a comprehensive evaluation. They may recommend therapy or medication.

- Be Supportive: Encourage small steps, like getting out of bed or eating a meal. Be patient—recovery takes time.

- Act Fast in a Crisis: If your teen talks about suicide, call 988 or go to the emergency room immediately.

- Promote Healthy Habits: Help with routines, like regular sleep and less screen time, especially if social media affects their mood.

Consistency and reassurance from parents play a major role in recovery. Teens often improve faster when they feel believed, supported, and not blamed for their struggles.

Please Act Now!

If depression isn't treated, it can get worse and mess with school, friends, and their health. In serious cases, it might even lead to thoughts of suicide. However, with help, most teens (70–90%) experience significant improvement and regain their energy.

ANXIETY DISORDER

An anxiety disorder is a mental health condition where worry, fear, or nervousness is so intense and persistent that it disrupts daily life, like school, friendships, or family time. It's more than just feeling stressed before a test—it can feel overwhelming and hard to control. Anxiety disorders often happen alongside depression, meaning many teens with anxiety might also feel sad or hopeless.

During the teenage years, anxiety can feel especially powerful because teens are still learning how to manage emotions and uncertainty. Pressure from school, social expectations, identity development, and future goals can make anxiety harder to escape without support.

What Does an Anxiety Disorder Feel Like?

For teens, an anxiety disorder might include:

- Worrying about things like grades, friends, or the future, even when there's no obvious reason.

- Feeling panicked, with a racing heart, sweating, or shaking.

- Avoiding situations, like parties or school, because they feel too scary.

- Trouble sleeping, feeling tired, or having headaches or stomach aches from stress.

- Feeling irritable, restless, or unable to focus because your mind is racing.

- If depression is also present, you might feel sad, lose interest in things you love, or feel worthless.

For parents, you might notice your teen:

- Worries a lot about small things or seems overly afraid.

- Skips school, activities, or time with friends.

- Complains about physical issues like stomach pain or tiredness with no clear cause.

- Gets panicky or upset in certain situations, like giving a presentation.

- Seems down, withdraws, or loses excitement for things they used to enjoy (a sign of depression).

-

Types of Anxiety Disorders

Common anxiety disorders include:

- Generalized Anxiety Disorder (GAD): Excessive worry about many things, like school or health, for 6 months or more.

- Social Anxiety Disorder: Intense fear of social situations, like speaking in class or meeting people.

- Panic Disorder: Sudden panic attacks with strong fear and physical symptoms, like a fast heartbeat.

- Specific Phobias: Extreme fear of something specific, like dogs or heights.

- Separation Anxiety Disorder: Fear of being away from parents or loved ones.

How Are Anxiety and Depression Connected?

Anxiety and depression often go hand in hand. About half of teens with an anxiety disorder also have depression. For example:

- Constant worry (anxiety) can make you feel hopeless or tired (depression).

- Feeling sad or worthless (depression) can make social situations scarier (anxiety).

- Both can cause trouble sleeping, focusing, or enjoying life, making it harder to cope.

How Common Are They?

The U.S. Census Bureau's 2023 data shows about 25.2 million teens aged 12–19 in the U.S., and around 1 in 5—roughly 4.84 million—have depression. About 1 in 5 U.S. teens also deal with anxiety disorders, which affect 58 million kids and teens worldwide out of 301 million teens. Girls are more likely to have these issues than boys, but both are common and can get better with the right help.

Despite how common anxiety is, many teens do not seek help because they believe their fears are normal or that they should be able to handle them alone. This delay can allow symptoms to grow stronger over time.

How Can You Get Help?

Anxiety and depression are treatable. Here's how to start:

For Teens:

- Share Your Feelings: Tell a parent, teacher, or counselor about your worries or sadness. Asking for help is brave.

- See a Professional: A therapist can teach skills like Cognitive Behavioral Therapy (CBT) to manage anxiety and depression. A doctor might suggest medication if needed.

- Take Care of Yourself: Eat well, sleep enough, and try small activities like walking or deep breathing to calm your mind.

- Get Help Now: If you're feeling panicked, hopeless, or thinking of hurting yourself, call or text 988 (Suicide & Crisis Lifeline) or talk to someone right away.

For Parents:

- Listen Calmly: Let your teen share their fears or sadness without judgment. Avoid saying "Just relax" or "Cheer up."

- Seek Help: Contact a doctor or therapist for therapy or, if necessary, medication to address both anxiety and depression.

- Support Healthy Habits: Encourage regular sleep, healthy meals, and less social media time.

- Act Fast in a Crisis: If your teen has panic attacks, seems very hopeless, or mentions suicide, call 988 or get emergency help.

Please Take Action Now:

Untreated anxiety and depression can make school, friendships, and health worse. They can also increase the risk of suicidal thoughts. But with treatment, most teens (70–80%) feel better and can enjoy life again.

With the right care, teens can learn to manage anxiety, regain confidence, and build resilience that supports their emotional well-being into adulthood.

BIPOLAR DISORDER

Bipolar disorder is a mental health condition that causes extreme mood swings, from high-energy "manic" periods where you feel overly happy or irritable to deep depressive lows where you feel sad or hopeless. These mood changes are more intense than typical ups and downs and can last days, weeks, or months, affecting school, friendships, and daily life. For teens, it can feel like an emotional rollercoaster. It often occurs alongside other conditions like anxiety or depression.

These mood shifts are not caused by laziness, attitude problems, or poor behavior. Bipolar disorder is linked to differences in brain chemistry, genetics, and how the brain regulates mood and energy. Stressful life events, lack of sleep, or substance use can trigger episodes, but they do not cause the disorder on their own.

For teens, bipolar disorder symptoms include:

- Manic or Hypomanic Episodes (highs):

- Feeling super happy, energetic, or irritable.

  - Talking fast, having racing thoughts, or feeling like you can do anything.

  - Needing less sleep (e.g., feeling rested after 2–3 hours).

  - Acting impulsively, such as spending too much money or taking risks.

  - In severe cases, seeing or hearing things that aren't there (hallucinations) or believing untrue things (delusions).

- Depressive Episodes (lows):

  - Feeling sad, empty, or hopeless for weeks.

  - Losing interest in things you love, like hobbies or friends.

  - Feeling tired, sleeping too much or too little, or having trouble focusing.

  - Feeling worthless or thinking about death or suicide.

- Mixed Episodes: Feeling manic and depressed at the same time, like being energized but sad or agitated, which can increase suicide risk.

For parents, you might notice their teens:

- Switches between being overly excited or irritable and very sad or withdrawn.

- Acts recklessly during high periods, like driving dangerously or overspending.

- Struggles with school or relationships due to mood swings.

- Complains of physical issues like headaches or stomachaches during low periods.

- Shows signs of anxiety or depression alongside mood swings.

How Common Is It?

About 2.8% of U.S. adults and 2.9% of teens (ages 13–18) have bipolar disorder. Globally, around 40 million people are affected. It's equally common in males and females, but females may have more depressive episodes. Symptoms often start in the teens or early 20s. However, your mood swings don't define you, and you're not alone. Getting help is brave and can make life easier.

How Can You Get Help?

Bipolar disorder is a lifelong condition, but treatment can help manage symptoms. Here's how:

For Teens:

- Talk to Someone: Tell a parent, counselor, or doctor about your mood swings. It's a strong step.

- See a Specialist: A psychiatrist can diagnose you and suggest treatments like mood stabilizers (e.g., lithium) or therapy, such as Cognitive Behavioral Therapy (CBT).

- Stay Healthy: Keep a regular sleep schedule, eat well, and avoid drugs or alcohol, which can trigger episodes.

For Parents:

- Listen Supportively: Avoid dismissing your teen's moods as "just a phase." Listen without judgment.

- Seek Professional Help: A psychiatrist can create a treatment plan with medication or therapy. Avoid antidepressants alone, as they can trigger mania.

- Encourage Routines: Help your teen stick to a sleep schedule and reduce stress.

- Watch for Crises: If your teen talks about suicide, call 988 or seek emergency care.

Why It's Important to Take Action

Untreated bipolar disorder can worsen, disrupting school, relationships, and health. It increases the risk of suicide (6% of people with bipolar disorder die by suicide over 20 years). With treatment, most teens (70–80%) can manage symptoms and live well.

Long-term treatment helps teens build coping skills, improve self-awareness, and gain confidence in managing their conditions. Many teens with bipolar disorder go on to graduate, build healthy relationships, and live meaningful, productive lives when they receive consistent support.

ATTENTION-DEFICIT/HYPERACTIVITY DISORDER (ADHD)

Attention-Deficit/Hyperactivity Disorder (ADHD) is a brain-based condition that makes it hard for someone to focus, stay organized, or control impulses. It's not just being distracted or active sometimes—ADHD symptoms are ongoing and can make school, friendships, and daily life challenging. For teens, it can feel like their brain is always "on," making it tough to keep up.

ADHD is considered a neurodevelopmental disorder, meaning it affects how the brain develops and functions over time. It is not caused by laziness, lack of discipline, or poor parenting.

For teens, ADHD might include:

Inattention:

- Trouble focusing on schoolwork, conversations, or details, leading to mistakes.

- Getting easily distracted by thoughts or things around you, like noises or your phone.

- Forgetting homework, losing items (like keys or books), or struggling to finish tasks.

- Daydreaming or feeling like your mind is "somewhere else."

Teens with inattention may be labeled as "unmotivated" or "not trying," even though they are often trying very hard but struggling internally.

Hyperactivity/Impulsivity:

- Feeling restless, fidgeting, or having trouble sitting still in class.

- Talking a lot, interrupting others, or blurting out answers without thinking.

- Acting impulsively, like making quick decisions that might cause trouble.

Hyperactivity may decrease as teens get older, but impulsivity and restlessness often remain and can affect decision-making and emotional control.

<u>**Other Signs**</u>: You might feel overwhelmed starting tasks, have mood swings, or struggle with time management. If you also have anxiety or depression, you might worry a lot or feel sad. For parents, you might notice your teen:

- Struggles with schoolwork, misses deadlines, or seems disorganized.

- Loses things often, like backpacks or assignments.

- Acts without thinking, like interrupting or taking risks.

- Seems restless, talks excessively, or can't stay seated during meals or class.

- Shows signs of anxiety (over-worrying) or depression (withdrawing or sadness).

<u>Types of ADHD</u>

ADHD shows up in three ways, depending on the main symptoms:

- Predominantly Inattentive: Mostly trouble focusing and organizing (e.g., forgetting tasks, being easily distracted).

- Predominantly Hyperactive-Impulsive: Mostly restlessness and impulsive actions (e.g., fidgeting, interrupting).

- Combined: A mix of both inattention and hyperactivity-impulsivity (the most common type).

The type of ADHD can change over time, especially during adolescence, as brain development continues.

How Is It Connected to Anxiety or Depression?

ADHD often comes with other conditions:

- Anxiety: Up to 50% of teens with ADHD have anxiety disorders, like excessive worry or panic, which can make focusing harder.

- Depression: About 20–30% of teens with ADHD experience depression, feeling sad or hopeless, which can worsen ADHD symptoms like low motivation.

- These conditions can overlap, making it harder to manage school or friendships, but treating ADHD can help with both.

Why Does ADHD Happen?

ADHD is caused by a mix of:

- Brain Differences: Areas of the brain that control attention, planning, and impulse control work differently. Chemicals like dopamine are often imbalanced.

- Genetics: ADHD runs in families—70–80% of cases have a genetic link.

- Environment: Factors like prenatal exposure to toxins (e.g., smoking), premature birth, or high stress can increase risk.

- Triggers: Lack of sleep, poor diet, or excessive screen time can worsen symptoms.

How Common Is It?

About 11.4% of U.S. children aged 3–17 (around 7 million) have been diagnosed with ADHD, with 2.9% of teens specifically affected. Boys (15%) are diagnosed more often than girls (8%), but girls are often underdiagnosed because their symptoms (like inattention) are less noticeable. Globally, about 5–7% of kids and teens have ADHD. Many teens remain undiagnosed until later adolescence or adulthood, especially those without obvious hyperactivity.

It's important to take action:

Untreated **ADHD** can lead to poor grades, strained friendships, low self-esteem, and higher risks of anxiety, depression, or risky behaviors (like substance use). About one-third of kids with **ADHD** have symptoms into adulthood, but early treatment can reduce this. With help, 70–80% of teens improve their focus, behavior, and quality of life.

EATING DISORDERS

Eating disorders are serious mental health issues where people have unhealthy thoughts about food, their body, or weight, leading to harmful actions like extreme dieting, overeating, or vomiting. Disorders like anorexia nervosa and bulimia nervosa are more than just worrying about looks—they can hurt your health, emotions, and life, like school or friendships. For teens, these problems can feel heavy or hard to share. For parents, knowing about eating disorders helps you support your teen. They often happen with other issues like anxiety, depression, or ADHD.

Eating disorders are not choices or habits; they are illnesses that affect both the mind and the body and require medical and psychological care.

<u>What Do Eating Disorders Feel Like?</u>

For teens, eating disorders might include:

- Anorexia Nervosa:

    - Intense fear of gaining weight, even when very thin.

    - Severely limiting food (e.g., eating tiny portions or skipping meals).

    - Seeing yourself as "fat" despite being underweight.

    - Feeling tired, dizzy, or cold, or noticing hair thinning.

Many teens with anorexia feel a strong sense of control when restricting food, even though their health is declining.

- Bulimia Nervosa:

  - Binge eating large amounts of food quickly, feeling out of control.

  - Purging by vomiting, using laxatives, or exercising excessively to avoid weight gain.

  - Feeling ashamed or hiding binging/purging habits.

  - Tooth damage or swollen cheeks from vomiting.

Bulimia often develops in secret, making it harder for adults to notice until physical symptoms appear.

- Other Symptoms (across disorders):

  - Obsessing over food, calories, or body shape.

  - Feeling guilty or anxious about eating.

  - Avoiding meals with others or eating in secret.

  - If anxiety, depression, or ADHD is present, you might also feel worried, sad, or have trouble focusing.

Some teens also experience "body checking," such as repeatedly weighing themselves or examining their bodies in mirrors.

For parents, you might notice your teen:

- Loses or gains weight rapidly or looks very thin.

- Skips meals, counts calories obsessively, or avoids certain foods.

- Goes to the bathroom right after eating (possible purging).

- Seems withdrawn, irritable, or overly focused on their body.

- Shows signs of anxiety (constant worry), depression (sadness), or ADHD (trouble focusing).

Types of Eating Disorders

- **Anorexia Nervosa**: Extreme food restriction, fear of weight gain, and distorted body image, often leading to dangerously low weight.

- **Bulimia Nervosa**: Cycles of binge eating followed by purging (vomiting, laxatives, or excessive exercise), with normal or varying weight.

- **Binge-Eating Disorder (BED)**: Frequent overeating with loss of control, without purging, often leading to guilt or weight gain.

- **Avoidant/Restrictive Food Intake Disorder (ARFID)**: Avoiding foods due to texture, smell, or fear (e.g., choking), not tied to body image, causing weight loss or nutritional issues.

- **Other Specified Feeding or Eating Disorder (OSFED)**: Eating issues that don't fully match other disorders but still cause distress, like atypical anorexia (restricting but not underweight).

<u>How Are They Connected to Anxiety, Depression, or ADHD?</u>

- Anxiety: Up to 65% of teens with eating disorders have anxiety disorders, like obsessive worry about food or body image, which can worsen behaviors like restricting or purging.

- Depression: About 40–50% of teens with eating disorders experience depression, feeling sad or worthless, which can fuel low self-esteem and body dissatisfaction.

- ADHD: Around 20–30% of teens with eating disorders have ADHD, where impulsivity or trouble focusing can lead to binge eating or chaotic eating habits.

- These conditions can make eating disorders harder to manage, but treating them together improves outcomes.

<u>Why Do Eating Disorders Happen?</u>

They're caused by a mix of:

- Genetics: If a family member has an eating disorder, anxiety, or depression, the risk is higher (50–80% genetic link).

- Brain Chemistry: Imbalances in chemicals like serotonin or dopamine affect mood, impulse control, and food behaviors.

- Environment: Pressure from social media, peers, or cultural ideals of thinness can trigger body image issues.

- Life Events: Trauma, bullying, or stress (e.g., family issues) can lead to using food or weight control to cope.

- Co-occurring Conditions: Anxiety, depression, or ADHD can amplify eating disorder symptoms.

<u>How Common Are They?</u>

About 9% of the U.S. population (28.8 million people) will have an eating disorder in their lifetime, with 6–8% of teens affected. Globally, 70 million people, including 13.9 million with anorexia or bulimia, have eating disorders. They're more common in girls (8.4% lifetime prevalence) than boys (2.2%), but anyone can be affected. Adolescents (ages 12–19) are at the highest risk. Many boys and nonbinary teens are underdiagnosed because eating disorders are often stereotyped as female illnesses.

Eating disorders are treatable, but early help is key. Here's how:

For Teens:

- Speak Up: Tell a parent, teacher, or counselor about your struggles with food or body image. It's a brave first step.

- See a Specialist: A doctor, therapist, or dietitian can help with therapy (e.g., Cognitive Behavioral Therapy), nutrition plans, or, for bulimia/BED, medication.

- Practice Self-Care: Try small, balanced meals, reduce social media use, and lean on supportive friends.

- Get Help Now: If you feel hopeless or suicidal, call or text 988 (Suicide & Crisis Lifeline) or tell someone immediately.

For Parents:

- Listen Without Judging: Avoid commenting on weight or saying "just eat." Show you care about their feelings.

- Seek Professional Help: Contact a doctor, therapist, or eating disorder specialist for therapy, nutrition counseling, or hospital care if severe.

- Support Routines: Encourage regular meals and limit triggers like diet talk or body-focused media.

- Act in a Crisis: If your teen is very underweight, purging often, or mentions suicide, call 988 or seek emergency care.

<u>Why It's Important to Act?</u>

Untreated eating disorders can cause serious health issues, like heart problems, bone loss, or infertility, and have the second-highest mortality rate of mental illnesses (after opioid addiction). Anorexia has a 5–10% death rate from starvation or suicide. But with treatment, 50–70% of teens recover fully or improve significantly.

SCHIZOPHRENIA

Schizophrenia is a serious mental health condition that changes how a person thinks, feels, and acts, making daily life, such as school, friendships, or family time, tough. It often causes hallucinations (seeing or hearing things that aren't real) or delusions (believing untrue things), which can feel confusing or scary for teens, as if reality is slipping away. It's less common than anxiety or depression, affecting about 0.3–0.7% of people worldwide (roughly 24 million, or 1 in 222 adults). In the U.S., about 0.25–0.64% of people have it. Symptoms usually start in the late teens to early 20s, earlier in boys (15–25) than girls, and teens often experience more visual hallucinations than adults.

Schizophrenia is not caused by bad parenting, weak character, or personal failure—it is a medical condition involving brain function.

For parents, you might notice your teen:

- Acts confused, talks about strange beliefs, or hears voices.

- Seems withdrawn, stops caring about hygiene, or struggles with school.

- Gets agitated, paranoid, or talks in a way that's hard to understand.

- Shows signs of anxiety (excessive worry), depression (sadness), or ADHD (restlessness).

Types of Schizophrenia Symptoms

- Positive Symptoms: Extra experiences, like hallucinations or delusions.

- Negative Symptoms: Missing normal behaviors, like a lack of emotion, motivation, or social interest.

- Cognitive Symptoms: Trouble with thinking, like poor memory or concentration.

- Disorganized Symptoms: Confused speech or behavior, like jumping between unrelated topics.

Negative and cognitive symptoms often affect school performance the most and may be mistaken for laziness or depression.

How Is It Connected to Anxiety, Depression, or ADHD?

- Anxiety: Up to 50% of people with schizophrenia have anxiety disorders, like constant worry or panic, which can worsen hallucinations or paranoia.

- Depression: About 25–40% experience depression, feeling hopeless or sad, which can overlap with negative symptoms like withdrawal.

- ADHD: Some teens with schizophrenia have ADHD (10–20%), where impulsivity or inattention can complicate disorganized thinking.

- These conditions can make schizophrenia harder to manage, but treating them together helps.

Why Does Schizophrenia Happen?

It's caused by a mix of:

- Genetics: If a family member has schizophrenia, the risk is higher (10% if a parent has it).

- Brain Chemistry: Imbalances in dopamine or glutamate affect how the brain processes reality.

- Environment: Stress, trauma, cannabis use, or prenatal issues (e.g., malnutrition) can trigger it.

- Development: Brain changes during adolescence may spark symptoms.

Symptoms include:

- **Hallucinations:**

  - Hearing voices that others don't hear, which might talk about you, give commands, or sound threatening.

  - Seeing things like people, shapes, or lights that aren't there.

  - Less often, smelling, tasting, or feeling things that aren't real (e.g., bugs crawling on your skin).

- **Delusions:**

  - Believing things that aren't true, like someone is out to harm you (paranoid delusions) or you have special powers (grandiose delusions).

  - Feeling like your thoughts are being controlled or broadcast to others.

- **Other Symptoms:**

  - Trouble organizing thoughts, making speech jumbled or hard to follow.

  - Feeling emotionless, unmotivated, or withdrawn (e.g., not wanting to socialize or care for yourself).

  - Struggling with focus, memory, or schoolwork.

  - If anxiety, depression, or ADHD is present, you might also feel worried, sad, or have trouble focusing.

<u>Why It's Important to Take Action:</u>

Untreated schizophrenia can disrupt school, relationships, and health, increasing risks of suicide (4.9% rate) or early death (2–3 times higher than others due to heart disease or diabetes). With treatment, 30–50% of people improve significantly, and 1 in 3 may fully recover.

<u>A Message to You!</u>

**Schizophrenia doesn't define you, and you're not alone.
Getting help is brave and can make life better.**

POST-TRAUMATIC STRESS DISORDER (PTSD)

Post-Traumatic Stress Disorder (PTSD) is a mental health condition that can develop after someone experiences or witnesses a traumatic event, like an accident, abuse, natural disaster, or violence. It's more than just feeling upset; it causes intense, ongoing symptoms like flashbacks, nightmares, or fear that make daily life, such as school or friendships, hard to manage. For teens, it can feel like the trauma is happening again or won't go away.

PTSD affects how the brain processes danger and safety, making the body stay in "survival mode" even when the threat is gone. This can make everyday situations feel overwhelming or unsafe.

Not everyone who experiences trauma develops PTSD, but when symptoms last longer than a month and interfere with daily life, professional support is often needed.

For teens, PTSD might include:

Reliving the Trauma:

- Flashbacks, where it feels like the traumatic event is happening again, with physical reactions like a racing heart or sweating.

- Nightmares about the trauma, making sleep scary or restless.

- Intrusive memories that pop up unexpectedly, causing distress.

These experiences are not memories alone; they can involve intense body reactions, making it feel impossible to just calm down.

Avoiding Reminders:

- Steering clear of places, people, or things tied to the trauma, like avoiding a street where an accident happened.

- Refusing to talk or think about the event can lead to isolation.

Avoidance may feel protective at first, but over time, it can shrink a teen's world and increase fear instead of reducing it.

Negative Thoughts and Mood:

- Feeling sad, guilty, or blaming yourself or others for the trauma (e.g., "It's my fault" or "I can't trust anyone").

- Losing interest in things you used to love, like sports or friends.

- Feeling detached, numb, or unable to feel happy.

Many teens struggle with shame or self-blame, even when the trauma was completely out of their control.

Feeling On Edge:

- Being jumpy, easily startled, or overly alert, like always watching for danger.

- Trouble sleeping, concentrating, or feeling irritable and angry.

- If anxiety, depression, or ADHD is present, you might also feel worried, hopeless, or struggle to focus.

This constant state of alertness can be exhausting and may lead to headaches, stomach issues, or chronic fatigue.

For parents, you might notice your teen:

- Seems scared, withdrawn, or avoids certain places or activities.

- Has nightmares, trouble sleeping, or sudden mood changes.

- Gets angry or upset easily, or seems "on guard" all the time.

- Struggles with school or pulls away from friends and family.

- Shows signs of anxiety (constant worry), depression (sadness), or ADHD (restlessness).

Types of PTSD

- **Standard PTSD:** Symptoms lasting over a month after a traumatic event, causing distress and disruption.

- **Complex PTSD (C-PTSD):** Develops from long-term trauma, like ongoing abuse, adding issues with emotions, relationships, or self-image.

- **Delayed-Onset PTSD:** Symptoms start more than 6 months after the trauma.

- **Acute Stress Disorder:** Similar symptoms within 3 days to 1 month after trauma, which may lead to PTSD if untreated.

Is It Connected to Anxiety, Depression, or ADHD?

- Anxiety: Up to 50% of teens with PTSD have anxiety disorders, like panic or excessive worry, which can worsen avoidance or hypervigilance.

- Depression: About 30–40% experience depression, feeling sad or worthless, which can overlap with PTSD's negative mood symptoms.

- ADHD: Around 10–20% have ADHD, where impulsivity or inattention can complicate PTSD symptoms like poor focus or irritability.

- Treating co-occurring conditions alongside PTSD improves recovery.

When these conditions overlap, symptoms can mask each other, making PTSD harder to recognize without professional assessment.

Why Does PTSD Happen?

PTSD is caused by:

- **Trauma:** Events like assault, accidents, war, or disasters that feel life-threatening or overwhelming.

- **Genetics:** Family history of mental health issues increases risk.

- **Brain Chemistry:** Changes in stress hormones or brain areas like the amygdala affect fear responses.

- **Environment:** Lack of support, ongoing stress, or past trauma (especially in childhood) raises the chance of PTSD.

- **Risk Factors:** Girls, those with prior mental health issues, or those facing extra stress (e.g., loss or injury) are more at risk.

How Common Is It?

About 3.9% of people worldwide (around 300 million) have had PTSD at some point, with 5–10% of those experiencing trauma developing it. In the U.S., about 4.1% of adults (over 8 million) and 5% of teens (ages 13–18) have PTSD in a given year. It's more common in girls (8%) than boys (2.3%) and is especially high after sexual violence or war (up to 15.3%).

How Can You Get Help?

PTSD is treatable, and early support makes a difference. Here's how:

For Teens:

- Talk to Someone: Share your feelings with a parent, counselor, or trusted adult. It's a brave step.

- See a Specialist: A therapist can use treatments like Cognitive Behavioral Therapy (CBT) or Eye Movement Desensitization and Reprocessing (EMDR) to help process trauma. A doctor may suggest antidepressants (e.g., sertraline) for severe symptoms.

- Practice Self-Care: Try relaxation techniques (e.g., deep breathing), regular sleep, and supportive friendships. Avoid drugs or alcohol, which worsen symptoms.

- Get Help Now: If you feel suicidal or overwhelmed, call or text 988 (Suicide & Crisis Lifeline) or tell someone immediately.

<u>For</u> Parents:

- Listen Without Judging: Don't push your teen to "get over it." Say, "I'm here for you," and validate their feelings.

- Seek Professional Help: Contact a therapist or psychiatrist for therapy or medication. School counselors can help with referrals.

- Support Routines: Encourage healthy habits like regular meals, sleep, and low-stress activities. Limit trauma triggers like violent media.

Act in a Crisis: If your teen talks about suicide or seems in **<u>danger</u>**, call 988 or seek emergency care.

Why It's Important to Take Action!

Untreated PTSD can worsen, affecting school, relationships, and health, and increasing risks of depression, substance use, or suicide (3–5% risk). With treatment, 40–60% of teens recover within a year, and most improve significantly.

A Message for You!

If you have PTSD, it doesn't mean you're weak; it's a response to something tough. Getting help is strong and can help you feel like yourself again.

You deserve safety, understanding, and support—and recovery is possible.

CHAPTER 3
Understanding the Numbers: A Statistical Look at Teenagers' Mental Health.

The mental health of adolescents has emerged as a critical public health concern, with increasing recognition of its impact on lifelong well-being, academic success, and social development. Recent data from 2023–2025 highlight the prevalence of mental health conditions among U.S. youth, including anxiety, depression, and behavioral disorders, alongside rising rates of suicidal behaviors and barriers to accessing care.

Recent national surveys show that nearly one in five teenagers experiences a diagnosable mental health condition each year, yet many do not receive treatment. Long waiting lists, financial barriers, and fear of stigma often prevent young people from getting the help they need. This gap between need and treatment remains one of the greatest challenges in youth mental health today.

Adolescence is a critical developmental period marked by rapid brain maturation, emotional regulation changes, and increased vulnerability to stress, making mental health conditions more likely to emerge during these years. Early mental health challenges often predict adult outcomes, with untreated adolescent disorders linked to higher risks of unemployment, substance use, chronic illness, and involvement with the justice system later in life.

During adolescence, the brain areas responsible for decision-making and impulse control are still developing. At the same time, emotional centers of the brain are highly active. This imbalance helps explain why teenagers may experience intense emotions, mood swings, or risk-taking behaviors. Understanding this developmental stage helps parents and teachers respond with patience and support instead of judgment.

This chapter synthesizes the latest research findings from authoritative sources, including the Centers for Disease Control and Prevention (CDC), the National Institute of Mental Health (NIMH), the Substance Abuse and Mental Health Services Administration (SAMHSA), and the American Psychiatric Association (APA). It examines major trends, differences based on gender, race, and socioeconomic background, and the impact of social factors such as schools and digital media. The chapter provides in-depth, evidence-based information to help educators and healthcare providers develop targeted strategies for supporting youth mental health.

Studies consistently show that girls report higher rates of anxiety and depression, while boys are more likely to display behavioral problems or avoid seeking help. Cultural expectations often discourage boys from expressing emotions, which can lead to untreated stress and emotional isolation. Understanding these differences helps professionals design better support systems for both groups.

Digital technology has also become a major influence on teen mental health. While online platforms can provide support and connection, excessive screen time and constant comparison with others can increase feelings of loneliness, anxiety, and low self-esteem. Healthy digital habits and balanced screen use are now considered important parts of mental health prevention.

In addition to prevalence rates, recent research emphasizes the importance of protective factors, such as strong family relationships, supportive school environments, and access to mental health education, in reducing symptom severity and improving resilience among teens.

Emerging data also highlights the role of structural inequities, including income instability, neighborhood safety, and access to healthcare, in shaping mental health outcomes across different adolescent populations.

2025 THE U.S. PREVALENCE OF MENTAL HEALTH CONDITIONS IN TEENAGERS

The map (Chart 2025 A1) from Mental Health America's 2025 State of Mental Health in America Report displays the prevalence of major depressive episodes (MDE) among U.S. teenagers aged 12–17 across all states and the District of Columbia. It draws on the latest available data, mainly 2022–2023 state-level estimates from SAMHSA's National Survey on Drug Use and Health (updated through 2024).

This map uses a green color scale: lighter green shades show lower rates (better outcomes), while darker green shades indicate higher rates (more concern). Prevalence ranges from a low of about 16.06% in Hawaii (ranked 1, lightest shade) to a high of 22.71% in New Hampshire (ranked near the bottom, darkest shade).

Nationally, the report points to encouraging improvement. In the most recent data, 15.4% of youth experienced at least one major depressive episode in the past year—a clear drop from 18.1% in 2023 and peaks near 20.8% in earlier years. This reverses the steady rise seen before 2024.

Other important numbers show that about 11.3% of youth (around 2.8 million) had MDE with severe impairment that seriously affected daily activities like school, home life, or friendships. Serious suicidal thoughts also fell to roughly 10.1%, impacting nearly 3 million teens.

These gains are likely due to greater availability of school-based mental health services, expanded crisis support such as the 988 Suicide & Crisis Lifeline, and stronger early intervention programs. That said, today's rates remain higher than pre-2020 norms (usually 11–13% for MDE in the late 2010s), so while the youth mental health crisis is easing, it is not yet over.

The MHA report ranks states based on 17 combined measures of mental health prevalence and access to care (primarily using 2022–2023 data for state comparisons). The top-performing states for youth mental health—those with lower depression rates plus better access to treatment—are led by New York, Hawaii, and New Jersey. The lowest-ranked states include Nevada, Arizona, and Alabama.

2025 data from MHA and NSDUH show meaningful progress in lowering teen depression and suicidality—possibly a turning point—though millions of adolescents continue to face substantial challenges. Persistent barriers like stigma, limited access, and low rates of help-seeking link to serious risks: academic difficulties, school absenteeism, social isolation, substance misuse, self-harm, and suicide. Ongoing policy emphasis on prevention, early screening, and equitable care is still crucial.

Youth With At Least One Major Depressive Episode (MDE) In The Past Year

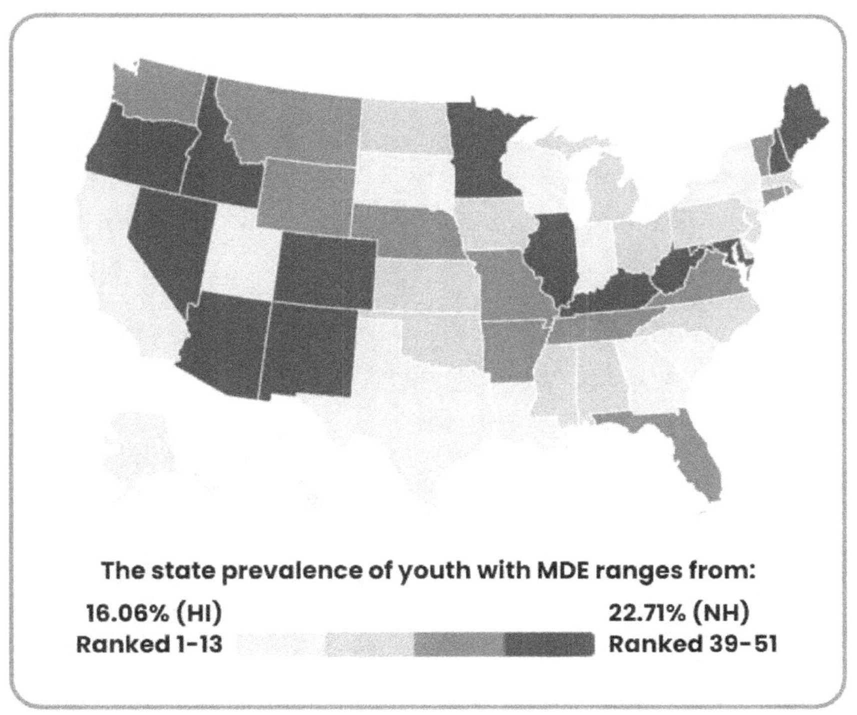

Chart 2025 A1

Rank	State	%	#
1	New York	11.30	155,000
2	District of Columbia	11.60	4,000
3	Connecticut	11.87	32,000
4	Texas	12.04	319,000
5	Utah	12.12	41,000
6	Mississippi	12.16	30,000
7	Georgia	12.17	111,000
8	Michigan	12.34	93,000
9	California	12.39	377,000
10	Oklahoma	12.39	42,000
11	North Carolina	12.51	103,000
12	Kentucky	12.58	45,000
13	New Jersey	12.59	89,000
14	Massachusetts	12.61	61,000
15	North Dakota	12.62	8,000
16	Kansas	12.62	31,000
17	South Carolina	12.66	51,000
18	Iowa	12.75	33,000
19	Missouri	12.88	62,000
20	Washington	12.92	74,000
21	Hawaii	12.92	13,000
22	Wisconsin	12.92	59,000
23	Louisiana	12.97	48,000
24	Florida	12.98	199,000
25	Indiana	13.10	73,000
26	Delaware	13.23	10,000

Rank	State	%	#
27	Arizona	13.37	77,000
28	Pennsylvania	13.38	125,000
29	Alaska	13.39	8,000
30	Colorado	13.45	59,000
31	Alabama	13.48	53,000
32	Rhode Island	13.52	10,000
33	Ohio	13.53	123,000
34	Arkansas	13.65	34,000
35	Montana	13.70	11,000
36	Oregon	13.72	42,000
37	Virginia	13.76	90,000
38	Illinois	13.79	136,000
39	Minnesota	13.98	64,000
40	Nebraska	14.06	23,000
41	Idaho	14.12	24,000
42	New Hampshire	14.19	13,000
43	Nevada	14.23	35,000
44	Wyoming	14.42	7,000
45	Tennessee	14.54	79,000
46	West Virginia	14.63	19,000
47	Maryland	14.66	70,000
48	Vermont	14.71	6,000
49	New Mexico	14.74	25,000
50	South Dakota	14.98	11,000
51	Maine	15.36	14,000
	National	12.87*	3,322,000*

Chart 2025 A2

Mental Health America's 2025 State of Mental Health in America report, drawing on the latest data from SAMHSA's National Survey on Drug Use and Health (NSDUH through 2024), highlights a significant national improvement in youth mental health. The percentage of U.S. teenagers aged 12–17 who experienced at least one major depressive episode (MDE) in the past year fell from 18.1% in 2023 to 15.4% in 2024, marking a clear reversal of the upward trend observed in previous years.

In 2024, 11.3% of youth—equating to an estimated 2.8 million adolescents had an MDE with severe impairment, meaning their depression seriously disrupted their ability to function in key areas such as school, home, or social life.

At the state level, several areas showed particularly strong progress. Alaska recorded the largest decline, with youth MDE rates dropping from 21.72% (based on 2021–2022 combined data) to 17.27% (2022–2023 combined data), a decrease of about 4.45 percentage points. Other states with statistically significant reductions in the percentage of youth experiencing an MDE in the past year include California, Indiana, New York, and Washington.

These improvements are encouraging and likely reflect expanded access to school-based mental health supports, increased availability of crisis intervention services such as the 988 Suicide & Crisis Lifeline, and broader early intervention efforts across the country. However, while the trend is moving in a positive direction, current rates remain above pre-2020 baselines (typically 11–13% for MDE in the late 2010s), indicating that the youth mental health crisis has begun to ease but is not yet fully resolved.

2025 Youth (12–17) With Substance Use Disorder (Sud) Rates In The U.S.

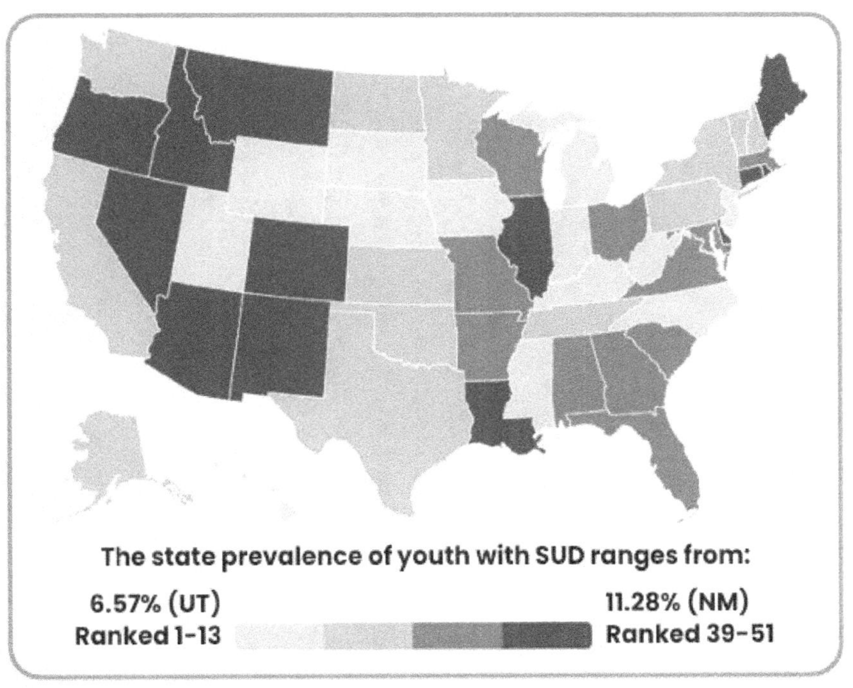

Chart 2025 A3

The percentage of U.S. teens (ages 12–17) with a past-year substance use disorder (SUD) fell from 9.2% in 2021 to 7.8% in 2024, according to Mental Health America's 2025 State of Mental Health in America report (based on federal NSDUH data). This drop shows real improvement in teen substance issues. Teen substance use dropped during the COVID-19 pandemic—probably because of less socializing and fewer in-person hangouts—and it has stayed fairly low even after kids returned to full-time school.

The Monitoring the Future (MTF) survey (2024–2025 data from the University of Michigan, funded by NIDA) found that abstinence from alcohol, marijuana, and nicotine among 8th–12th graders reached record highs since tracking began in 2017. In 2024, abstinence rates in the past 30 days were stable or increased (e.g., ~89–91% for 8th-grader students, higher for older grades in some measures), with use of most substances remaining low or declining slightly.

Rank	State	%	#
1	Utah	6.57	22,000
2	Hawaii	6.84	7,000
3	Iowa	7.09	18,000
4	North Carolina	7.58	63,000
5	Mississippi	7.58	19,000
6	South Dakota	7.70	6,000
7	New Jersey	7.79	55,000
8	Nebraska	7.86	13,000
9	Kentucky	7.90	28,000
10	Wyoming	8.00	4,000
11	Michigan	8.03	61,000
12	West Virginia	8.05	10,000
13	Indiana	8.07	45,000
14	New Hampshire	8.09	8,000
15	New York	8.17	112,000
16	Texas	8.17	216,000
17	California	8.18	249,000
18	Oklahoma	8.21	28,000
19	Minnesota	8.24	38,000
20	Tennessee	8.25	45,000
21	Vermont	8.33	4,000
22	Alaska	8.34	5,000
23	North Dakota	8.39	5,000
24	Pennsylvania	8.52	80,000
25	Washington	8.57	49,000
26	Kansas	8.61	21,000

Rank	State	%	#
27	Ohio	8.63	78,000
28	Virginia	8.69	57,000
29	South Carolina	8.77	36,000
30	Arkansas	8.79	22,000
31	Maryland	8.82	42,000
32	Alabama	8.86	35,000
33	Missouri	8.90	43,000
34	Massachusetts	8.95	43,000
35	Georgia	9.11	83,000
36	District of Columbia	9.13	3,000
37	Florida	9.16	141,000
38	Wisconsin	9.20	42,000
39	Idaho	9.24	16,000
40	Rhode Island	9.30	7,000
41	Illinois	9.32	92,000
42	Montana	9.35	8,000
43	Louisiana	9.52	35,000
44	Maine	9.57	9,000
45	Connecticut	9.72	26,000
46	Colorado	9.88	43,000
47	Oregon	10.02	30,000
48	Nevada	10.05	25,000
49	Arizona	10.15	58,000
50	Delaware	10.34	8,000
51	New Mexico	11.28	19,000
	National	8.56*	2,210,000*

Chart 2025 A4

However, mental health challenges remain a key risk factor. Youth with a past-year major depressive episode (MDE) were 21% more likely to use illicit drugs than those without MDE. Similarly, those with moderate-to-severe anxiety symptoms showed 16% higher illicit drug use rates. This highlights a strong link between untreated or poorly managed mental health issues and substance use—especially illicit drugs—suggesting that while overall SUD trends are improving, sustaining gains requires prioritizing youth mental health support.

2025 Youth With Serious Thoughts Of Suicide In The Past Year

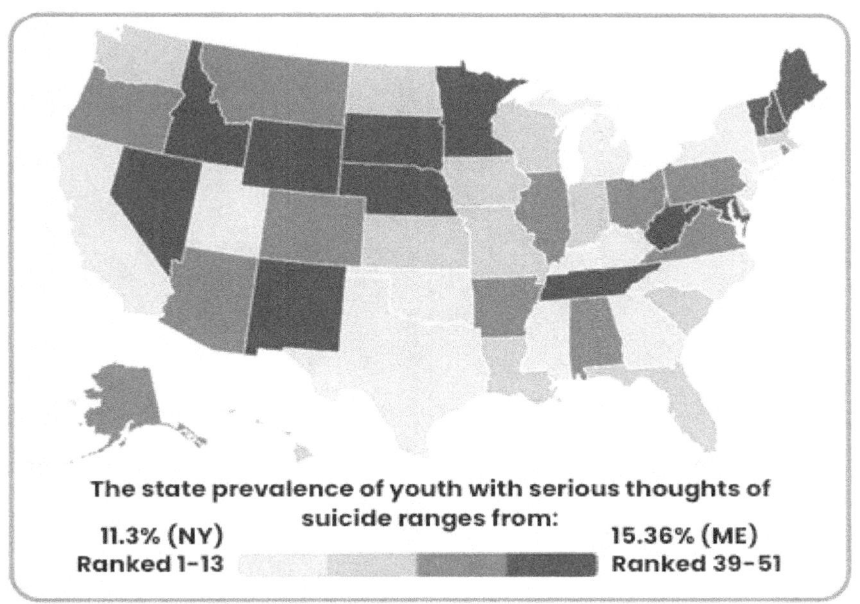

Chart 2025 A5

The national rate of U.S. teens (ages 12–17) reporting serious thoughts of suicide (suicidal ideation) in the past year decreased from 12.3% in 2023 to 10.1% in 2024, according to Mental Health America's 2025 State of Mental

Health in America report (based on federal NSDUH data). Even so, this still means nearly 3 million young people were affected.

The overall drop in suicidal thoughts among youth is very positive and hopeful news. This improvement probably comes from greater access to mental health resources and crisis support, such as the wider availability of the 988 Suicide & Crisis Lifeline and the increased funding and investments in mental health services that took place from 2021 to 2023.

Rank	State	%	#
1	New York	11.30	155,000
2	District of Columbia	11.60	4,000
3	Connecticut	11.87	32,000
4	Texas	12.04	319,000
5	Utah	12.12	41,000
6	Mississippi	12.16	30,000
7	Georgia	12.17	111,000
8	Michigan	12.34	93,000
9	California	12.39	377,000
10	Oklahoma	12.39	42,000
11	North Carolina	12.51	103,000
12	Kentucky	12.58	45,000
13	New Jersey	12.59	89,000
14	Massachusetts	12.61	61,000
15	North Dakota	12.62	8,000
16	Kansas	12.62	31,000
17	South Carolina	12.66	51,000
18	Iowa	12.75	33,000
19	Missouri	12.88	62,000
20	Washington	12.92	74,000
21	Hawaii	12.92	13,000
22	Wisconsin	12.92	59,000
23	Louisiana	12.97	48,000
24	Florida	12.98	199,000
25	Indiana	13.10	73,000
26	Delaware	13.23	10,000

Rank	State	%	#
27	Arizona	13.37	77,000
28	Pennsylvania	13.38	125,000
29	Alaska	13.39	8,000
30	Colorado	13.45	59,000
31	Alabama	13.48	53,000
32	Rhode Island	13.52	10,000
33	Ohio	13.53	123,000
34	Arkansas	13.65	34,000
35	Montana	13.70	11,000
36	Oregon	13.72	42,000
37	Virginia	13.76	90,000
38	Illinois	13.79	136,000
39	Minnesota	13.98	64,000
40	Nebraska	14.06	23,000
41	Idaho	14.12	24,000
42	New Hampshire	14.19	13,000
43	Nevada	14.23	35,000
44	Wyoming	14.42	7,000
45	Tennessee	14.54	79,000
46	West Virginia	14.63	19,000
47	Maryland	14.66	70,000
48	Vermont	14.71	6,000
49	New Mexico	14.74	25,000
50	South Dakota	14.98	11,000
51	Maine	15.36	14,000
	National	12.87*	3,322,000*

Chart 2025 A6

2025 Youth With MDE Who Did Not Receive Mental Health Services In The U.S.

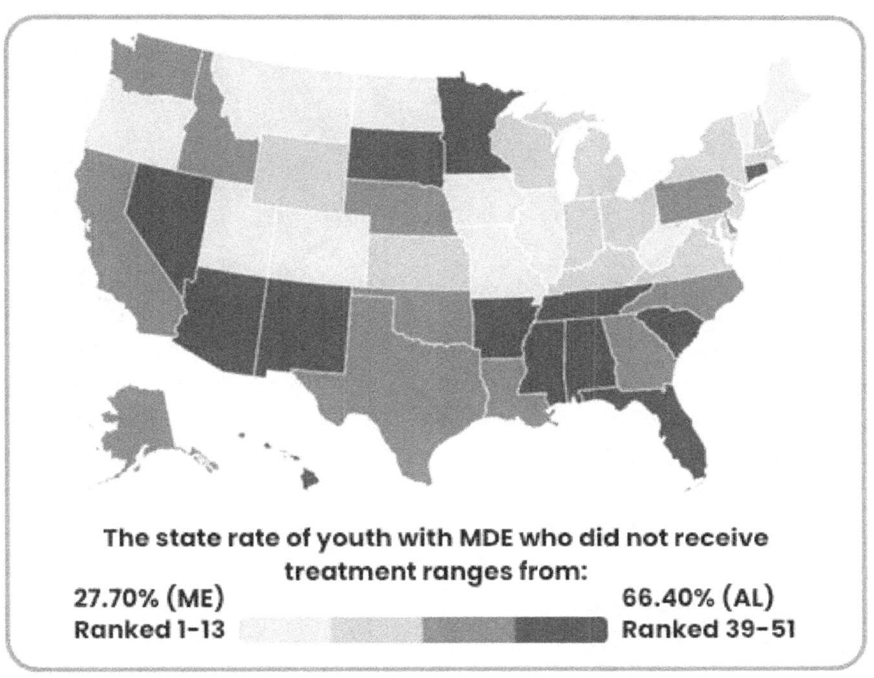

Chart 2025 A7

Rank	State	%	#
1	Maine	27.70	5,000
2	Missouri	37.70	38,000
3	Vermont	37.80	3,000
4	Illinois	38.20	78,000
5	Iowa	39.80	17,000
6	Colorado	40.00	42,000
7	North Dakota	41.50	5,000
8	Utah	41.50	21,000
9	Oregon	42.50	27,000
10	Montana	43.00	7,000
11	Rhode Island	43.30	6,000
12	West Virginia	44.40	11,000
13	District of Columbia	45.20	2,000
14	Ohio	45.60	77,000
15	Kentucky	45.70	34,000
16	New York	46.70	95,000
17	Wisconsin	46.80	27,000
18	Michigan	47.70	66,000
19	Wyoming	47.80	4,000
20	Virginia	47.90	63,000
21	Massachusetts	48.00	37,000
22	Indiana	48.30	39,000
23	Maryland	48.50	57,000
24	Kansas	49.10	24,000
25	New Jersey	49.10	59,000
26	New Hampshire	49.80	11,000

Rank	State	%	#
27	North Carolina	50.10	78,000
28	Pennsylvania	50.40	88,000
29	Delaware	50.80	7,000
30	Georgia	51.10	70,000
31	Idaho	51.10	20,000
32	Nebraska	52.10	19,000
33	Texas	52.20	216,000
34	California	52.40	267,000
35	Louisiana	52.70	34,000
36	Oklahoma	53.10	30,000
37	Washington	53.40	59,000
38	Alaska	55.00	5,000
39	New Mexico	56.70	22,000
40	Florida	57.10	166,000
41	Hawaii	57.10	6,000
42	South Carolina	57.80	38,000
43	Arkansas	59.00	29,000
44	Nevada	59.50	39,000
45	South Dakota	59.80	5,000
46	Mississippi	60.30	26,000
47	Arizona	61.50	81,000
48	Connecticut	61.90	26,000
49	Tennessee	63.70	61,000
50	Minnesota	64.10	67,000
51	Alabama	66.40	46,000
	National	50.80	2,360,000

Chart 2025 A8

In 2022–2023 (combined data), Mental Health America, discussing Youth with Major Depressive Episode Who Did Not Receive Mental Health

Services, in their report named 2025 State of Mental Health in America ranked U.S. states and the District of Columbia by the percentage of youth ages 12–17 who experienced a major depressive episode (MDE) in the past year but received no treatment or counseling. The data comes from combined 2022–2023 estimates, primarily sourced from SAMHSA's National Survey on Drug Use and Health.

Nationally, more than half—50.80%—of teens with an MDE went without any mental health care during that period. This represents a modest improvement of about 5% compared to the 2021–2022 combined data, which is a positive step forward. Even so, it still leaves over 2 million young people struggling with depression without professional support. This gap between need and care suggests that awareness alone is not enough; many communities still lack accessible providers, affordable treatment options, or youth-focused services that feel safe and approachable to adolescents.

State-level differences are striking. In the lowest-ranked state, Alabama (rank 51), nearly two-thirds of youth with MDE received no treatment at all, highlighting particularly wide gaps in access or willingness to seek help in certain regions.

Common barriers keep many teens from getting care. In 2023 data, around 85.30% of affected youth said they did not seek help because they believed they should be able to handle their mental health problems, emotions, or challenges on their own. Nearly 3 in 5 (58.90%) worried about stigma—what others might think or say if they got treatment—and a similar proportion (58.20%) feared that what they shared would not stay confidential. Many adolescents also struggle to recognize the difference between normal emotional ups and downs and symptoms of clinical depression, which can delay help-seeking until the situation becomes severe. In addition, some teens report not knowing where to go for help or how to begin the process of finding a counselor or therapist.

Fear of forced or involuntary treatment was another major concern: 46.20% of youth avoided care because they were afraid of being committed to a hospital or pushed into treatment against their will. These deeply held fears and misconceptions help explain why so many teens continue to suffer in silence, even when they need support the most.

Tackling these barriers head-on could truly transform outcomes for young people. By expanding access to teen-friendly mental health services, actively working to reduce stigma through education, open dialogue, and positive role modeling, and by clearly communicating strong privacy safeguards along with the fact that treatment is always voluntary, we can help far more adolescents feel secure and empowered to reach out for—and actually receive—the support they need and deserve.

2024 THE U.S. PREVALENCE OF MENTAL HEALTH CONDITIONS IN TEENAGERS

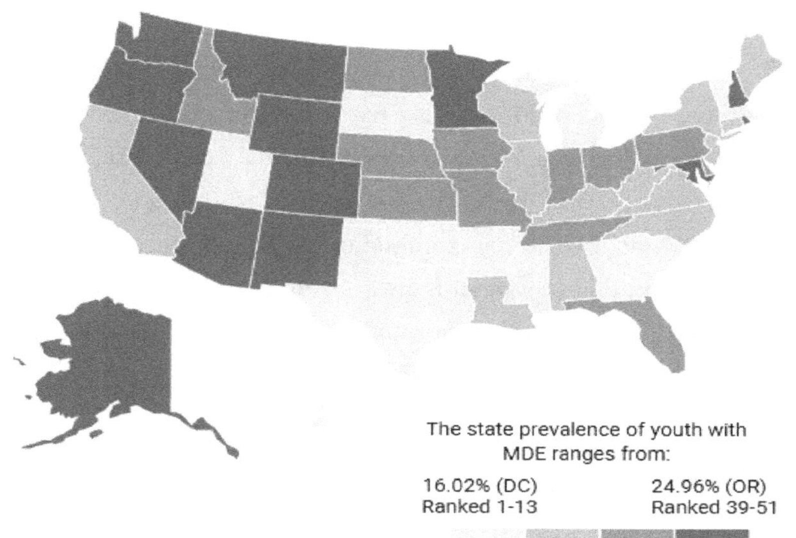

Chart 2024 A1

These findings reflect a continued upward trend compared to pre-pandemic levels, suggesting that adolescent depression has not returned to baseline despite the easing of COVID-19-related disruptions.

Major depressive episodes during adolescence are strongly associated with academic decline, increased absenteeism, social withdrawal, and a higher risk for substance use and self-harm behaviors.

Research also indicates that teens experiencing severe depressive episodes are less likely to seek help on their own, often due to stigma, fear of judgment, or difficulty recognizing symptoms as a mental health condition.

Rank	State	%	#
1	District of Columbia	16.02	5,000
2	Hawaii	17.15	17,000
3	Georgia	17.39	159,000
4	South Carolina	17.88	72,000
5	Utah	18.33	62,000
6	Texas	18.40	483,000
7	Michigan	18.65	142,000
8	Mississippi	18.73	47,000
9	Oklahoma	18.76	63,000
10	Arkansas	18.97	47,000
11	Massachusetts	19.18	93,000
12	South Dakota	19.21	14,000
13	Vermont	19.25	8,000
14	Alabama	19.41	76,000
15	Wisconsin	19.41	89,000
16	North Carolina	19.46	160,000
17	Kentucky	19.50	69,000
18	New York	19.58	272,000
19	New Jersey	19.70	141,000
20	Connecticut	19.83	54,000
21	West Virginia	19.85	25,000
22	Louisiana	19.91	74,000
23	Maine	19.93	18,000
24	California	20.01	616,000
25	Illinois	20.21	202,000
26	Virginia	20.22	133,000

Rank	State	%	#
27	Kansas	20.34	50,000
28	Indiana	20.44	114,000
29	Tennessee	20.50	111,000
30	Pennsylvania	20.50	193,000
31	Delaware	20.55	15,000
32	Ohio	20.79	190,000
33	Iowa	20.88	54,000
34	Nebraska	21.12	35,000
35	Florida	21.43	325,000
36	Idaho	21.50	37,000
37	North Dakota	21.56	13,000
38	Missouri	21.59	105,000
39	New Hampshire	21.63	20,000
40	Wyoming	21.70	10,000
41	Alaska	21.72	13,000
42	Montana	21.89	18,000
43	Minnesota	22.07	102,000
44	Rhode Island	22.15	16,000
45	Maryland	22.17	105,000
46	New Mexico	23.23	40,000
47	Colorado	23.32	103,000
48	Washington	23.39	135,000
49	Nevada	23.51	58,000
50	Arizona	23.96	139,000
51	Oregon	24.96	76,000
	National	20.17	5,217,000

Chart 2024 A2

The map (Chart 2024 A2) from Mental Health America's 2024 Report shows the rates of major depressive episodes (MDE) among American teens aged 12–17 in every state and the District of Columbia, using survey data from 2021–2022. The percentages vary from a minimum of 16.02% in D.C.

(rank 1, palest shade) to a maximum of 24.96% in Oregon *(rank 51, deepest shade),* with blue colors indicating levels—lighter tones for lower rates *(positive results)* and darker tones for higher rates *(negative results).*

The second chart sourced from Mental Health America's 2024 report, ranks U.S. states and the District of Columbia by the percentage of youth (ages 12–17) who experienced at least one major depressive episode (MDE). The rankings range from 1 to 51, with the District of Columbia at 16.02% (5,000 youth) and Oregon at 24.96% (76,000 youth). The national average is 20.17%, affecting approximately **5,217,000** youth. States with the lowest prevalence include the District of Columbia (16.02%), Hawaii (17.15%), Georgia (17.39%), South Carolina (17.88%), and Utah (18.33%). The highest prevalence states are Oregon (24.96%), New Mexico (23.51%), Washington (23.39%), Colorado (23.32%), and Nevada (23.32%).

2024 Youth With Substance Use Disorder Report In The U.S.

According to Mental Health America (2024), a survey conducted from 2014 to 2022 among 13–18-year-olds assessed for substance use disorder treatment found that the primary reasons for substance use were to relax or unwind (73%), to have fun or experiment (50%), and to improve sleep (44%). Additionally, substance use was employed to manage depression or anxiety. These findings suggest that many adolescents turn to substances not primarily out of rebellion, but as a form of self-medication or emotional regulation when healthier coping strategies are not available or well understood. Prevention efforts could focus on these triggers by directly addressing youth stress, improving family sleep routines, and building strong mental health and coping skills. Furthermore, approximately 8.95% of U.S. youth experienced a substance use disorder in the past year, with 3.2% affected by an alcohol use disorder and 7.17% by a drug use disorder.

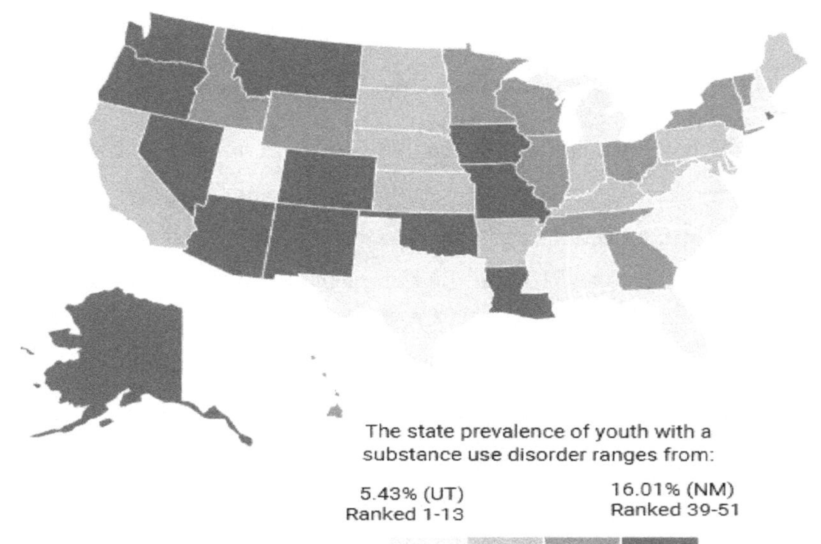

Chart 2024 A3

These findings suggest that substance use among teens is often a coping strategy rather than purely recreational behavior, closely tied to unmet mental health needs. Early initiation of substance use during adolescence is associated with changes in brain development, increasing the likelihood of long-term addiction and worsening mental health outcomes in adulthood.

Youth with co-occurring mental health conditions, such as depression or anxiety, are significantly more likely to develop substance use disorders than their peers without these conditions. Environmental influences also play an important role. Teens who are exposed to peer pressure, family members who use substances, or communities where drugs and alcohol are easily available face a greater risk of developing substance-related problems. Access and availability often shape patterns of use just as strongly as personal emotional struggles.

Rank	State	%	#
1	Utah	5.43	18,000
2	New Hampshire	7.13	7,000
3	New Jersey	7.25	52,000
4	North Carolina	7.42	61,000
5	South Carolina	7.44	30,000
6	Connecticut	7.66	21,000
7	Mississippi	7.69	19,000
8	Virginia	7.69	50,000
9	Texas	7.79	204,000
10	Alabama	7.82	31,000
11	Michigan	8.12	62,000
12	Massachusetts	8.14	39,000
13	Florida	8.19	124,000
14	California	8.21	253,000
15	South Dakota	8.23	6,000
16	Maryland	8.31	39,000
17	Kentucky	8.40	30,000
18	Pennsylvania	8.55	80,000
19	Maine	8.66	8,000
20	Arkansas	8.77	22,000
21	Indiana	8.78	49,000
22	Kansas	8.81	22,000
23	Nebraska	8.86	15,000
24	West Virginia	8.96	11,000
25	North Dakota	8.97	5,000
26	Delaware	9.09	7,000

Rank	State	%	#
27	Georgia	9.29	85,000
28	Illinois	9.33	93,000
29	Ohio	9.41	86,000
30	Wyoming	9.43	5,000
31	Hawaii	9.44	9,000
32	Tennessee	9.47	51,000
33	New York	9.53	132,000
34	Idaho	9.86	17,000
35	Vermont	10.10	4,000
36	Wisconsin	10.28	47,000
37	Minnesota	10.30	47,000
38	District of Columbia	10.34	4,000
39	Arizona	10.68	62,000
40	Montana	10.93	9,000
41	Iowa	10.95	28,000
42	Washington	10.96	63,000
43	Rhode Island	11.03	8,000
44	Missouri	11.15	54,000
45	Colorado	11.27	50,000
46	Oklahoma	11.49	38,000
47	Alaska	11.51	7,000
48	Oregon	12.52	38,000
49	Louisiana	13.40	50,000
50	Nevada	14.09	35,000
51	New Mexico	16.01	27,000
	National	8.95	2,316,000

Chart 2024 A4

The charts (Charts 2024 A3 & A4) from Mental Health America, 2024, are based on a survey from the 2024 report and rank U.S. states and the District of Columbia by the percentage of youth with a substance use disorder (SUD). The rankings range from 1 to 51, with Utah at 5.43% (18,000 youth) and New Mexico at 16.01% (27,000 youth). The national average is 8.95%, affecting approximately 2,316,000 youth. States with the lowest prevalence include Utah (5.43%), New Hampshire (7.13%), New Jersey (7.25%), North Carolina (7.42%), and South Carolina (7.44%). The highest prevalence states are New Mexico (16.01%), Nevada (14.09%), Louisiana (13.40%), Oregon (12.52%), and Alaska (11.51%).

2024 Youth With Serious Thoughts Of Suicide In The U.S.

The map shows (Chart 2024 A5) how common substance use disorders are among U.S. teens, which can hint at their mental health struggles. The lowest rate is 5.43% in Utah (ranked 1–13), and the highest is 16.01% in New Mexico (ranked 39–51). States like New Mexico, Louisiana, Alaska, Arizona, Nevada, and Iowa (darker colors) have more teens with these issues, which might indicate more problems like anxiety, depression, or suicidal thoughts. States like Utah, Texas, and Vermont (lighter colors) have fewer cases, suggesting better mental health there.

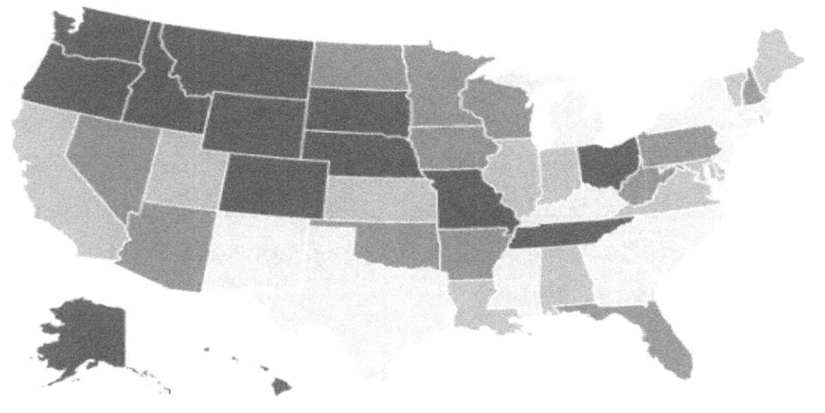

Chart 2024 A5

The 2021 YRBS found that 45% of LGBQ+ high school students in the U.S. seriously considered attempting suicide, compared to 15% of their heterosexual peers.

Rank	State	%	#
1	District of Columbia	10.68	4,000
2	Connecticut	11.00	30,000
3	Michigan	11.85	90,000
4	Texas	12.05	316,000
5	Massachusetts	12.24	59,000
6	New York	12.25	170,000
7	Georgia	12.34	113,000
8	Mississippi	12.37	31,000
9	South Carolina	12.55	50,000
10	New Jersey	12.71	91,000
11	North Carolina	12.79	105,000
12	Kentucky	12.94	46,000
13	New Mexico	12.95	22,000
14	Rhode Island	12.98	10,000
15	Utah	13.04	44,000
16	Delaware	13.06	10,000
17	Vermont	13.07	6,000
18	Kansas	13.09	32,000
19	Louisiana	13.20	49,000
20	Illinois	13.21	132,000
21	Alabama	13.23	52,000
22	Maryland	13.32	63,000
23	Maine	13.34	12,000
24	Indiana	13.34	74,000
25	California	13.34	411,000
26	Virginia	13.37	88,000

Rank	State	%	#
27	Florida	13.40	203,000
28	Pennsylvania	13.46	127,000
29	New Hampshire	13.58	13,000
30	Arizona	13.61	79,000
31	North Dakota	13.63	8,000
32	Wisconsin	13.69	63,000
33	Oklahoma	13.71	46,000
34	Nevada	13.80	34,000
35	Iowa	13.80	36,000
36	West Virginia	13.90	18,000
37	Minnesota	13.94	64,000
38	Arkansas	14.03	35,000
39	Hawaii	14.04	14,000
40	Tennessee	14.16	77,000
41	Nebraska	14.18	24,000
42	Ohio	14.25	130,000
43	Colorado	14.26	63,000
44	South Dakota	14.33	11,000
45	Wyoming	14.34	7,000
46	Missouri	14.43	70,000
47	Alaska	14.52	9,000
48	Montana	14.64	12,000
49	Washington	14.79	85,000
50	Idaho	14.89	25,000
51	Oregon	15.00	46,000
	National	13.16	3,406,000

Chart 2024 A6

Over 3.4 million youth, or 13.16%, reported having serious suicidal thoughts. Prevalence varied by state, with Oregon at 15.00% (ranked 39–51) and Washington, D.C., at 10.68% (ranked 1–13). Significant racial disparities exist in youth suicidality. In 2021–2022, Native Hawaiian or Other Pacific Islander youth (25%) and multiracial youth (20%) reported the highest rates of suicidal ideation. American Indian and Alaska Native youth and young adults aged 10–24 had the highest suicide rates (36.3 per 100,000). Between 2018 and 2021, suicide rates among Black youth and young adults rose by 37%, the largest increase across racial/ethnic groups.

2024 Youth With MDE Who Did Not Receive Mental Health Services In The U.S.

In 2022, teens with major depressive episodes (MDE) were asked if they felt they needed mental health treatment but didn't get it. Nearly half—48.3%, or about 987,000 teens in the U.S.—said they had an unmet need. The top reason they didn't seek help was that they thought they should handle it on their own (86.9%). Other big reasons included worrying about what others might think or say.

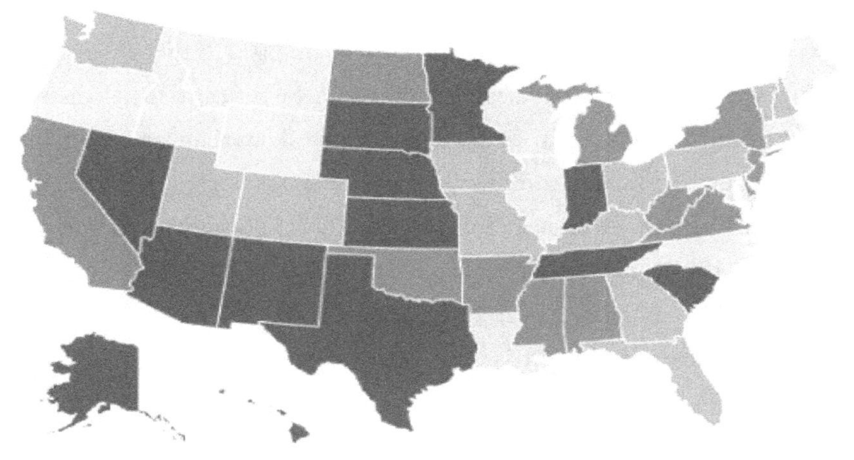

Chart 2024 A7

Over half of teens with major depression—56.1%—didn't get any mental health support. This means they didn't see a doctor or professional for treatment or counseling, nor did they take medication for major depressive episodes (MDE).

Rank	State	%	#
1	District of Columbia	31.50	2,000
2	Maine	34.60	6,000
3	Louisiana	38.90	31,000
4	Illinois	39.30	79,000
5	Idaho	42.60	14,000
6	Rhode Island	43.20	8,000
7	Oregon	44.70	37,000
8	Maryland	46.00	49,000
9	Massachusetts	46.10	35,000
10	Montana	46.60	9,000
11	Wisconsin	47.00	37,000
12	North Carolina	47.20	71,000
13	Wyoming	47.20	4,000
14	Utah	47.90	24,000
15	Florida	49.70	155,000
16	Iowa	51.20	28,000
17	Ohio	52.00	97,000
18	Colorado	52.90	64,000
19	Connecticut	53.00	24,000
20	New Hampshire	53.00	11,000
21	Vermont	53.00	3,000
22	Missouri	53.30	65,000
23	Georgia	53.70	75,000
24	Pennsylvania	53.70	104,000
25	Washington	54.00	79,000
26	Kentucky	54.10	32,000

Rank	State	%	#
27	Virginia	54.50	75,000
28	Michigan	55.70	71,000
29	New Jersey	56.40	71,000
30	Mississippi	56.60	26,000
31	Oklahoma	56.60	28,000
32	Delaware	56.80	9,000
33	West Virginia	57.10	14,000
34	New York	57.20	149,000
35	Arkansas	58.30	24,000
36	Alabama	58.70	42,000
37	North Dakota	61.30	9,000
38	California	62.40	346,000
39	Tennessee	62.40	69,000
40	Minnesota	63.50	70,000
41	Nebraska	65.10	24,000
42	Indiana	66.40	65,000
43	Alaska	66.70	9,000
44	Kansas	66.70	34,000
45	Arizona	67.20	101,000
46	Texas	67.60	284,000
47	South Carolina	67.70	39,000
48	New Mexico	69.60	31,000
49	Hawaii	69.90	8,000
50	Nevada	73.70	47,000
51	South Dakota	82.10	8,000
	National	56.10	2,793,000

Chart 2024 A8

YOUTH WITH AT LEAST ONE MAJOR DEPRESSIVE EPISODE(MDE) IN 2023

According to Mental Health America (2023), the CDC's Adolescent Behaviors and Experiences Survey (ABES) revealed that U.S. high school students faced significant challenges during the COVID-19 pandemic. Approximately 67% found schoolwork more challenging, 55% reported emotional abuse at home, 11% experienced physical abuse, and 24% faced food insecurity, all of which can negatively impact mental health.

These stressors are strongly associated with higher rates of major depressive episodes among teens, as prolonged exposure to academic pressure, unsafe home environments, and unmet basic needs increases emotional distress and feelings of helplessness.

Food insecurity, in particular, has been linked to higher levels of depression and anxiety in adolescents, as uncertainty about meals can contribute to chronic stress and poor concentration in school.

Emotional abuse at home is one of the strongest predictors of adolescent depression, often leading to low self-esteem, feelings of worthlessness, and difficulty trusting others. Teens who struggled academically during the pandemic were also more likely to report symptoms of depression, such as loss of motivation, fatigue, and difficulty concentrating, which can persist even after schools reopened.

Social isolation during the pandemic also played a major role in adolescent depression. Many teenagers lost regular contact with friends, teachers, coaches, and mentors who normally provide emotional support and stability. Without these connections, feelings of loneliness and disconnection increased significantly, contributing to depressive symptoms.

Increased screen time and online activity during the pandemic may have further affected teen mental health. While digital communication helped some teens stay connected, excessive social media use has been associated with sleep disruption, negative self-comparisons, and exposure to harmful online content, all of which can worsen depressive symptoms.

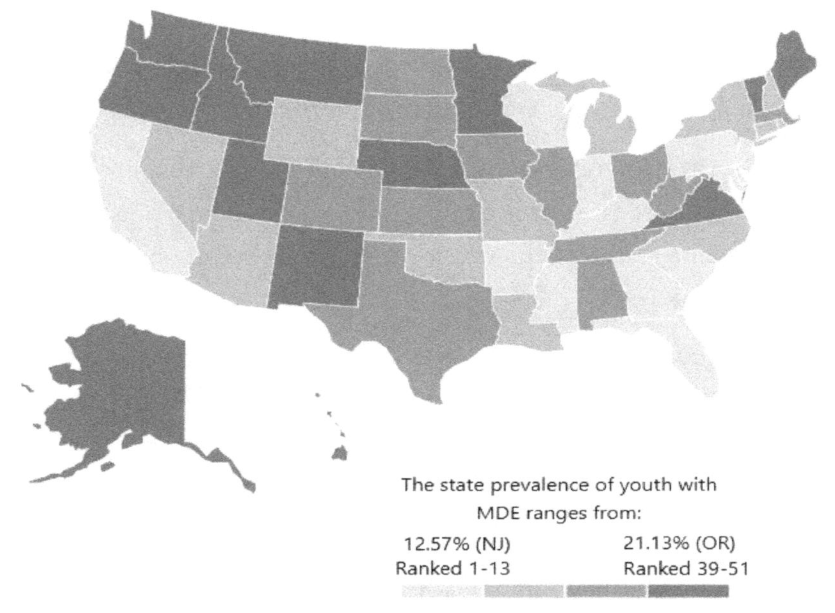

Chart 2023 A1

The map illustrates the state prevalence of youth with Major

Depressive Episodes (MDE) in the United States for 2023, based on the provided data. The prevalence ranges from 12.57% in New Jersey (NJ), ranked 1–13, to 21.13% in Oregon (OR), ranked 39–51.

Approximately 16.39% of young people aged 12–17 experienced at least one major depressive episode (MDE) within the past year.

Rank	State	%	#
1	New Jersey	12.57	84,000
2	South Carolina	13.41	51,000
3	Pennsylvania	14.04	127,000
4	Wisconsin	14.16	63,000
5	Delaware	14.24	10,000
6	Georgia	14.49	127,000
7	California	14.83	447,000
8	Kentucky	14.89	51,000
9	Arkansas	14.97	36,000
10	Mississippi	15.08	37,000
11	Maryland	15.37	69,000
12	Indiana	15.45	83,000
13	Florida	15.51	225,000
14	North Carolina	15.56	124,000
15	Connecticut	15.64	42,000
16	Rhode Island	15.90	11,000
17	Oklahoma	15.97	51,000
18	Michigan	15.99	119,000
19	Nevada	16.02	38,000
20	New York	16.03	214,000
21	Louisiana	16.18	58,000
22	District of Columbia	16.32	5,000
23	Wyoming	16.78	8,000
24	Missouri	16.84	79,000
25	Arizona	16.90	96,000
26	New Hampshire	17.02	16,000

Rank	State	%	#
27	Colorado	17.05	74,000
28	Texas	17.08	429,000
29	Iowa	17.10	42,000
30	Tennessee	17.32	89,000
31	Alabama	17.56	65,000
32	Massachusetts	17.74	84,000
33	North Dakota	17.77	10,000
34	West Virginia	17.92	22,000
35	Kansas	17.94	43,000
36	South Dakota	17.96	13,000
37	Illinois	18.10	177,000
38	Ohio	18.25	162,000
39	Alaska	18.36	10,000
40	Hawaii	18.36	17,000
41	Utah	19.08	61,000
42	New Mexico	19.32	32,000
43	Minnesota	19.39	86,000
44	Virginia	19.56	124,000
45	Washington	19.57	108,000
46	Maine	19.85	18,000
47	Nebraska	20.08	32,000
48	Montana	20.18	16,000
49	Vermont	20.64	8,000
50	Idaho	20.88	33,000
51	Oregon	21.13	63,000
	National	16.39	4,087,000

Chart 2023 A2

The table provides data on the percentage and number of youth (aged 12–17) experiencing at least one major depressive episode (MDE) in the past year across U.S. states and the District of Columbia, ranked from lowest to highest prevalence.

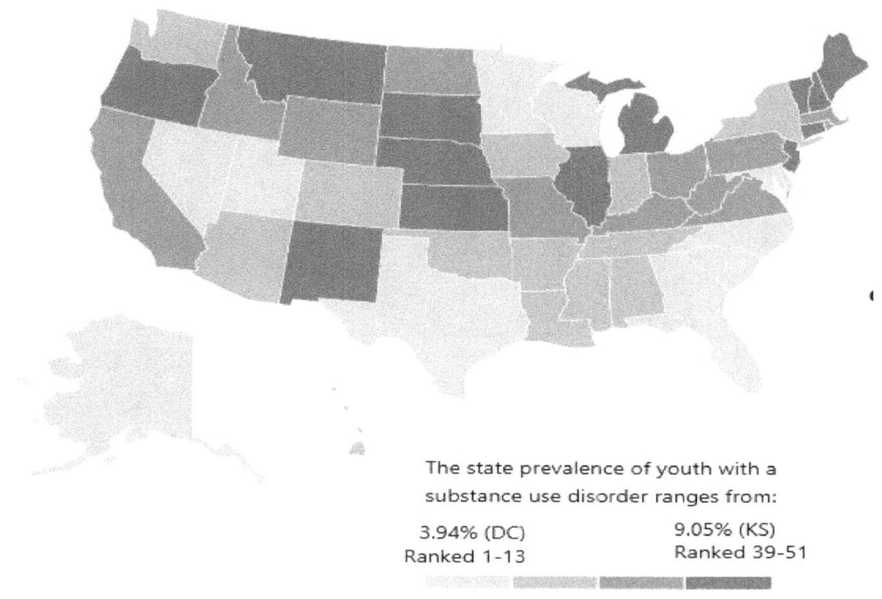

Chart 2023 A3

Approximately 6.34% of U.S. youth reported a substance use disorder in the past year, affecting an estimated 1,584,000 young people nationwide, according to recent national data. Illicit drug use disorders were more prevalent than alcohol use disorders, with 4.85% of youth affected by illicit drugs compared to 2.85% with alcohol use disorder.

The state-level prevalence of youth with a substance use disorder varies widely, ranging from a low of 3.94% in the District of Columbia (ranked 1, lightest shade) to a high of 9.05% in Kansas (ranked 51, darkest shade). States with the lowest rates (generally ranked 1–13, lighter purple shades) include the District of Columbia (3.94%), Georgia (4.65%), Nevada (4.85%), Alaska (5.06%), and North Carolina (5.13%), showing notably better outcomes in these areas.

Rank	State	%	#
1	District of Columbia	3.94	1,000
2	Georgia	4.30	38,000
3	Nevada	4.65	11,000
4	Alaska	5.06	3,000
5	North Carolina	5.13	41,000
6	Delaware	5.13	4,000
7	South Carolina	5.26	20,000
8	Maryland	5.27	24,000
9	Wisconsin	5.66	25,000
10	Utah	5.70	18,000
11	Minnesota	5.73	25,000
12	Texas	5.79	146,000
13	Florida	5.99	87,000
14	Louisiana	6.00	22,000
15	Arizona	6.06	35,000
16	Oklahoma	6.07	20,000
17	Hawaii	6.08	6,000
18	Alabama	6.11	23,000
19	Tennessee	6.13	32,000
20	Washington	6.27	35,000
21	Arkansas	6.29	15,000
22	Colorado	6.37	28,000
23	Mississippi	6.48	16,000
24	New York	6.49	86,000
25	Indiana	6.49	35,000
26	Iowa	6.52	16,000

Rank	State	%	#
27	Colorado	17.05	74,000
28	Texas	17.08	429,000
29	Iowa	17.10	42,000
30	Tennessee	17.32	89,000
31	Alabama	17.56	65,000
32	Massachusetts	17.74	84,000
33	North Dakota	17.77	10,000
34	West Virginia	17.92	22,000
35	Kansas	17.94	43,000
36	South Dakota	17.96	13,000
37	Illinois	18.10	177,000
38	Ohio	18.25	162,000
39	Alaska	18.36	10,000
40	Hawaii	18.36	17,000
41	Utah	19.08	61,000
42	New Mexico	19.32	32,000
43	Minnesota	19.39	86,000
44	Virginia	19.56	124,000
45	Washington	19.57	108,000
46	Maine	19.85	18,000
47	Nebraska	20.08	32,000
48	Montana	20.18	16,000
49	Vermont	20.64	8,000
50	Idaho	20.88	33,000
51	Oregon	21.13	63,000
	National	16.39	4,087,000

Chart 2023 A4

In contrast, states with the highest prevalence (ranked 39–51, darker purple shades) include Kansas (9.05%), Montana (8.60%), Oregon (7.97%), Vermont (7.91%), and New Mexico (7.75%), indicating significantly greater challenges in these regions. The prevalence in the highest-ranked state (Kansas) is more than double that of the lowest (District of Columbia), highlighting substantial geographic differences in youth substance use disorders across the country.

These patterns reveal clear regional trends: the Southeast (including Georgia, North Carolina, and South Carolina) and certain other states like Utah and the District of Columbia tend to have lower rates, while several Midwestern, Western, and Northern states face much higher burdens.

Youth with Severe Major Depressive Episode in 2023

Approximately 11.5% of youth, totaling over 2.7 million individuals, experienced severe major depression. The prevalence of severe major depressive episodes (MDE) among youth varies significantly across states, ranging from a low of 5.2% in South Carolina (SC), ranked 1–13, to a high of 19.9% in South Dakota (SD), ranked 39–51. Notable racial and geographic disparities are evident among youth with severe MDE. The highest rates are observed among youth identifying with multiple races, at 16.5%, impacting approximately 123,000 individuals. Furthermore, the prevalence of severe MDE in South Dakota, ranked 51, is nearly four times higher than that in South Carolina, ranked 1.

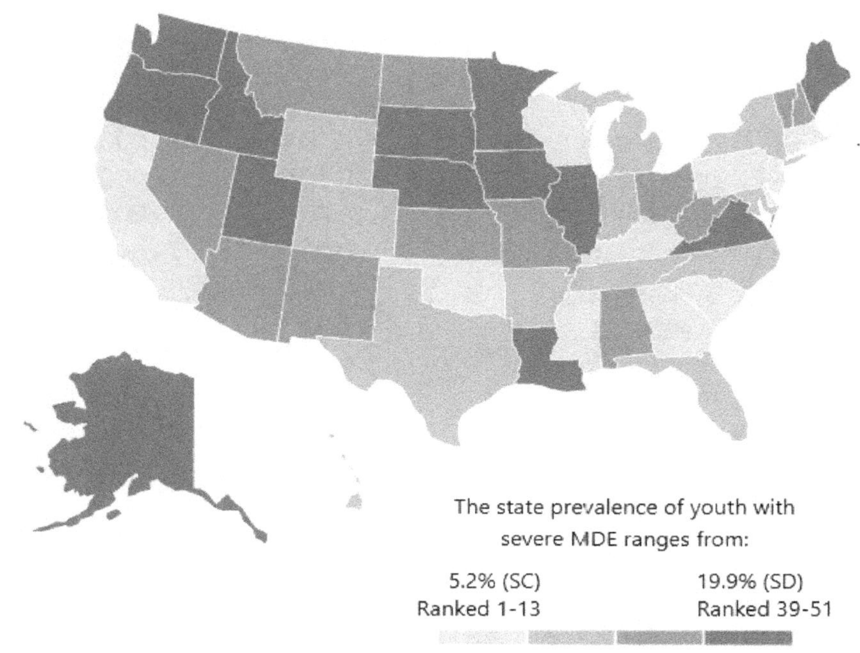

Chart 2023 A5

Around 16.39% of kids aged 12–17 dealt with at least one major depressive episode (MDE) in the last year.

Rank	State	%	#
1	South Carolina	5.20	19,000
2	New Jersey	7.50	48,000
3	Mississippi	8.10	19,000
4	Wisconsin	8.50	37,000
5	Massachusetts	8.80	40,000
6	Pennsylvania	9.20	79,000
7	California	9.20	269,000
8	Kentucky	9.30	30,000
9	Rhode Island	9.90	7,000
10	Georgia	10.00	85,000
11	Delaware	10.10	7,000
12	Connecticut	10.20	26,000
13	Oklahoma	10.30	32,000
14	District of Columbia	10.60	3,000
15	Arkansas	10.60	25,000
16	Tennessee	10.60	54,000
17	North Carolina	10.60	82,000
18	Wyoming	10.70	5,000
19	New York	10.80	137,000
20	Texas	10.80	261,000
21	Hawaii	10.90	10,000
22	Colorado	10.90	46,000
23	Indiana	11.20	57,000
24	Michigan	11.30	83,000
25	Florida	12.30	174,000
26	Maryland	12.40	55,000

Rank	State	%	#
27	New Mexico	12.80	21,000
28	West Virginia	13.00	16,000
29	Kansas	13.00	30,000
30	Arizona	13.10	72,000
31	Alabama	13.20	48,000
32	New Hampshire	13.30	12,000
33	Montana	13.40	10,000
34	North Dakota	13.60	7,000
35	Nevada	13.80	32,000
36	Missouri	13.80	64,000
37	Vermont	13.90	5,000
38	Ohio	13.90	119,000
39	Washington	14.00	74,000
40	Illinois	14.40	136,000
41	Alaska	14.80	8,000
42	Iowa	15.00	36,000
43	Minnesota	15.20	64,000
44	Nebraska	15.70	23,000
45	Virginia	15.70	97,000
46	Maine	16.30	14,000
47	Utah	16.40	50,000
48	Louisiana	16.60	59,000
49	Idaho	17.50	27,000
50	Oregon	19.00	55,000
51	South Dakota	19.90	14,000
	National	11.50	2,782,000

Chart 2023 A6

Youth with MDE Who Did Not Receive Mental Health Services in 2023

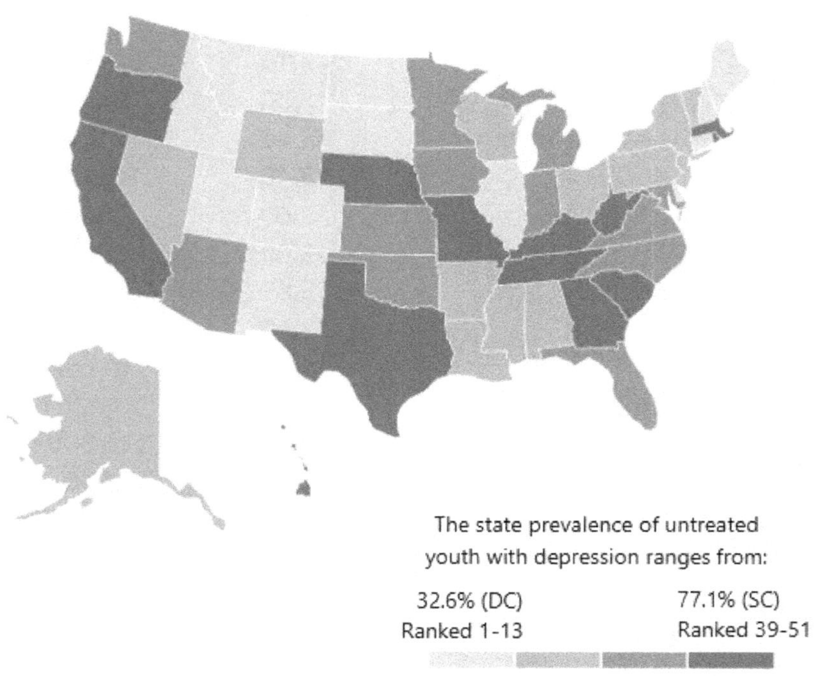

Chart 2023 A7

Approximately 59.80% of U.S. youth with a major depressive episode (MDE) in the past year did not receive any specialty mental health care or treatment, affecting an estimated 2,331,000 young people nationwide, according to recent national data from Mental Health America's report.

The state-level prevalence of youth with MDE who did not receive mental health services varies significantly, ranging from a low of 32.60% in the District of Columbia (ranked 1, lightest shade) to a high of 77.10% in South Carolina (ranked 51, darkest shade). States with the lowest rates of untreated youth (generally ranked 1–13, lighter purple shades) include the District of Columbia (32.60%), Colorado (34.40%), New Hampshire (35.90%), Montana (37.10%), and New Mexico (38.30%), indicating relatively better access to care in these areas.

Rank	State	%	#
1	District of Columbia	32.60	1,000
2	Colorado	34.40	20,000
3	New Hampshire	35.90	6,000
4	Montana	37.10	5,000
5	New Mexico	38.30	11,000
6	Illinois	39.90	65,000
7	Connecticut	42.90	16,000
8	South Dakota	43.40	7,000
9	Utah	44.40	26,000
10	North Dakota	44.90	5,000
11	Idaho	47.80	18,000
12	Delaware	47.90	4,000
13	Maine	49.70	8,000
14	Wyoming	50.40	3,000
15	Nevada	50.70	22,000
16	Vermont	51.00	3,000
17	Louisiana	52.80	37,000
18	New York	53.10	105,000
19	Wisconsin	53.40	23,000
20	Alabama	53.50	31,000
21	Ohio	53.50	86,000
22	New Jersey	54.10	36,000
23	Mississippi	54.50	20,000
24	Pennsylvania	54.60	59,000
25	Arkansas	55.10	22,000
26	Alaska	55.60	6,000

Rank	State	%	#
27	Indiana	55.60	39,000
28	Arizona	55.90	51,000
29	Kansas	56.50	23,000
30	Iowa	56.50	25,000
31	Minnesota	56.80	54,000
32	Oklahoma	57.40	23,000
33	Washington	57.70	61,000
34	Maryland	59.20	47,000
35	Virginia	60.20	90,000
36	Michigan	60.30	71,000
37	North Carolina	61.70	64,000
38	Florida	61.80	146,000
39	Rhode Island	62.10	7,000
40	Nebraska	63.70	19,000
41	Massachusetts	63.90	47,000
42	Oregon	64.30	43,000
43	Missouri	65.30	49,000
44	Georgia	66.60	76,000
45	West Virginia	68.80	16,000
46	California	69.50	287,000
47	Tennessee	71.10	72,000
48	Kentucky	74.70	29,000
49	Hawaii	74.90	12,000
50	Texas	74.90	306,000
51	South Carolina	77.10	29,000
	National	59.80	2,331,000

Chart 2023 A8

In contrast, states with the highest rates of untreated youth (ranked 39–51, darker purple shades) include South Carolina (77.10%), Texas (74.90%), Kentucky (74.70%), Hawaii (74.90%, note: Hawaii is listed at 74.90% but ranked 49), and Tennessee (71.10%), showing much larger gaps in treatment access. The rate in the highest state (South Carolina) is more than double that of the lowest (District of Columbia), underscoring stark geographic disparities in youth mental health care.

Racial and ethnic disparities are also evident: Asian youth with MDE were least likely to receive care, with 78% going without services, followed closely by multiracial youth (68%) and Black or African American youth (68%). In specific states like Kentucky, Hawaii, and Texas, about three-quarters of youth with major depression did not receive treatment, while in South Carolina—the lowest-ranked state—nearly 8 in 10 affected youth went without care.

These patterns highlight clear regional and demographic trends: certain Northeastern and Western states (such as the District of Columbia, Colorado, and New Hampshire) show better treatment access, while Southern states like South Carolina, Texas, and Kentucky face the greatest barriers, compounded by racial inequities in who receives help.

Access to Mental Health Treatment

Access to mental health care remained a critical challenge. In 2022, 56.1% of U.S. teens with major depression (approximately 2.9 million) received no mental health support, such as therapy or medication, a trend that likely persisted into 2024. The share of untreated teens varied by state, ranging from 32.6% in Washington, D.C., to 77.1% in South Carolina, with three-quarters of teens in states like Kentucky, Hawaii, and Texas also going without treatment. Only 28% of teens with severe depression received consistent care (7–25+ visits per year). Common barriers included cost, stigma, and 86.9% of teens feeling they should handle problems independently.

2022–2025 PREVALENCE OF MENTAL HEALTH ISSUES AMONG TEENAGERS IN NEW YORK STATE/CITY

New York City (2022–2025 Trends)

- In the NYC Department of Health and Mental Hygiene's State of Mental Health reports (updated through 2024–2025), nearly half (48–50%) of surveyed NYC teenagers reported some level of depressive symptoms in 2023–2024 data: mild symptoms in about 27%, moderate in 14–16%, and severe in 11%. This is consistent with earlier 2022–2023 findings, where 50% of teens showed mild to severe depression symptoms.

- Among daily social media users (which includes ~90% of NYC teens regularly using at least one platform), 28% reported moderate to severe depressive symptoms in 2023–2024 surveys, with girls disproportionately affected by increased anxiety, loneliness, and body-image issues linked to heavy platform use.

- Persistent sadness or hopelessness among NYC high school students remained elevated (around 38–40% in 2021–2023 Youth Risk Behavior Survey data), with suicidal ideation and attempts higher than pre-pandemic levels in some years. However, 2024–2025 city-level tracking shows modest stabilization or slight declines in crisis calls and emergency department visits for youth mental health, likely due to expanded school-based therapists, teen mental health hotlines, and citywide anti-stigma campaigns.

- Adult psychological distress (a related proxy) dropped noticeably in NYC in 2024–2025 (anxiety/depression symptoms fell to ~18–19%

overall), suggesting broader recovery trends that may gradually benefit adolescents.

- In 2023, 50% of NYC teenagers surveyed reported mild to severe symptoms of depression, with 28% of daily social media users reporting moderate to severe depressive symptoms.

- A 2022 survey found 14% of adult New Yorkers experienced serious psychological distress (SPD), a proxy for mental health issues, with adolescents likely facing similar or higher rates due to social media and pandemic-related stressors.

- Social media use is a significant factor, with 90% of NYC teens using at least one platform regularly, linked to increased depression, anxiety, and loneliness, particularly among girls.

- Urban stressors unique to New York City may also contribute to adolescent mental health challenges. Factors such as crowded living conditions, academic competition, neighborhood safety concerns, and long commuting times to school can create chronic stress that affects emotional well-being. Teens living in high-density urban environments may have fewer quiet or private spaces to relax, study, or reflect, which can increase emotional strain over time.

- Another important factor is academic pressure. Many New York City students attend highly competitive schools where expectations for grades, college admission, and extracurricular achievement are extremely high. Constant comparison with high-achieving peers can increase anxiety and self-doubt, especially among students already vulnerable to depression.

New York State (2022–2025 Trends)

- In Mental Health America's 2025 State of Mental Health in America report (using primarily 2022–2023 data extended into 2024–2025 reporting), New York ranks highly (often #1 or top 5) in overall youth mental health, driven by lower prevalence of severe major depressive episode (MDE) with impairment and better access to care compared to most states.

- Youth MDE prevalence in New York remained around 16–17% in 2024–2025 estimates (affecting roughly 230,000–250,000 youth), with notable declines in serious suicidal thoughts and severe impairment observed from 2023 to 2025.

- Treatment gaps persisted: Approximately 55–57% of New York youth with major depression did not receive mental health services in 2024–2025 data, though this improved slightly from earlier years and performed better than the national average of ~60% untreated.

- Social media and digital stressors continued to contribute, but statewide initiatives (including social media safety regulations enacted in 2023–2024 and expanded school mental health programs through 2025) helped stabilize or reduce rates compared to peak pandemic levels in 2021–2022.

- Over 1 in 5 New Yorkers (including adolescents) experience mental disorder symptoms annually, with 1 in 10 facing challenges severe enough to impair functioning. Half of lifetime mental illness cases begin by age 14.

- According to the CDC, nearly 1 in 4 teens in NYS have considered suicide, with 1 in 3 teenage girls reporting this in 2023, a significant rise over the past decade.

- In 2022, the NYS Office of Mental Health (OMH) reported that mental health issues are a leading health challenge for children, with untreated disorders linked to school failure and disability.

Suicide is now one of the leading causes of death among adolescents in New York State, with rising rates particularly among youth of color and LGBTQ+ teens. Cultural attitudes toward mental health also influence treatment rates across New York State. In some communities, families may prefer handling emotional problems privately rather than seeking professional help, which can delay early intervention and allow symptoms to worsen.

Early identification programs in schools have become increasingly important across New York State. Screening programs and mental health awareness training for teachers help identify students at risk and connect them with services before crises develop.

Access to Mental Health Treatment in New York City:

NYC Teenspace: Launched in 2023, this free tele-mental health service for teenagers 13–17 served nearly 7,000 youth in its first six months, with 80% identifying as people of color from underserved neighborhoods. Of users, 65% reported symptom relief, and 64% noted improved mental health. The platform offers therapy via phone, video, and text, with 96% using text and over 40% using both text and video. Text-based therapy has proven especially effective for teens who are hesitant to speak openly, helping reduce stigma and increase engagement in mental health care.

School-Based Clinics: In 2024, NYC announced 16 new mental health clinics in public schools, serving over 20,000 students in high-need areas like the South Bronx and Central Brooklyn. An additional 34 schools have rapid referral access to NYC Health + Hospitals outpatient clinics. These initiatives are funded by a $5 million Mental Health Continuum partnership and $700,000 in state grants. School-based clinics reduce absenteeism, disciplinary actions, and emergency mental health crises by providing early, on-site intervention.

In 2022, 34% of NYC adults with mental health diagnoses reported unmet treatment needs due to cost, stigma, or access issues. Adolescents face similar barriers, with Asian New Yorkers accessing care the least.

A 2022 RAND study found that low geographic access to Medicaid-accepting facilities in parts of the Bronx, Queens, Staten Island, Manhattan, and Brooklyn results in poorer coverage.

Even when services are available, many teens do not know how to access them or may feel overwhelmed by the process of scheduling appointments, completing paperwork, or discussing mental health concerns with unfamiliar professionals. Simplifying referral systems and increasing awareness of available services can help reduce these practical barriers.

New York State: School-Based Mental Health Clinics: Governor Hochul's $1 billion mental health plan (2023–2024) funded 137 new school-based clinic satellites, bringing the statewide total to over 1,200.

In 2024, $20 million in startup funding was allocated to expand clinics to any school requesting one, with enhanced reimbursement rates for commercial insurance.

In May 2025, Hochul announced $4.5 million to establish 10 new Youth ACT teams (including five in NYC), building on earlier expansions to 42 teams across 31 counties (with 23 operational by 2025). The goal is to support around 360 additional youth, reduce reliance on inpatient care, and keep young people stable in their communities.

These large-scale investments reflect a broader shift in New York's mental health strategy—from crisis response to early intervention and community-based stabilization. By embedding services directly within schools and neighborhoods, the state aims to identify problems sooner and reduce the need for hospitalization. Research consistently shows that when treatment is delivered in familiar settings, such as schools, youth engagement and follow-through improve significantly.

Residential and Crisis Services: NYS offers Children's Community Residences (CCRs) and Residential Treatment Facilities (RTFs) for youth with complex needs, providing temporary supervised care and on-site treatment. Crisis residences stabilize acute distress with stays up to twenty-one days.

- In 2024, $30 million was allocated to expand residential treatment facilities, and $50 million to increase inpatient mental health services for children and adults.

- A 2024 survey by the NYS Attorney General found that 86% of listed in-network mental health providers were "ghosts" (unreachable, not in-network, or not accepting patients), severely limiting access.

The "ghost network" problem highlights a critical disconnect between insurance directories and real-world access to care. Even when families believe they have coverage, they may spend weeks calling providers who are unavailable, delaying urgent treatment for vulnerable youth. This administrative barrier often discourages families and increases the likelihood that teens' conditions worsen before they receive help.

- In 2025, $10 million was made available for Teen Mental Health First Aid training, using peer ambassadors to engage disconnected teens.

- The FY 2025 budget (enacted in 2024) allocated $55 million to create 200 new inpatient psychiatric beds at state-operated psychiatric facilities, with portions supporting youth and children's services as part of broader inpatient expansions.

- Additional investments included $18 million in capital and $30 million in operating funds to add 150 new inpatient beds in state-operated psychiatric hospitals, contributing to overall capacity growth for children and adults in crisis.

- Teen Mental Health First Aid Training (2025 Update) In January 2025, Governor Hochul announced $10 million available statewide to support Youth and Teen Mental Health First Aid training programs. This initiative empowers teachers, caregivers, parents, and teens themselves to recognize signs of mental health challenges, provide initial support, and connect peers to professional help. The funding aims to train thousands annually (including about 2,500 adults and teens per year in some projections) and create around 200 new instructors statewide each year. It has been expanded in high schools, with peer ambassadors engaging disconnected or at-risk teens to reduce stigma and promote early intervention.

- In January 2026 (reflecting 2025–2026 planning), Governor Hochul announced $43 million to expand inpatient and emergency psychiatric services statewide, including $20 million in capital and $3 million in start-up funding specifically for new or expanded Comprehensive Psychiatric Emergency Programs (CPEPs) serving children/youth or adding youth capacity to adult programs. This builds on prior efforts, such as a 2024 investment that established or expanded CPEPs receiving over 110,000 visits from October

2024 to September 2025. The expansion of Comprehensive Psychiatric Emergency Programs (CPEPs) reflects growing recognition that emergency mental health services must be specialized for youth. Adolescents experiencing psychiatric crises often require developmentally appropriate care, family involvement, and trauma-informed approaches that differ significantly from adult emergency treatment models.

Barriers to Access

New York City:

- **Geographic Disparities:** Areas like the northern Bronx, eastern Queens, and Staten Island have fewer Medicaid-accepting facilities, limiting access for low-income teens.

- **Stigma and Cost:** Stigma, high costs, and lack of awareness prevent many teens from seeking care. Daily social media use (90% of teens) exacerbates mental health issues, yet only half of those with symptoms access treatment.

- **Provider Shortages:** Low reimbursement rates and inaccurate provider directories ("ghost networks") hinder access, particularly for insured teens seeking in-network care.

New York State:

- **Insurance and Provider Issues:** The "ghost network" problem affects statewide access, with only 14% of listed providers offering in-network appointments.

- **Workforce Shortages:** A lack of child psychiatrists and youth-trained clinicians is a persistent issue. Hochul's 2024 loan repayment program aims to address this, but shortages remain.

- **Stigma and Delays:** Stigma and delayed recognition of symptoms result in care access nine years after issues emerge, on average.

- **Rural Access:** Rural areas face greater provider shortages and longer travel distances to facilities compared to urban areas like NYC.

Key Initiatives and Policy Efforts

New York City:

- Care, Community, Action (2023): NYC's mental health agenda focuses on youth through Teenspace, school-based clinics, and social media education.

- Telehealth Expansion: Teenspace and telehealth strategies address access gaps, though quality concerns persist.

- State of Mental Health Report (2024): The first-ever report tracks mental health across age groups, highlighting teen resilience (69% report high/medium resilience) but persistent treatment gaps.

- Care, Community, Action (2025): NYC's mental health agenda continued as an ongoing plan from 2023 under the Mayor's Office of Community Mental Health, focusing on youth through Teenspace telehealth, school-based clinics via the Mental Health Continuum partnership, and expanded community supports—including crisis respite centers (now 11 citywide, with $3 million allocated in the FY2026 budget).

- Telehealth Expansion: Teenspace, the free virtual therapy program for NYC teens ages 13–17 powered by Talkspace, stayed active and promoted in 2025–2026, providing unlimited messaging plus scheduled sessions with licensed therapists for issues like anxiety, depression, and stress; the program was extended through at least November 2026 and featured in school and youth resources.

Additional 2025 Highlights for NYC Youth and Mental Health:

- Emphasis on school-based mental health clinics, with expansions through the Mental Health Continuum partnership (DOE, NYC Health + Hospitals, DOHMH) and new clinics serving thousands of students.

- Crisis infrastructure growth, including B-HEARD (911 mental health response), handling nearly 35,000 calls through June 2025; in November 2025, Mayor Adams announced its transition to full operation by NYC Health + Hospitals (effective spring 2026) for a streamlined, health-led model, reassigning FDNY EMTs to improve general emergency response times.

- State-level impacts on NYC: Opening of a new 21-bed youth inpatient psychiatric facility at NYC Children's Center (Bronx, November 2025), five new Youth Assertive Community Treatment teams in NYC (May 2025), and supportive housing expansions.

New York State:

- **Social Media Protections (2025):** Governor Hochul advanced protections against social media harms by signing legislation in December 2025 requiring warning labels on platforms with addictive features (such as infinite scroll and autoplay) to alert young users to mental health risks. This was built on the SAFE for Kids Act (passed in 2024, with proposed rules issued in 2025), which restricts addictive feeds and notifications for minors without parental consent, while continuing to provide educational resources for caregivers and issuing digital safety proclamations.

- **Crisis and Access Expansions (2025):** In May 2025, $4.5 million was allocated for 10 new Youth Assertive Community Treatment (ACT) teams statewide, serving youth with serious emotional disturbances who are at risk of or transitioning from high-intensity care. Broader investments included $20 million for Project RISE in December 2025, supporting violence prevention, youth development, and mental health services in targeted communities.

- **State-level youth-focused highlights (2025–2026):** In the 2025–2026 State of the State address, Governor Hochul proposed several first-in-the-nation initiatives, including mandatory Teen Mental Health First Aid training for all 10th graders, expanded youth clubhouses, and stronger online protections against predators, scammers, and harmful AI content. The ongoing $1 billion mental health investment continued to deliver results, such as additional inpatient beds, increased supportive housing, and expanded school-based services to address the youth behavioral health crisis.

- **Governor Hochul's $1 Billion Plan (2023–2024):** Includes school-based clinics, Youth ACT, residential treatment expansion, and workforce development.

- **Youth Mental Health Advisory Board (2024):** Engages teens in shaping mental health policies, following a 2023 statewide listening tour.

- **988 Suicide & Crisis Lifeline:** Implemented in 2022, it provides immediate support via call, text, or chat.

Rising Demand For Services (Updated In 2025)

The youth mental health crisis in New York City continued to be severe in 2025, with persistently high levels of sadness, hopelessness, and suicide-related behaviors fueling greater demand for services. Vulnerable populations—including LGBTQ+ teens (who often experience rates 2–3 times higher), racially minoritized youth (such as Latino and Black students, who show elevated prevalence), and those in low-income or underserved communities—faced disproportionately greater challenges and barriers to accessing care.

The youth mental health crisis intensified, with hospital visits for mental health issues among teens increasing by 124% from 2016 to 2022. Vulnerable groups, including LGBTQ+ teens, Native American teens, and those in low-income or rural areas, faced greater mental health challenges and had less access to care.

One significant but often overlooked driver of rising demand is the shortage of child and adolescent psychiatrists. New York, like much of the country, faces a workforce gap in youth mental health specialists, leading to extended wait times for evaluations and medication management. In some areas, families report waiting several months for an initial psychiatric appointment, delaying critical early intervention.

- **In 2023** (latest NYC Youth Risk Behavior Survey data, cited in 2025 reports), 35% of public high school students reported persistent sadness or hopelessness interfering with daily activities (down slightly from 38% in 2021 but up from 27% in 2013). Suicidal ideation rose to 18% and suicide attempts to 14% (from 9.2% in 2021), per the NYC Health Department's September 2025 Epi Data Brief. These upward trends from 2013 to 2023 continued to drive high post-COVID service demand.

- Among middle school students, persistent sadness and hopelessness reached 48% in 2022 (up from 34% in 2018), with similar increases in non-suicidal self-injury, suicidal ideation, and attempts; these trends were further detailed in the 2025 Epi Data Brief.

- **A December 2025 NYC Comptroller Brad Lander report** called the youth mental health crisis in public schools a "record high," with nearly 40% of high school students reporting persistent sadness or hopelessness, the highest in over a decade. It highlighted fragmented care, severe staffing shortages (e.g., 70% of schools below national social worker standards), and unequal access, leaving many needs unmet.

- **Social media continued as a major contributing factor:** Nearly 90% of teens used it daily, with heavy use strongly linked to higher levels of depression and anxiety. 2025 reports and resources consistently highlighted the connection between excessive social media engagement and moderate-to-severe depressive symptoms, further increasing demand for services amid ongoing pandemic-related and societal stressors.

New York City

Increased Prevalence Driving Demand:

- In 2023, 50% of NYC teenagers surveyed reported mild to severe depressive symptoms, with 28% of daily social media users (90% of teens) experiencing moderate to severe depression, indicating a significant mental health burden fueling demand for services.

- A 2022 survey found 14% of NYC adults experienced serious psychological distress (SPD), with adolescents likely facing higher rates due to social media and pandemic stressors, further driving service needs.

- In 2021, 38% of NYC high school students reported persistent sadness or hopelessness that disrupted normal activities, with 9.2% attempting suicide in the past year, per the 2021 Youth Risk Behavior Survey. These figures, though slightly pre-2022, were cited in 2023 reports as evidence of sustained high demand post-COVID.

Service Utilization and Demand (Updates from 2025)

- **NYC Teenspace:** The program continued to experience strong demand in 2025. Figures from late 2024 (still cited in 2025 promotions) showed over 16,000 teens had enrolled and received services, with approximately 65% reporting mental health improvements. Representation from underserved communities remained high, and Teenspace was actively promoted in 2025 school communications and youth resources, despite persistent privacy concerns raised by advocacy groups.

- **Systemic Indicators of Demand:** The December 2025 report from NYC Comptroller Brad Lander labeled the youth mental health crisis in public schools a "record high," noting that close to 40% of high school students experienced persistent sadness or hopelessness—the highest rate in more than ten years. It pointed to severe staffing shortages (over 70% of schools falling short of national social worker benchmarks, requiring approximately 2,137 additional social workers and 1,220 guidance counselors at an estimated annual cost of $402–$426 million), fragmented service delivery, and persistent inequities in access that left substantial needs unaddressed.

Service Utilization and Demand (2023-2024)

- **NYC Teenspace:** This free online therapy program for teens aged 13–17 (powered by Talkspace and launched in 2023) continued to be very popular in 2025. By the end of 2024 (numbers still used in 2025 reports and hearings), more than 19,000 NYC teens had signed up, and over 16,000 had actually received help. Many users came from underserved neighborhoods (over 80% identified as people of color in some reports), and about 65% said their symptoms improved. The program was still actively promoted in schools and youth resources in 2025, though some advocacy groups continued to raise concerns about privacy and data sharing.

- **School-Based Mental Health Clinics:** In March 2025, New York City opened 16 new mental health clinics in public schools as part of the Mental Health Continuum partnership (between the Department of Education, NYC Health + Hospitals, and the Department of Health and Mental Hygiene). These clinics directly helped more than 6,000 students in high-need areas such as the South Bronx and Central Brooklyn. Overall, the program supported over 20,000 students across 50 schools with counseling, quick referrals to outside services, staff training, and crisis help. Funding stayed temporary at about $5 million for FY2026, creating worries about long-term stability due to staffing shortages and calls from advocates for steady, permanent funding.

- **A 2022 RAND report** showed that many people in NYC needed mental health help but weren't getting it. This pattern continued in 2025. The December 2025 report by NYC Comptroller Brad Lander pointed out that demand for services far exceeded what was available, due to broken systems, not enough staff, and unequal access—especially in underserved parts of the city—leaving many young people without the support they needed in schools.

Systemic Indicators of Demand (2022–2025):

- In 2025, ongoing inequities in access to youth mental health treatment and growing demand for services in New York City were clearly documented in multiple authoritative sources. The Mayor's Office of Community Mental Health (OCMH) published its 2025 Annual Report in February, which noted continued advancements while pointing out major remaining gaps in equitable care.

- The OCMH white paper "Bridging the Gap," released in January, examined key challenges in the behavioral health workforce. Meanwhile, the December 2025 report by NYC Comptroller Brad Lander on youth mental health in public schools highlighted fragmented care delivery, widespread unmet needs, and a notably high rate of persistent sadness or hopelessness among high school students, approximately 40%, marking the highest level seen in more than ten years.

- The 2024 NYC State of Mental Health Report highlighted deep inequities in treatment access despite rising demand, with teens showing resilience (69% reported high/medium resilience) but high worry (90% among daily social media users), underscoring the need for expanded services.

- Workforce shortages and low Medicaid acceptance exacerbate unmet demand, with informants in a 2022 study noting that increased service needs post-COVID overwhelmed providers, particularly for non-English-speaking teens.

New York State

Increased Prevalence Driving Demand (Updated for 2025)

- The most recent data (from 2022–2024 national surveys, summarized in 2025 reports by NAMI and Mental Health America) show that about 21.3% of New York adults—more than 3.2 million people—experience any mental illness each year. Around 5.2–5.6% (roughly 800,000–900,000 adults) have serious mental illness (SMI). For young adults aged 18–25, mental health issues remain common at higher rates. However, recent national trends for youth are improving slightly: major depressive episodes and serious thoughts of suicide among teens aged 12–17 have decreased (for example, serious suicidal thoughts dropped to about 10% nationally in 2024).

- Suicide continues to be a leading concern (2025): It ranks as the third leading cause of death for ages 10–24 in New York State. The 2025 Prevention Agenda updates and OMH references cite 2023 YRBSS data showing 18.5% of high school students statewide seriously considered suicide in the past year, and 10.9% attempted suicide. New York maintains one of the lowest overall suicide rates nationally (~7.9 per 100,000), but risks remain high for youth, especially among LGBTQ+ teens and certain racial/ethnic groups.

- In 2025, over 20% of New Yorkers experience mental health symptoms each year, and half of all lifetime disorders begin by age 14. According to Mental Health America's 2025 report, New York ranks #1 nationwide for overall mental health due to lower prevalence and strong access to care. However, youth service demand remains high because of COVID-19 impacts, social media pressures, and inequities. Nationally, youth major depressive episodes declined to 15.4% in 2024 (from 18.1%), and serious suicidal thoughts dropped to 10.1% (from 12.3%), showing progress but ongoing need for support.

- The CDC reported in 2023 that nearly 25% of NYS teens had considered suicide, with 33% of teenage girls reporting this, a significant rise over the past decade, driving urgent demand for crisis and preventive services.

Service Utilization and Demand (New York State—Updates from 2025)

- Mental health continued to be a major issue for children and teens in 2025, with untreated problems often leading to school struggles and higher risks. The Office of Mental Health (OMH) focused on early help by expanding Youth Safe Spaces (peer-led programs for ages 12–24), rolling out Youth and Teen Mental Health First Aid training statewide ($10 million funded early 2025), and strengthening community-based supports.

- In 2025, New York State expanded its public mental health system by adding over 1,000 psychiatric beds, including new youth beds, like the 21-bed unit at NYC Children's Center that opened in November 2025. Teens and young people used these services a lot, thanks to more awareness, easier eligibility, and stronger early intervention efforts.

- **School-Based Clinics:** Governor Hochul's $1 billion mental health plan and 2025–2026 priorities kept focusing on school-based mental health services. This included plans to add Teen Mental Health First Aid training and support for any school requesting help. Teen usage stayed high, but no new specific numbers for added clinics were reported in 2025 beyond earlier expansions.

- **Youth Assertive Community Treatment (ACT):** In May 2025, $4.5 million funded 10 new Youth ACT teams (5 in NYC, 2 on Long Island, 3 upstate), serving ~360 additional youth with serious emotional disturbances through multidisciplinary wraparound care (therapy, crisis support, community-based intensive services), reflecting strong demand for these supports.

- **The 988 Suicide & Crisis Lifeline:** Usage remained high in 2025, with continued integration into youth crisis resources. Funding increased (e.g., $60 million in FY2025 budget), maintaining strong in-state answer rates (~90%) and emphasis on youth diversion and follow-up, amid sustained crisis demand.

Service Utilization and Demand (2022–2024):

- From 2013 to 2022, the NYS public mental health system saw a 23% increase in individuals served, reaching nearly 900,000 residents, with adolescents contributing significantly due to expanded eligibility and awareness.

- The NYS Office of Mental Health (OMH) reported in 2022 that mental health issues are a leading health challenge for children, with untreated disorders linked to school failure and increasing demand for early intervention services.

- School-Based Clinics: Governor Hochul's $1 billion mental health plan (2022–2024) added 137 school-based clinic satellites in 2023, bringing the total to over 1,200, with high utilization reflecting teen demand. In 2024, $20 million was allocated to further expand clinics to any requesting school.

- **Youth Assertive Community Treatment (ACT):** Expanded in 2024, this program saw increased uptake for wraparound care (therapy, crisis support) among teens, indicating demand for intensive community-based services.

- The 988 Suicide & Crisis Lifeline, implemented in 2022, saw significant use among teens, with the 2024 OMH report detailing high call/text volumes, reflecting crisis service demand.

Systemic Indicators of Demand (Updates in 2025)

- In 2025, the capacity concerns were addressed through continued expansions under Governor Hochul. More than 1,000 psychiatric beds have been added statewide since she took office, including 125 new beds announced for state-operated centers in April 2025 and a new 21-bed youth unit at NYC Children's Center that opened in November 2025. These additions helped ease earlier shortages and reduced pressure on inpatient services.

- The 2024 New York Health Foundation report indicated a 40% decrease in self-reported anxiety and depression symptoms (dropping from 31.9% in July 2023 to 18.9% in July 2024), though 24.4% of adults aged 18–34 (including older teens) continued to report these symptoms. No comparable statewide survey was published in 2025, but demand for youth mental health services remained strong, as evidenced by ongoing reports from the Office of Mental Health (OMH) and the NYC Comptroller highlighting high levels of persistent sadness or hopelessness and ongoing unmet needs among young people.

- **Workforce shortages and "ghost networks"** continued to restrict access in 2025, especially in rural areas and for underserved communities. New rules effective July 2025 required health plans to offer initial outpatient behavioral health appointments within 10 business days, keep provider directories current and accurate, remove misleading information, and provide dedicated staff to assist with finding in-network providers—all aimed at cutting down ghost networks and boosting access. Ongoing shortages were highlighted in reports like the OCMH "Bridging the Gap" white paper (January 2025) and national forecasts, with demand still exceeding available supply in many regions.

Systemic Indicators of Demand (2022–2024):

- A 2024 Comptroller report noted a 10.5% drop in inpatient psychiatric beds (990 beds lost from 2014–2023) despite a 23% rise in demand, with only 222 of 843 offline beds reopened by April 2023, highlighting capacity strain.

- The 2024 New York Health Foundation report showed a 40% drop in reported anxiety/depression symptoms from July 2023 (31.9%) to July 2024 (18.9%), but 24.4% of 18–34-year-olds (including older teens) still reported symptoms, sustaining demand.

- Workforce shortages and "ghost networks" (86% of listed providers unreachable in 2024) limit service access, with demand outpacing supply, especially in rural areas.

Key Drivers of Rising Demand (Both NYC and NYS—Updates from 2025)

- **COVID-19 Impact:** The effects of the pandemic still affected young people's mental health in 2025. Things like feeling alone, money worries, sadness from loss, and big changes in life kept causing high levels of sadness and hopelessness (for example, about 40% of high school students in NYC, according to the December

2025 Comptroller report). Both NYC and New York State worked on early help to fix these ongoing problems.

- **Social Media:** In 2025, daily social media use remained a big stressor for teens. Nearly 90% used it heavily every day, and it was linked to more depression, anxiety, loneliness, body image problems, and addiction-like habits. In NYC, heavy use was tied to worse depressive symptoms. Statewide, Governor Hochul signed a law in December 2025 requiring warning labels on apps with addictive features (like endless scrolling or auto-play) to warn young users about mental health risks, building on earlier SAFE for Kids Act rules.

- **Awareness and Destigmatization:** In 2025, greater awareness and less stigma encouraged more young people to seek mental health help. Key efforts included the Youth Safe Spaces program (funding awarded in September 2025 for peer-led, non-clinical support for ages 12–24) and the statewide rollout of Youth and Teen Mental Health First Aid training ($10 million announced early 2025), which promoted wellness, self-advocacy, and easier access to services.

- **School and Community Stressors**: Academic pressure, bullying, exposure to violence, and fragmented care continued to increase demand in 2025. The NYC Comptroller's December 2025 report described a "record-high" youth mental health crisis in public schools, with nearly 40% of high school students reporting persistent sadness or hopelessness—the highest rate in over a decade—tied to staffing shortages, unequal access, and broader societal pressures. In New York State, efforts focused on creating safe spaces and community supports to reduce isolation and build positive relationships.

Limitations and Data Gaps (Updates from 2025)

- NYC data mainly focuses on teens (e.g., Teenspace and Youth Risk Behavior Survey trends cited in 2025 reports) but lacks a comprehensive new citywide survey on teen service utilization after 2023; the December 2025 Comptroller report provided important insights on school mental health needs while pointing out fragmented systems and transparency problems.

- NYS data includes teens but often aggregates them with young adults (ages 18–25), limiting teen-specific metrics. Rural demand is less documented than in urban areas, though 2025 efforts by the Office of Mental Health (OMH) focused on improving access in local communities.

- Parental reporting and surveys may underestimate teen symptoms, while provider shortages and "ghost networks" (inaccurate directories) continue to skew perceived access.

Limitations and Data Gaps (Updates from 2022–2024)

- NYC data is often adolescent-specific (e.g., Teenspace, Youth Risk Behavior Survey) but lacks comprehensive 2024 updates for citywide teen service utilization.

- NYS data includes teens but often aggregates with young adults (18–25), limiting teen-specific metrics. Rural demand is less documented than urban.

- Parental reporting (e.g., 2022 Household Pulse Survey) may underestimate teen symptoms, while provider shortages skew reported access.

- "Ghost network" issues inflate perceived service availability, masking true demand.

TEENAGERS' DEPRESSION (MDE) IN THE U.S. (2022–2025)

Depression is a common mental health issue that causes long-lasting sadness, hopelessness, and a loss of interest in daily life, affecting millions of people in the U.S. It's one of the top mental health problems for both adults and teens. According to Mental Health America's State of Mental Health in America 2025 report (using 2024 NSDUH data), about 15.4% of U.S. youth aged 12–17 experienced at least one major depressive episode (MDE) in the past year (down from 18.1% in 2023). This equates to millions affected, with 11.3% experiencing MDE with severe impairment (severely impacting school, work, or home life)—an estimated 2.8 million youth. The report notes gradual national declines in youth MDEs and serious suicidal thoughts (from 12.3% in 2023 to 10.1% in 2024), though many still go untreated.

While these slight declines are encouraging, experts caution that depression rates among adolescents remain significantly higher than they were a decade ago, suggesting that today's youth are navigating more complex social, academic, and digital pressures than previous generations.

The Substance Abuse and Mental Health Services Administration (SAMHSA) 2024 NSDUH (released 2025) confirms a decline in past-year MDEs among teens aged 12–17 to 15.4% (from higher rates like 20.8% in 2021), representing about 1.4 million fewer affected teens compared to prior peaks. Severe impairment from depression remains a concern for a subset. The CDC's Youth Risk Behavior Survey trends (latest 2023 data, referenced in 2025 reports) show persistent challenges: About 40% of high school students reported ongoing sadness or hopelessness (with early signs of slight improvement from 2021 peaks), and depression symptoms were higher in females (e.g., 26.5% in ages 12–19 per 2021–2023 NHANES data) and certain groups like LGBTQ+ youth.

Gender differences in depression are believed to be influenced by both biological and social factors. Hormonal changes during adolescence, combined with higher exposure to social comparison and relational stress, may partially explain why girls report higher rates of depressive symptoms. However, boys may underreport emotional distress, which can result in underdiagnosis.

In 2024, Mental Health America (MHA) found that about 20.17% of U.S. teens, or roughly 5.22 million, had at least one major depressive episode (MDE). Around 15% of these teens struggled significantly with daily tasks like school, work, or home life due to their depression. The rate of MDEs varied across states, from 16.02% in Washington, D.C. (5,000 teens) to almost 25% in Oregon (76,000 teens). MHA also reported that 56.1% of teens with MDEs got no mental health help, such as therapy or medication.

In 2023, about 8.4% of U.S. teens aged 12–17 were diagnosed with depression, but the real number might be higher because some cases are not reported. Symptoms like feeling tired, having trouble focusing, being irritable, or avoiding friends can make school and relationships tough for young people. Depression often starts in the teen years or early adulthood, and it's hard to identify in teens since it can look like normal mood changes. Getting help early with things like talking to a counselor, making lifestyle changes, or taking medication is important to manage symptoms and feel better.

According to MHA's 2023 State of Mental Health Report, about 11.5% of U.S. youth, or more than 2.7 million teens, faced severe depression. The rates of severe MDEs ranged from a low of 5.2% in South Carolina to a high of 19.9% in South Dakota. Multiracial (Polyethnic) teens had the highest rates of severe depression in 2023, with 16.5% affected, or about 123,000 individuals. In 2022, the Substance Abuse and Mental Health Services Administration (SAMHSA) reported that 19.5% of U.S. teens, or 4.8 million, experienced an MDE. Of those, 14.6% (3.6 million teens) had severe symptoms that disrupted their daily lives. White teens had the highest MDE rates at 21%, followed by Hispanic teens at 19.5%, and multiracial teens at 19.1%. Cultural, socioeconomic, and environmental stressors may contribute to these disparities. Experiences such as discrimination, community violence, economic instability, and limited access to culturally responsive mental health services can increase vulnerability among certain racial and ethnic groups. Addressing these broader social determinants of health is essential for reducing long-term inequities in adolescent depression rates.

Statistics On Treatment Rates Among Teenagers With Depression In The U.S.

Depression treatment rates among U.S. teens remain a major concern, with many not receiving care despite high needs. The most recent data come from reputable sources like the Substance Abuse and Mental Health Services Administration (SAMHSA) 2024 National Survey on Drug Use and Health (NSDUH, released in 2025) and Mental Health America (MHA)'s State of Mental Health in America 2025 report (using 2024 NSDUH data).

In 2024, among U.S. adolescents aged 12–17 who experienced a major depressive episode (MDE) in the past year, 60.6% (approximately 2.3 million teens) received some form of mental health treatment, leaving about 39.4% without any treatment. Overall, 28.5% of all adolescents in this age group (roughly 7.4 million) received any mental health care during the year, regardless of diagnosis. According to Mental Health America's 2025 report (based on 2024 data), among teens who did receive treatment for a major depressive episode, 65% found it at least somewhat helpful, and 36% described it as very or extremely effective. However, perceived helpfulness varied widely by location: Washington, D.C. had the highest rate at 84.6%, while Iowa had the lowest at 32.5%, creating a 52 percentage-point gap between the top and bottom states. These figures reflect both some progress in treatment access and persistent barriers for many teens.

The variation in perceived effectiveness may reflect differences in provider availability, appointment wait times, insurance coverage, and access to specialized child and adolescent mental health professionals. In some areas, long waitlists and workforce shortages can delay care for months, reducing the likelihood of early intervention.

In 2023, MHA reported that just 28% of teens with severe depression got regular treatment, meaning they had 7 to 25 visits in a year. Even in the best state, South Dakota, only 58% of teens received this minimum level of care. Moreover, 59.8% of teens with major depression received no mental health care at all in 2023, and 14.7% only saw a doctor 1 to 6 times the whole year. Asian teens were the least likely to get help, with 78% missing out on depression treatment, followed by multiracial and African American teens, both at 68%. In states like Kentucky, Hawaii, and Texas, about 75% of teens with depression didn't get treatment, and in South Carolina, nearly 80% went without proper care. In 2022, almost half (48.3%) of teens with major depression said they didn't receive the mental health care they needed. The top reason? A whopping 86.9% felt they had to handle their mental health on their own.

Teen Depression in New York State and New York City (2022–2025)

Prevalence of Teen Depression in New York City (2022–2025):

According to a 2023 report from the New York City Department of Health and Mental Hygiene, published in the inaugural State of Mental Health of New Yorkers, 48% of NYC teens reported depressive symptoms in 2023. These ranged from mild (27%) to severe (11%), indicating a substantial mental health challenge among adolescents. Moreover, 28% of teens who used social media daily experienced moderate to severe depression symptoms, due to the influence of social media on mental health.

In 2022, 14% of adult New Yorkers reported serious psychological distress, up from 5% before the pandemic, reflecting a broader mental health crisis that likely affected teens. By 2023, this figure dropped to 8%, suggesting a gradual recovery that may extend to adolescents. Among children aged 3–13 in NYC, 3% had diagnosed depression in 2021, compared to 8% with anxiety, indicating that depression is present even in younger age groups and may increase in prevalence among teenagers.

New York State (2022–2025):

A 2024 New York Health Foundation report found that 31.5% of New Yorkers reported poor mental health in March 2023, an increase from 26.0% in March 2020, driven by the ongoing effects of the COVID-19 pandemic. Among young adults (ages 18–34), 24.4% reported anxiety and/or depression in early 2024, double the rate of older adults (12.3% for ages 65+). However, data focuses on young adults, suggesting that teens (ages 12–17) likely face similar or higher rates due to their susceptibility to social and environmental stressors. From 2023 to 2024, symptoms of anxiety and/or depression decreased for some groups, notably those with household incomes of $50,000–$99,999 (from 32.3% to 13.5%). However, disparities remained, with Hispanic New Yorkers reporting the highest rates of poor mental health (25.3% in 2024). These patterns likely influence teens, as family income and racial/ethnic disparities are known to impact adolescent mental health.

The U.S. National Context Relevant to New York (2023–2025):

In the U.S. national context relevant to New York, recent data from 2024–2025 sources indicate a slight easing in some youth mental health metrics compared to earlier peaks, though rates remain elevated and concerning—particularly for depressive symptoms and major depressive episodes (MDE) among adolescents.

According to the Mental Health America (MHA) State of Mental Health in America 2025 report and SAMHSA's National Survey on Drug Use and Health (NSDUH) 2024 (released in 2025), the percentage of U.S. youth aged 12–17 experiencing at least one major depressive episode in the past year decreased from 18.10% in 2023 to 15.40% in 2024 (approximately 3.8 million adolescents), with 11.30% (about 2.8 million) facing severe impairment that significantly affected functioning at school, work, or home. This decline represents a positive trend since higher rates like 20.8% in 2021, though New York's rates are typically moderate to high based on state variations (e.g., historically higher in states like Oregon at around 25%, lower in the District of Columbia at around 16%).

Despite the national decline, researchers note that depressive episodes among adolescents remain significantly higher than pre-2016 baselines, suggesting that structural stressors—such as academic pressure, economic instability, and social media exposure—continue to shape youth mental health nationwide. Urban states like New York may also face added pressures related to the cost of living, overcrowded schools, and service demand exceeding provider capacity.

For diagnosed depression, the National Survey of Children's Health (NSCH) data through 2023 (latest detailed in 2024–2025 analyses) shows that 8.4% of adolescents aged 12–17 had a current diagnosis, with females more affected (10.9%) than males (6.0%)—a 45% increase from 5.8% in 2016—highlighting ongoing growth in diagnosed cases.

A 2024 KFF analysis of the Teen National Health Interview Survey (July 2021–December 2022) found that 17% of U.S. adolescents aged 12–17 reported depressive symptoms in the past two weeks, with females (25%) more than twice as likely as males (10%) to report these symptoms. This aligns with the elevated rates of depressive symptoms among NYC teens, particularly young girls.

The CDC's 2023 Youth Risk Behavior Survey (YRBS) further reports that 39.7%–40% of high school students experienced persistent feelings of sadness or hopelessness (down slightly from 42% in 2021, with females at 52.6%–53% and LGBTQ+ youth at 65.7%), 28.5% had poor mental health, 20.4% seriously considered suicide, and 9.5% attempted it. These national figures underscore persistent challenges, with gender disparities (females higher), protective factors like family and school support linked to lower risks, and some recovery signals in 2024.

Anxiety Disorder

Anxiety disorders involve intense, persistent feelings of worry, fear, or nervousness that can significantly interfere with daily life, making them one of the most common mental health challenges for both adults and teens in the United States. Recent 2024–2025 data confirm that anxiety remains highly prevalent among adolescents, with lifetime estimates from the

National Institute of Mental Health (NIMH) indicating that about 31.9% of U.S. adolescents (ages 13–18) have experienced any anxiety disorder, higher among females (38.0%) than males (26.1%), and often with severe impairment in around 8.3% of cases.

Current symptoms and diagnosed rates also stay elevated. According to SAMHSA's NSDUH 2024 (released 2025), nearly 1 in 5 adolescents aged 12–17 reported moderate or severe generalized anxiety disorder (GAD) symptoms in the past two weeks (18.8%: 10.6% moderate, 8.2% severe), a new measure underscoring ongoing burden. CDC data from the National Health Interview Survey–Teen (NHIS-Teen, 2021–2023, referenced in 2025 updates) show about 20% of teens aged 12–17 experienced anxiety symptoms in the past two weeks, with females disproportionately affected—aligning with patterns in NYC and broader youth trends.

Short-term symptom reporting is particularly important because anxiety often fluctuates in intensity. Even when not meeting full diagnostic criteria, moderate symptoms can impair concentration, sleep quality, and peer relationships, contributing to academic decline and social withdrawal.

Diagnosed anxiety affects around 11% of children ages 3–17 (per NSCH/CDC), often beginning early (e.g., specific phobias, the most common type, around age 7). Contributing factors like academic pressure, social media, bullying, and lingering post-pandemic effects continue to drive these high levels, while adult anxiety/depression symptoms have declined more noticeably (e.g., from 34% in late 2023 to 21% in April 2024 per CDC). Treatment gaps persist, with only about 1 in 4 people with anxiety disorders receiving care.

Teen Anxiety Disorders in New York State and New York City (2022–2024)

Prevalence of Teen Anxiety Disorders Among Children and Teens

- According to the 2023 National Survey of Children's Health (NSCH), 11% of New York children and adolescents aged 3–17 had a diagnosed anxiety disorder in 2022–2023. This includes 12% of females and 9% of males. Nationally, 21% of teens aged 12–17 reported anxiety symptoms in the past two weeks (2021–2022, Teen National Health Interview Survey), and New York's rates are likely similar.

- A 2024 New York Health Foundation report found that 24.4% of young adults (ages 18–34) in New York reported anxiety and/or depression in early 2024, compared to 12.3% of older adults. Teens may face similar or higher rates due to stressors like school pressure and social media. Hispanic New Yorkers reported the highest rates of poor mental health (25.3%), indicating disparities that likely impact teens.

- **National Trends Relevant to New York:** A 2024 KFF analysis of the NHIS-Teen (2021–2022) showed that 21% of U.S. teens aged 12–17 experienced anxiety symptoms, with higher rates among females (31%) and LGBTQ+ teens (43%). These trends likely mirror New York's diverse, urban teen population, especially in New York City.

- The 2024 Mental Health America report noted that 31.9% of U.S. youth aged 13–18 have an anxiety disorder, with untreated cases at risk for issues like poor school performance, social isolation, and substance abuse. New York's rates are likely similar, with urban areas like NYC potentially facing higher rates due to environmental stressors.

- **Impact of COVID-19:** The COVID-19 pandemic significantly increased stress for teens in New York State and New York City. Trilliant Health (2023) reported a 107.4% increase in behavioral health visits (including anxiety and depression) from 2018 to 2022, with teens aged 15–19 being the most affected population. Social isolation, grief, and economic challenges were major contributing factors.

Teen and Child Anxiety in New York City (2022–2023)

- **Anxiety in Children and Teens:** The 2023 State of Mental Health of New Yorkers report by the New York City Department of Health and Mental Hygiene identified anxiety as the most common mental health diagnosis among children aged 3–13, with 8% diagnosed with anxiety in 2021, compared to 3% with depression. In addition, this data focuses on younger children; it suggests anxiety is prevalent in preadolescents and likely increases among teens (ages 12–17) due to developmental and social pressures. The report noted that most NYC teens worry about the future or fear something bad happening to themselves or their families, which may indicate anxiety symptoms, though specific teen prevalence data was not provided.

- **Co-occurring Mental Health Issues:** A 2023 survey found that 48% of NYC teens reported depressive symptoms. Given that nearly half of individuals with depression also have an anxiety disorder, a significant portion of these teens report experiencing anxiety symptoms.

- **Post-Pandemic:** In 2022, 14% of NYC adults reported serious psychological distress, a sharp rise from 5% pre-pandemic, likely reflecting similar challenges among teens, including anxiety. By 2023, adult distress dropped to 8%, indicating some recovery, but teens continued to face difficulties due to ongoing factors like social media use and post-pandemic adjustment.

Bipolar Disorder

Bipolar disorder is a serious mental health condition characterized by extreme mood swings, including manic or hypomanic highs (euphoric, irritable, or energetic states) and depressive lows (profound sadness, hopelessness, or low energy). These episodes can severely impair daily functioning, relationships, school or work performance, and elevate suicide risk—often 10–30 times higher than in peers without the condition for affected teens. Teens may present atypically, with irritability, destructive outbursts, or mixed symptoms rather than classic euphoria during mania, complicating diagnosis due to overlap with depression, ADHD, anxiety, or disruptive mood dysregulation disorder.

Because symptoms can fluctuate rapidly during adolescence, bipolar disorder is sometimes misdiagnosed initially as major depressive disorder. This is especially concerning because antidepressant treatment alone, without mood stabilization, can potentially trigger manic episodes in vulnerable youth. Careful longitudinal assessment is therefore critical in distinguishing bipolar disorder from other mood conditions.

In the United States, the most reliable statistics from the National Institute of Mental Health (NIMH) (based on the National Comorbidity Survey Replication for adults and NCS-A for adolescents) show no major updates from new national surveys in 2025 or 2026, altering the established benchmarks. For adults aged 18 and older, past-year prevalence is approximately 2.8% (affecting roughly 5.7–6.1 million people), with lifetime prevalence around 4.4%. Rates are similar across genders (2.9% for males, 2.8% for females), but severe impairment affects 82.9% of those with the condition—the highest rate among mood disorders.

Among adolescents aged 13–18, lifetime prevalence is 2.9%, with 2.6% experiencing severe impairment (using DSM-IV criteria). Rates are slightly higher in females (3.3%) than males (2.6%) and rise with age: 1.9% at ages 13–14, 3.1% at 15–16, and 4.3% at 17–18. Bipolar remains less common than anxiety (around 16–20% with symptoms) or depression (8–15% with major depressive episodes) but often requires early intervention with therapy, medication, and support to reduce long-term risks like strained relationships, poor academic outcomes, social withdrawal, physical complaints (e.g., headaches or stomachaches), and potential progression from depression.

Family history is one of the strongest risk factors for bipolar disorder. Adolescents with a parent or close relative diagnosed with bipolar disorder face a significantly elevated risk, suggesting both genetic and environmental contributions. Early warning signs may include sleep disturbance, sudden mood reactivity, increased goal-directed activity, or irritability that is episodic rather than chronic.

Globally, the World Health Organization (WHO) (updated September 8, 2025) estimates 37 million people live with bipolar disorder (about 0.5% prevalence, or 1 in 200), primarily among working-age individuals but also youth, with significant disability burden—including earlier mortality (on average 13 years) and risks for suicide, anxiety, and substance use disorders. Some U.S. treatment trends show declining bipolar diagnoses in favor of anxiety/depression classifications.

Bipolar Disorder Among Teenagers in New York State and New York City (2021–2024)

The 2024 State of Mental Health of New Yorkers report by the NYC Department of Health and Mental Hygiene noted that 3% of NYC adults (roughly 181,000 individuals) have a diagnosed bipolar disorder, but specific data for teens was not included. A 2021 analysis of New York State's SPARCS data showed a 5.4% rise in mental health disorders among youth aged 0–17 from 2009 to 2016, with bipolar disorder likely contributing, especially in Westchester County, where mental health issues increased by 32%.

Disparities and Treatment Gaps: In New York City, Hispanic and Asian teens face significant barriers to mental health care, including stigma, high costs, and limited access. The 2024 NYC report found that 34% of adults with mental health diagnoses, including bipolar disorder, had unmet treatment needs, with Asian New Yorkers accessing care the least. Teens likely face similar obstacles, with national data indicating that only 28% of youth with severe depression (which often co-occurs with bipolar disorder) receive regular treatment (7–25+ visits per year).

In New York State, a 2024 State Comptroller report highlighted a 23% increase in individuals using public mental health services from 2013 to 2022, with nearly 900,000 residents served, reflecting a growing need among teens. Governor Hochul's $1 billion investment in mental health services announced in 2022 aims to improve access, but the challenges still remain, such as limited psychiatric beds and barriers for underserved communities.

Addressing these disparities requires expanding school-based mental health programs, increasing bilingual and culturally competent providers, strengthening early screening initiatives, and ensuring sustained funding for community-based treatment models. Without targeted interventions, treatment gaps among Hispanic and Asian youth may persist despite broader statewide investments.

Resilience and Coping: Despite these challenges, 69% of NYC teens reported high or medium resilience in 2023, using coping strategies like listening to music and humor to manage symptoms. However, excessive social media use, linked to increased worry and mental health concerns, remains a challenge for teens with bipolar disorder.

Attention-Deficit/Hyperactivity Disorder (ADHD)

Based on the 2022 National Survey of Children's Health (NSCH), about 14.3% of U.S. teens aged 12–17 (around 2.8–3.5 million) have been diagnosed with ADHD. This is higher than in younger kids, where only 8.6% of those aged 5–11 have an ADHD diagnosis. Boys (17.1%) are more likely to be diagnosed than girls (11.2%). However, girls often show inattentive symptoms, which can be harder to spot and may lead to missed diagnoses. There are also differences across racial and ethnic groups. White non-Hispanic teens have the highest diagnosis rate at 16.3%, followed by Black non-Hispanic teens at 12.8%, Hispanic teens at 10.7%, and Asian teens at 4.5%. American Indian/Alaska Native teens have a diagnosis rate of about 10%.

The higher rates among adolescents compared to younger children may reflect improved detection as academic demands increase in middle and high school, where sustained attention, organization, and time management become more critical. Symptoms that were manageable in elementary school may become more impairing during adolescence.

A 2023 global study found that 5.6% of teens aged 12–18 have ADHD (with a range of 4.8–7%), but U.S. numbers from the NSCH are noticeably higher. The 2022 National Survey of Children's Health (NSCH), reviewed in 2023–

2024, offers the latest data on ADHD among U.S. teenagers (ages 12–17). About 11.4% of children aged 3–17, roughly 7.1 million, have ever been diagnosed with ADHD, with 10.5%, or 6.5 million, currently living with the condition. This reflects a 1 million increase in diagnoses since 2016. Among teens, diagnosis rates vary by state, ranging from 6% to 16%. Boys are diagnosed at a higher rate (15%) than girls (8%), and Black and White teens (12% each) are diagnosed more often than Asian teens (4%). These differences point to variations in healthcare access and diagnostic practices across regions and communities.

A 2023 study in Psychiatric Research and Clinical Practice noted that new ADHD diagnoses in teens decreased slightly from 2016 to 2018 but remained steady from 2018 to 2023. In contrast, adult diagnoses increased after 2020, likely due to expanded telehealth services during the COVID-19 pandemic.

The expansion of telehealth has improved access to evaluation for many families, particularly those in rural or underserved areas. However, concerns have also been raised about ensuring thorough diagnostic assessments and preventing overreliance on brief virtual screenings without comprehensive clinical histories.

Research funded by the National Institute of Mental Health (NIMH) in 2023–2024 has provided fresh insights into how ADHD affects the brains of teenagers. A March 2024 study published in the American Journal of Psychiatry examined over 10,000 brain scans from young people with ADHD. It showed that ADHD symptoms are connected to unusual interactions between the frontal cortex, which controls attention and behavior, and deeper brain regions like the caudate, putamen, and nucleus accumbens, which are involved in learning, movement, rewards, and emotions. These stronger connections could explain why teens with ADHD often struggle with focus and impulse control.

These findings support the understanding of ADHD as a neurodevelopmental disorder rather than simply a behavioral issue, helping to reduce stigma and reinforce the importance of evidence-based treatment approaches.

The study's large dataset helped clear up inconsistencies from smaller studies, offering more solid evidence. There is another 2024 study in Translational Psychiatry that highlighted genetics as a key factor in ADHD. It found that a specific part of the SLC6A3 gene, known as the VNTR intron 8, is linked to a higher risk of ADHD in kids and teens. By comparing 95 teens with ADHD to 95 without, researchers noticed that the 5R/5R genotype and 5R allele were more common in the ADHD group, pointing to a role in dopamine regulation. Environmental factors like exposure to smoking or alcohol during pregnancy or lead exposure in early childhood are also being explored as possible contributors, but genetics appears to be the main driver.

ADHD in teens often co-occurs with other mental, behavioral, or developmental disorders, complicating diagnosis and treatment. A 2024 study in the Disability and Health Journal found that teens with ADHD often have co-occurring conditions like anxiety, depression, autism spectrum disorder, or conduct problems, which can worsen ADHD symptoms and lead to greater challenges in daily life. These co-occurring conditions increase the risk of academic struggles, social difficulties, and family stress. Untreated ADHD in teens is associated with a greater chance of risky behaviors, such as substance use, with a 2024 CDC report highlighting increased risks of accidental injuries and poor academic performance.

Attention-Deficit/Hyperactivity Disorder (ADHD) Among Teenagers in New York State and New York City (2022–2025)

- **ADHD Prevalence in New York State** According to the 2022 National Survey of Children's Health (NSCH), 11.4% of U.S. children aged 3–17 (about 7 million) have been diagnosed with ADHD, with 10.5% (6.5 million) currently diagnosed. New York State's rates are likely similar, though teen-specific data (ages 12–17) is not available. Boys (15%) are diagnosed more frequently than girls (8%), and non-Hispanic children (12%) have higher rates than Hispanic children (10%).

- **Mental Health Challenges** A 2024 New York Health Foundation report found that 24.4% of young adults (ages 18–34) in New York reported anxiety and/or depression. Teens likely face similar or higher rates of mental health issues, including ADHD, due to stressors like school demands and social media.

- **National Trends Relevant to New York** A 2024 study in the Journal of Clinical Child & Adolescent Psychology reported that 11.4% of U.S. children and teens aged 3–17 had an ADHD diagnosis in 2022, up from 9.8% in 2016. For teens aged 12–17, ADHD rates range from 6% to 16% across states, with New York likely within this range. Urban areas like NYC may have higher rates due to environmental stressors. The 2024 Mental Health America report noted that 78% of children with ADHD have at least one co-occurring condition, such as behavioral problems (48%), anxiety (40%), or depression (15%), which complicates diagnosis and treatment in New York's diverse teen population.

- **Impact of COVID-19:** The COVID-19 pandemic worsened mental health challenges, including ADHD, in New York. A 2023 Trilliant Health report documented a 107.4% increase in behavioral health visits among teens aged 15–19 from 2018 to 2022, driven by social isolation, grief, and economic challenges, with ADHD likely contributing. In NYC, a 2022 survey showed serious psychological distress among adults rose to 14% (from 5% pre-pandemic), likely reflecting similar trends among teens with ADHD.

Schizophrenia

According to the National Institute of Mental Health (NIMH), schizophrenia and related psychotic disorders affect approximately 0.25% to 0.64% of non-institutionalized individuals in the U.S., with adolescents representing a small portion of this group. Determining the exact prevalence in teens is difficult due to diagnostic challenges and symptom overlap with conditions like depression or ADHD.

Schizophrenia typically emerges in late adolescence or early adulthood, with males often showing earlier onset than females. Early-onset schizophrenia (before age 18) is rare but tends to be associated with more severe symptoms and greater long-term functional impairment.

Many adolescents with schizophrenia remain undiagnosed due to stigma, limited healthcare access, or residing in non-household settings such as institutions or homeless environments. Globally, about 50% of individuals in mental health facilities are diagnosed with schizophrenia, yet only 31.3% of those with psychosis receive specialized mental health care, indicating a significant treatment gap. In teenagers, schizophrenia manifests with a mix of positive, negative, and cognitive symptoms, which are often more severe than in adults.

Early Signs: Schizophrenia in teens often begins with subtle changes, such as declining grades, social withdrawal, irregular sleep patterns, poor personal hygiene, or difficulty concentrating, which may be mistaken for typical teen behavior or confused with conditions like ADHD or depression.

Increasingly Severe Symptoms: As the condition develops, teens may experience hallucinations (like hearing voices or seeing things that aren't real), false beliefs (delusions), confused speech, or a lack of emotion or motivation. Memory problems, especially with organizing thoughts or remembering details, are common and can make schoolwork challenging.

Brain Development: Schizophrenia symptoms in teens may be linked to problems with brain development. Some children show mild thinking or behavior changes years before a diagnosis is made in adolescence.

Risk Factors:

Genetics: Having a family member with schizophrenia increases a teen's risk, as genes play a big role.

Environment: Stressful experiences like trauma, abuse, or poverty during pregnancy or early childhood can raise the risk. Using substances like cannabis during the teen years can also trigger or worsen symptoms in those already at risk.

Social and Emotional Factors:

Teens facing violence, bullying, or rejection are more likely to develop mental health issues, including schizophrenia. According to the 2023 Youth Risk Behavior Survey, school violence is rising, with 9% of students reporting being threatened or injured with a weapon at school (up from 7% in 2021), which can make mental health problems worse.

Mental Health Implications

Around half of teens with schizophrenia also deal with other mental health issues, like anxiety (affecting 16.1% of teens) or depression (affecting 8.4%), based on 2023 data from the National Survey of Children's Health. These additional conditions can make it harder for doctors to diagnose and treat schizophrenia.

Suicide Risk: Teens with schizophrenia are at a much higher risk of suicide. Around 4.9% may die by suicide, and 20% may attempt it, especially early on. According to the 2023 Youth Risk Behavior Survey, suicide attempts slightly decreased among Black teens (from 14% in 2021 to 10% in 2023) and Hispanic teens (with 16% making a suicide plan in 2023, down from 19% in 2021), but the risk remains high for teens with schizophrenia.

Stigma and Social Challenges: Schizophrenia often comes with unfair judgment, which can lead to teens feeling left out or struggling to connect with others. This is especially tough for teens, who may face bullying (19% of students reported being bullied at school in 2023, up from 15% in 2021) or find it hard to make friends.

Health and Lifespan: Teens with schizophrenia are 2–3 times more likely to pass away early due to health problems like heart or metabolic issues, or from suicide. On average, they may lose about 28.5 years of life compared to others.

According to the 2023 National Survey of Children's Health (NSCH), 61% of teens with mental health conditions, including schizophrenia, struggled to get the treatment they needed, a 35% increase since 2018. Only 80% of teens who needed mental health care received it, due to barriers like high costs, limited services, and stigma. The 2023 Youth Risk Behavior Survey (YRBS) showed a small improvement in teen mental health, with fewer teens feeling persistently sad or hopeless (down from 42% in 2021 to 40% in 2023).

However, teens with schizophrenia don't see as much improvement because the condition is more severe and long-lasting.

School Challenges: School safety concerns have risen, with 13% of students missing school in 2023 due to feeling unsafe, up from 9% in 2021. This can make mental health struggles worse for teens with schizophrenia, who are especially sensitive to stress and social issues. Female teenagers face higher rates of mental health challenges, including symptoms related to psychosis, and are more likely to experience bullying or violence, which can worsen schizophrenia symptoms.

Prevalence And Diagnosis Of Teenagers In New York State And New York City (2022–2025)

Schizophrenia usually develops in late adolescence or early adulthood, with symptoms commonly appearing between ages 16 and 30. Identifying the condition early in teenagers is crucial but difficult because its symptoms often resemble those of other disorders, such as depression, anxiety, or substance use issues.

New York City Data (2024–2025):

In 2025, several reports reinforced ongoing mental health challenges for NYC youth. The NYC Comptroller Brad Lander's December 2025 report described a "record-high" youth mental health crisis in public schools, with nearly 40% of high school students reporting persistent sadness or hopelessness—the highest level in over a decade. This was linked to fragmented care systems, severe staffing shortages (more than 70% of schools falling below national standards for social workers), and persistent inequities, all of which can delay recognition and treatment of serious conditions such as early psychosis.

Limited school-based staffing is particularly concerning for early identification of schizophrenia-spectrum disorders, as teachers and counselors are often the first to notice behavioral changes. When support staff is overstretched, subtle warning signs such as social withdrawal or unusual thinking may go unaddressed until a crisis occurs.

Additionally, the NYC Department of Health and Mental Hygiene's September 2025 Epi Data Brief No. 149, based on 2023 Youth Risk Behavior Survey data, highlighted sustained high rates of mental health burdens among public school students. Persistent sadness or hopelessness affected 35% of high school students and 48% of middle school students. Suicidal ideation was reported by 18% of high school students, and 14% of high school students reported having made a suicide attempt. These figures underscore the ongoing and serious emotional distress experienced by many NYC youth.

While resilience factors such as peer support and creative expression are protective, reliance on online spaces may sometimes intensify social comparison, sleep disruption, or exposure to harmful content, which can exacerbate vulnerability among teens already at risk for serious mental illness.

New York State Data (2025):

For young adults aged 18–25—the bridge between late adolescence and early adulthood—the prevalence of any mental illness (AMI) in New York State is generally similar to or slightly lower than national levels. Nationally, 32.2% of U.S. young adults in this age group experienced AMI in 2024, based on SAMHSA's 2024 NSDUH data (released 2025). New York-specific statistics often group this age range with broader young adults (ages 18–34), where serious mental illness (SMI) prevalence was about 8.3% among Medicaid-enrolled individuals, showing considerable variation by location (per 2025 analyses).

New York City Data (2024):

The New York City State of Mental Health Report (released May 2024) provides insights into mental health across age groups, including teenagers. The report highlights that mental health challenges are significant, with 28% of teens who use social media daily reporting moderate to severe depressive symptoms, which can complicate early schizophrenia diagnosis. The report highlighted that teenagers show resilience, with 69% describing high or medium resilience levels, often using coping mechanisms like music, social media, and humor. However, these mechanisms may mask early psychotic symptoms, delaying intervention.

The Office of the New York State Comptroller report (March 2024) indicates that 21.1% of adults in New York State had any mental illness (AMI) in 2021–2022, with 5.1% experiencing serious mental illness (SMI), including schizophrenia. Among 18- to 25-year-olds, AMI prevalence was higher at 30%, suggesting a significant mental health burden in late adolescence. The report also notes that mental health needs have risen, with a 23% increase in individuals served by the state's public mental health system (2013–2022), including younger populations.

Symptoms in Teens:

According to NYC Health (2022–2025), schizophrenia symptoms in teenagers include positive symptoms (hallucinations, delusions), negative symptoms (reduced emotional expression, social withdrawal), and cognitive symptoms (difficulty with memory or concentration). Teens may hear voices, develop paranoid thoughts, or struggle with school and social functioning. These symptoms often mimic typical adolescent behavior, making diagnosis by specialized clinicians essential.

New York State and City have expanded mental health infrastructure, but challenges persist, particularly for teenagers with schizophrenia.

NYC Initiatives (2025):

- No new standalone "NYC State of Mental Health Report" was released in 2025 to update the May 2024 version. As a result, the deep inequities in treatment access described in the 2024 report continued to exist throughout 2025.

- Black and Latino teenagers were less likely to receive timely mental health care. Several barriers contributed to this ongoing problem: stigma and shame surrounding mental health issues, economic challenges such as high costs or lack of insurance, shortages of available providers, and broader systemic issues within the healthcare system.

- The December 2025 report from NYC Comptroller Brad Lander confirmed that serious problems in youth mental health care are still happening. The report called the situation in New York City public schools a "record-high" crisis and listed three main issues:1) Mental health support is broken up and not well connected, so it doesn't work smoothly. 2) There are very serious shortages of staff—more than 70% of schools do not have enough social workers to meet national standards. 3) Access to help is very unequal, meaning many young people cannot get the services they need.

- Low-income or underserved neighborhoods and teenagers dealing with serious mental health conditions such as schizophrenia or early psychosis, often face significant barriers to accessing proper mental health support.

NYC Initiatives (2024):

- The NYC State of Mental Health Report highlights deep inequities in treatment access, with Black and Latino teens less likely to receive timely care due to stigma, economic barriers, and provider shortages. The city has expanded 988 Suicide & Crisis Lifeline services, offering 24/7 multilingual support for teens in crisis, including those with psychotic symptoms.

- Health Information Tool for Empowerment (HITE) connects New Yorkers to over 5,000 free or low-cost services, including schizophrenia treatment. NAMI-NYC provides free support and education for families, crucial for teens navigating a diagnosis.

New York State Efforts (2023–2025):

- The State Comptroller's Report notes a 10.5% drop in inpatient psychiatric beds (2014–2023), limiting options for teens in acute psychotic episodes. However, the 2023–24 State Budget allocated $1 billion for mental health, including efforts to restore 850 offline beds and increase Medicaid reimbursement rates by 20% to incentivize hospitals to reopen psychiatric units. As of December 2023, nearly 500 beds were restored, improving access for severe cases.

- The New York State Office of Mental Health (OMH) promotes early intervention through programs like **OnTrackNY**, which supports young people (16–30) with first-episode psychosis. **OnTrackNY**, available statewide, offers coordinated care, including medication, therapy, and peer support, with a focus on keeping teens in school and community settings.

- **Treatment Centers (2025):** Recovery.com's 2025–2026 listings show 56 schizophrenia treatment centers in New York State (up from 32 in 2024). These facilities offer virtual, outpatient (including PHP and IOP programs), residential, and inpatient care. Many use evidence-based treatments like CBT, DBT, medication management, family therapy, and early psychosis coordinated care. A large number accept Medicaid, Medicare, private insurance, and some provide sliding-scale or low-cost options. Outpatient programs are especially important for teens transitioning from inpatient care to support ongoing recovery.

- **Treatment Centers (2024):** Recovery.com lists 32 schizophrenia treatment centers in New York, offering virtual, outpatient, and residential options. These centers use evidence-based approaches like CBT, DBT, and medication management, with many accepting insurances, including Medicaid. Outpatient programs (PHP, IOP) are critical for teens transitioning from inpatient care, ensuring continuity.

Critical Note: Even with more funding, mental health services are hard to access due to a lack of staff and long wait times, especially in rural New York State. Teens in underserved communities face extra challenges, like not trusting healthcare providers and dealing with cultural stigma, which can delay a schizophrenia diagnosis for up to nine years.

- **Social and Environmental Influences on Teen Schizophrenia:** Teenagers with schizophrenia are significantly affected by environmental stressors, which are more intense in urban areas like New York City (NYC).

IMPACT OF THE COVID-19 PANDEMIC (2022–2025)

Impact of the COVID-19 Pandemic (2025 Updates):

In 2025, the effects of COVID-19 still impacted teen mental health in New York City and State. Ongoing social isolation, money worries, grief, and major life changes continued to cause high levels of sadness and hopelessness. For example, the December 2025 report by NYC Comptroller Brad Lander called the youth mental health situation in public schools a "record-high" crisis, blaming it on post-pandemic stress, broken care systems, staff shortages, and unequal access to help.

Mental health professionals also observed that the pandemic disrupted critical developmental milestones, such as peer bonding, extracurricular engagement, and early work experiences, which are protective factors during adolescence. The loss of these stabilizing routines contributed to delayed emotional regulation skills and heightened vulnerability to anxiety and mood instability.

In New York State, the Office of Mental Health (OMH) and Governor Hochul prioritized early support. They expanded programs like Youth Safe Spaces, Teen Mental Health First Aid training, and community-based services to help reduce isolation and support teens recovering from pandemic-related challenges.

Social Media Use (2025)

In 2025, daily social media use continued to be a major stressor for teens. Almost 90% used it heavily every day, and heavy use was strongly linked to increased depression, anxiety, loneliness, body image issues, and addiction-like behaviors. In New York City, heavy use was tied to more severe depressive symptoms.

Sleep disruption from late-night screen exposure further compounded these effects, as inadequate sleep is strongly associated with worsening mood symptoms and, in vulnerable adolescents, increased risk for psychotic-like experiences.

In New York State, Governor Hochul signed a law in December 2025 requiring warning labels on apps and platforms with addictive features (such as endless scrolling or auto-play videos) to alert young users to mental health risks. This was built on previous SAFE for Kids Act rules. While social media can provide creative outlets and social connections, its role in worsening mental health—especially for teens at risk of psychotic symptoms—remained a serious concern.

In 2025, alcohol and cannabis use remained important risk factors for teens in New York City. Cannabis use during adolescence was especially concerning because studies showed it increases the risk of schizophrenia and psychosis, particularly for teens with a family history or genetic vulnerability. Across New York State, NYSDOH and OMH reports in 2025 emphasized prevention education and early intervention to reduce these risks, especially since post-pandemic stress continued to affect many young people.

Key Insight:

In 2025, urban challenges such as poverty, unstable housing, and exposure to violence continued to affect NYC teens the most, raising their risk of psychosis and other mental health issues. Public health efforts mainly focused on individual treatments but often failed to tackle these larger social problems, which reduced their overall effectiveness.

The NYC Comptroller's December 2025 report and the DOHMH's September 2025 Epi Data Brief No. 149 showed persistently high rates: sadness or hopelessness affected 35% of high school students and 48% of middle school students, while 18% reported suicidal thoughts and 14% reported suicide attempts. These figures highlighted how structural issues made it harder for teens to recover from pandemic effects and manage serious conditions like psychosis.

Impact of the COVID-19 Pandemic (2022–2024)

According to the NYC State of Mental Health Report, the COVID-19 pandemic increased feelings of loneliness, financial strain, and social inequalities, worsening mental health challenges for teens. A 2022 survey showed that 14% of adult New Yorkers faced serious psychological distress, and teens likely experienced similar or greater difficulties due to disrupted schooling and social isolation.

During this earlier phase, telehealth rapidly expanded across New York, increasing access to therapy and psychiatric consultations. While virtual care improved convenience for many families, it also revealed digital divides for low-income households without reliable internet access.

Social Media Use

Daily social media use is linked to heightened anxiety (90% of teens) and depressive symptoms (28%), which may intensify psychotic symptoms in teens with schizophrenia. It also provides a space for creative outlets and social connections, emphasizing its complex role in mental health.

Researchers during this period began examining the relationship between algorithm-driven content, exposure, and worsening self-esteem, especially among adolescent girls and LGBTQ+ youth.

Substance Use

In NYC, alcohol (used by 45% of adults) and cannabis (used by 23%) are used widely. Cannabis use during adolescence is particularly concerning, as it increases the risk of schizophrenia, especially in those with a family history, showing the importance of focused prevention education.

Key Insight:

Urban challenges such as poverty, unstable housing, and exposure to violence disproportionately impact NYC teens, raising their risk of psychosis. Public health efforts often focus on individual treatments rather than addressing these broader social factors, limiting their effectiveness.

Eating Disorder

Healthcare visits and hospitalizations for eating disorders among U.S. teens and adolescents remained significantly elevated in 2024 and 2025, although the sharpest pandemic-related surges (2020–2022) have moderated somewhat. No new national survey has provided an exact update to the 107.4% rise in visits from approximately 50,000 in 2018 to over 100,000 in 2022 for those under 17. However, recent studies and ongoing reports continue to confirm persistently high demand for eating disorder treatment services.

Clinicians in 2024–2025 have also reported an increase in the medical severity of cases at first presentation, with more teens requiring inpatient stabilization for complications such as bradycardia, electrolyte imbalances, dehydration, and acute malnutrition. This suggests that delays in early detection may be contributing to more critical health risks at the time of diagnosis.

A 2025 study published in the Journal of Adolescent Health (August 2025) examined long-term trends in emergency department (ED) visits and hospitalizations for eating disorders among adolescents and young adults. Rates peaked dramatically in 2021, reaching 170% above expected levels for new-onset cases in ages 10–17. By 2023, rates were still elevated compared to pre-pandemic expectations: 37% above expected for new presentations and 53% above expected for pre-existing cases. ED visit rates for new eating disorders stood at 4.35 per 100,000 population among adolescents in 2023, indicating partial stabilization but no complete return to pre-2020 baseline levels.

Researchers also observed shifts in diagnostic patterns, with a notable rise in avoidant/restrictive food intake disorder (ARFID) and atypical anorexia nervosa, conditions that may not always present with visibly low body weight but still carry serious medical and psychological consequences.

Eating disorders among teenagers (ages 13–18) have significantly increased in recent years, with U.S. healthcare visits for these conditions rising by 107.4% from approximately 50,000 in 2018 to over 100,000 in 2022. Teens aged 15–19 continue to show the highest rates, with up to 12% affected by an eating disorder as reported in 2023 data. Eating disorders, such as anorexia nervosa and bulimia nervosa, are serious mental health conditions that significantly impact teenagers. Below are key details about each:

Anorexia Nervosa: Anorexia nervosa affects about 0.3% of U.S. teenagers (ages 13–18), with females (0.9%) more affected than males (0.3%). It is the third most common chronic illness among U.S. adolescents.

Symptoms: Extreme weight loss, fatigue, delayed puberty, brittle hair/nails, low heart rate, and low blood pressure. Emotional signs include anxiety, depression, and social withdrawal. Some teens exhibit psychotic-like symptoms, which may overlap with schizophrenia.

- Anorexia nervosa has the highest mortality rate of any eating disorder and is widely regarded as one of the most deadly psychiatric illnesses in 2025.

- In 2025, the crude mortality rate (CMR) is approximately 5–10.4% (often cited around 5.9% in long-term studies; some reviews note up to 10.4% as the highest among mental disorders).

- In 2025, eating disorders overall cause about 10,200 deaths per year in the U.S. (one death every 52 minutes), with anorexia contributing significantly.

- Hospitalizations for anorexia among adolescent girls doubled during the COVID-19 pandemic and remain high in 2023–2024.

- In 2022, about 55% of teens with anorexia also have mental health conditions like anxiety or depression, and some show symptoms, such as distorted body image, that resemble delusions and may overlap with schizophrenia.

- Anorexia has the highest death rate among eating disorders at approximately 4.0%, with 60 U.S. males aged 15–19 dying from the condition in 2018–2019

New research from a 2024 Yale University study revealed that genetic and brain-related factors linked to anorexia nervosa can emerge as early as age 9, with smaller caudate brain regions associated with the disorder (Effective School Solutions, 2024). A 2025 meta-analysis showed that anorexia incidence in primary care remains steady at 6–7 cases per 100,000 person-years, but rates are rising among teens under 15, indicating earlier onset or improved detection (PMC, 2025).

<u>Bulimia Nervosa:</u> Bulimia nervosa is a serious eating disorder affecting approximately 0.9% of U.S. teenagers (ages 13–18), with females (1.5%) more affected than males (0.5%).

It involves repeated episodes of binge eating followed by actions like vomiting, fasting, or excessive exercise to prevent weight gain.

<u>Symptoms</u>: Common signs include sore throat, tooth decay, stomach problems, irregular periods, and feelings of shame, guilt, or secrecy around eating.

Bulimia Nervosa (2025 Updates – Key Points)

- Teens and young adults with bulimia have a significantly higher risk of suicidal behavior.

- They are 7–8 times more likely to attempt suicide compared to peers without eating disorders.

- Lifetime suicidal ideation is reported by 50–60% of individuals with bulimia.

- Among LGBTQ+ youth with bulimia, suicidal thoughts are even more common, often reaching 50–70%.

- Suicide continues to be one of the leading causes of death in this population.

- Early intervention and comprehensive support are urgently needed to reduce these risks.

Bulimia Nervosa (2022–2024)

- Teens with bulimia face a death rate of about 3.9%, with risks from heart problems, electrolyte imbalances, and suicide.

- They are 7.5 times more likely to attempt suicide than their peers, and 53% of teens with bulimia, particularly LGBTQ+ youth, report suicidal thoughts in 2024.

- In 2024, about 88% of teens with bulimia also have mental health conditions like depression (88%) or anxiety (66%), which often complicates diagnosis and treatment due to the disorder's hidden nature.

- Pandemic Impact: Hospitalizations for bulimia among adolescent girls doubled during the COVID-19 pandemic, with high rates continuing into 2023–2025. Healthcare visits for eating disorders surged by 107.4% from 2018 to 2022.

- A 2024 study found that bulimia cases have slightly decreased in primary care settings, such as UK general practices, but the condition has become more severe, with teens showing more complex mental health symptoms (PMC, 2025). Another 2023 review highlighted that ethnic discrimination is an increasing risk factor, making minority teens three times more likely to engage in binge eating.

TEEN EATING DISORDERS IN NEW YORK STATE AND NEW YORK CITY (2022–2025)

<u>Eating</u> Disorders in New York: What's Happening and Why It Matters The Big Picture with a New York Twist

- Eating disorders are becoming a bigger issue among young people in the U.S., and New York is no exception. From 2018 to 2022, health visits for eating disorders among kids under 17 more than doubled nationwide, jumping 107.4%—from about 50,000 to over 100,000 visits. Anorexia nervosa cases, which can be deadly, spiked by 129.26%. New York City and State are likely seeing similar trends because of their large populations and urban stresses.

- A 2025 study published in the Journal of Adolescent Health (August 2025) found that emergency department (ED) visit rates for new eating disorders among adolescents were 4.35 per 100,000 population in 2023. These rates remained elevated compared to pre-pandemic levels: 37% higher than expected for new cases and 53% higher for pre-existing cases. Teens aged 15–19 continue to experience the highest rates, with up to 12% affected by some form of eating disorder, according to 2025 statistics from NEDA and ANAD. New York City and State are likely seeing similar patterns, driven by large populations, urban stressors, social media pressures, and barriers to accessing care.

<u>What's Driving This in New York?</u>

The COVID-19 pandemic made things worse. Teens in New York City, stuck at home during lockdowns, faced more stress, isolation, and social media pressure—think TikTok and Snapchat pushing unrealistic body ideals.

For some, like one NYC teen, staying home meant less pressure to eat normally, letting eating disorders grow in secret.

New York's Response

In 2025, New York State and New York City continued to strengthen their responses to youth eating disorders and broader mental health needs. Senate Bill S5225, introduced during the 2023–2024 legislative session to require eating disorder screenings as part of routine school health checks, did not pass in 2025. However, it remains an important sign of growing legislative attention to the issue and serves as a reference point for future policy discussions. At the same time, the state expanded early intervention and prevention programs, including:

- $7.5 million awarded in September 2025 to establish Youth Safe Spaces—peer-led, non-clinical community programs for ages 12–24 to reduce isolation and promote wellness.

- $10 million announced early in 2025 for the statewide rollout of Youth and Teen Mental Health First Aid training to help teens and adults recognize and respond to mental health crises, including signs of eating disorders.

- New York State is stepping up with Senate Bill S5225 (2023–2024), which could require eating disorder screenings in school health checks. It's a sign people are starting to take this seriously, though we don't know yet how it's playing out.

- The NYC Comptroller Brad Lander's December 2025 report described a "record-high" youth mental health crisis in public schools, with nearly 40% of high school students reporting persistent sadness or hopelessness—often overlapping with body image issues and eating disorder symptoms. The DOHMH's

September 2025 Epi Data Brief No. 149 (using 2023 YRBS data) showed sustained high rates of sadness/hopelessness (35% high school, 48% middle school), linking post-pandemic stress, social media influence, and urban challenges to mental health struggles, including eating disorders.

Who's Affected?

- Nationally, about 2.7% of teens deal with eating disorders, and it's probably higher in places like NYC, where social pressures hit hard. Around 62% of teenage girls and 29% of boys try to lose weight, and over half of girls and a quarter of boys engage in dieting behaviors that can lead to eating disorders. In a diverse city like New York, teens facing racial or ethnic discrimination (like Black, Hispanic, or Asian American kids) are three times more likely to develop binge-eating disorder. LGBTQ+ youth, especially transgender and non-binary teens, are also at higher risk—12% of trans boys and 11% of non-binary kids assigned female at birth reported eating disorder diagnoses.

The COVID Effect

- The pandemic was rough globally, with 22% of kids and teens showing disordered eating behaviors, according to a 2023 study. In NYC, long lockdowns and heavy social media use are likely to make this worse. It's a tough issue, but awareness is growing, and New York's working on ways to tackle it.

Post-Traumatic Stress Disorder (PTSD)

A 2024 study conducted by the Adolescent Brain and Cognitive Development (ABCD) Study investigated the prevalence of post-traumatic stress disorder (PTSD) among U.S. preadolescents aged 9–10. The findings revealed a lifetime PTSD prevalence of 2.17% in this age group. Significant risk factors included sexual minority status, multiracial identity, having unmarried parents, and residing in households with economic instability.

The study identified separation anxiety as the psychiatric condition most strongly associated with PTSD, with broader psychopathology increasing the likelihood of its occurrence. Notably, approximately one-third of children with a history of PTSD did not receive mental health treatment, underscoring a critical gap in access to care. Furthermore, even after PTSD remission, these children remained at elevated risk for subsequent mental health challenges.

Neuroimaging research has shown that early trauma exposure is associated with alterations in brain regions involved in emotion regulation and threat processing, including the amygdala and prefrontal cortex. These neurodevelopmental changes may partially explain why some youth experience persistent hyperarousal, difficulty concentrating, or impulsivity even after traumatic events have ended.

Between 15% and 43% of U.S. teenagers encounter at least one traumatic event, such as abuse, violence, or natural disasters. Of these, 3% to 15% of girls and 1% to 6% of boys develop post-traumatic stress disorder (PTSD), with sexual trauma being the most significant risk factor, affecting up to 40% of those exposed, according to the National Center for PTSD (2025).

Community-level violence and exposure to neighborhood crime have also emerged as major contributors to trauma symptoms among urban adolescents, particularly in densely populated areas such as New York City. Chronic exposure to unsafe environments can lead to cumulative trauma, sometimes referred to as "complex trauma," which may not stem from a single event but from repeated stressors over time.

The COVID-19 pandemic intensified trauma for teens due to social isolation, grief, and family stress, resulting in a 107.4% surge in behavioral health visits, including for PTSD, from 2018 to 2022, with 15- to 19-year-olds most affected, as reported by Trilliant Health. Elevated PTSD symptoms persisted into 2023–2024, per NBC News. According to the DSM-5-TR, teens with PTSD experience symptoms that significantly disrupt their daily functioning.

<u>**Symptoms of PTSD:**</u>

- **Intrusion:** Unwanted memories, nightmares, or flashbacks of a traumatic event, making teens feel like they're reliving it (e.g., reacting strongly to sounds or images tied to the trauma).

- **Avoidance:** Steering clear of people, places, or activities that remind them of the trauma, which can lead to social withdrawal or skipping school.

- **Negative Mood and Thoughts:** Ongoing sadness, guilt, or negative beliefs (e.g., "I'm worthless"). Teens may lose interest in hobbies or feel disconnected from others.

- **Hyperarousal:** Feeling irritable, jumpy, or having trouble sleeping or focusing.

- **Teen-Specific Signs:** Teens may act out with aggression, defiance, or risky behaviors like substance use or self-harm. Younger teens might seem clingy, while older teens may take bigger risks. Academic performance may also drop.

- **Duration:** For a PTSD diagnosis, symptoms must last more than a month and significantly affect teen's life. If similar symptoms last 3 days to a month, it's called acute stress disorder (ASD). About 19%

to 50% of teens with ASD from interpersonal violence may develop PTSD.

Certain factors make teens more likely to develop PTSD:

- **Type of Trauma:** Sexual violence (15%–40% develop PTSD), physical abuse, or witnessing violence (like school shootings) carries the highest risks.

- **Genetic/Biological Factors:** A family history of mental health issues or changes in how the brain handles stress (e.g., an overactive amygdala) can increase risk.

- **Environmental Factors:** Growing up with challenges like poverty, discrimination, or childhood adversity can triple the risk of PTSD. School violence is also a factor, with 9% of teens reporting weapon-related threats in 2023, up from 7% in 2021.

- **Social Factors:** Lack of support from family or community after a trauma raises the chance of developing PTSD.

- **Demographic Factors:** Girls are twice as likely to develop PTSD, often due to higher rates of sexual trauma. LGBTQ+ and minority teens face greater risks due to discrimination.

More than 80% of teens with post-traumatic stress disorder (PTSD) also have other mental health issues, which can make things more challenging:

- **Depression:** About 37% of teens with PTSD experience severe depression, feeling deeply sad or hopeless.

- **Anxiety Disorders:** Many teens develop conditions like generalized anxiety or panic disorder.

- **Substance Use:** Some teens turn to consuming alcohol or drugs to cope with PTSD, which can increase the risk of addiction.

- **Eating Disorders:** Nearly half (49.3%) of teens in residential eating disorder programs have PTSD. Trauma can lead to unhealthy eating habits, like restricting food (anorexia) or bingeing and purging (bulimia), as a way to cope. These eating disorders can also worsen PTSD symptoms due to stress about body image.

- **Schizophrenia:** PTSD and schizophrenia share some risk factors, like trauma and genetics. Severe PTSD flashbacks or eating disorder-related distorted thoughts (e.g., about body image) can sometimes look like schizophrenia symptoms, making diagnosis tricky. About 10% of people with schizophrenia also show eating disorder symptoms, but data specific to teens is limited.

- **Suicide Risk:** Teens with PTSD are 31 times more likely to attempt suicide. For those with both PTSD and eating disorders, the risk is even higher: 53% of teens with bulimia and 92% with anorexia report thinking about suicide, with LGBTQ+ youth being especially vulnerable.

- **Long-term Effects:** If PTSD goes untreated, it can cause ongoing problems with school, friendships, and future jobs. About 36.6% of PTSD cases in teens are considered severe, meaning they significantly disrupt daily life.

Teen PTSD in New York State and New York City (2022–2024)

PTSD, or post-traumatic stress disorder, is becoming more common among young people, and New York's teens are likely to feel the impact. A 2024 study showed PTSD diagnoses among U.S. college students doubled from

3.4% in 2017 to 7.5% in 2022. Older teens (18–22) in places like New York City probably face similar spikes, given the stress of school, social pressures, and urban life.

What We Know About Teens and PTSD?

Back in 2001–2004, about 5% of U.S. teens aged 13–18 had dealt with PTSD at some point, with girls (8%) affected more than boys (2.3%). A 2023 review said the COVID-19 pandemic made things worse, with teens facing stress from isolation, fear, or seeing traumatic stuff online. Globally, about 5.6% of teens exposed to trauma have PTSD, but in high-stress places like war zones, it can hit 15.3%. In NYC, the urban chaos likely pushes numbers up as well.

Why Are Teens at Risk?

Globally, about 24% of people exposed to trauma develop PTSD, but for teens, the risk is often tied to personal traumas like sexual violence, which can trigger PTSD in up to 40% of victims. In New York City, 1,800 sexual assault cases were reported in 2022. By 2024, NYPD data showed 1,341 reported rapes plus 8,612 other sex crimes, with increases partly attributed to the 2024 "Rape is Rape" law (which expanded definitions of rape) and improved reporting practices. Teens remain especially vulnerable to these experiences and the resulting PTSD risk.

In New York's Story

There's no exact data on PTSD rates for New York teens from 2022–2024, but clues point to a real problem. The 2021 NYC Youth Risk Behavior Survey found 10.2% of high schoolers felt ongoing sadness or hopelessness, which can signal PTSD risk.

Living in NYC can be tough on teens' mental health. Community violence, racial discrimination, and the disruptions from COVID-19 lockdowns all make the situation worse. A 2023 report highlighted how NYC teens dealt with trauma from being isolated and seeing violent or upsetting content online during the pandemic. Plus, gun violence in the city jumped 13% from 2019 to 2022, according to NYPD data, putting teens in areas like the Bronx and Brooklyn at higher risk. It's a heavy load for NYC teens, and the city's unique stresses make PTSD a growing concern.

What Puts New York Teens at Risk for PTSD?

Life in the City: Stress and Trauma

Living in New York City can be intense, especially for teens in certain neighborhoods. Places like the South Bronx or East New York see a lot of violent crime, and the 2022 NYC Community Health Survey said 15% of people in high-poverty areas have seen violence up close. For teens witnessing things like shootings, assaults, or gang activity, PTSD rates could hit 15–20%, based on national studies. Repeated exposure to trauma can also disrupt sleep, impair attention, and affect school performance.

Discrimination and Its Impact

NYC is a diverse city in the U.S.—70% of its teens are Black, Indigenous, or People of Color (BIPOC). A 2023 study found that teens facing racial discrimination are 2–3 times more likely to develop PTSD symptoms, especially Black and Hispanic kids, who make up half of the city's teen population. Over-policing in these communities only adds to the trauma. Microaggressions and daily experiences of bias also contribute to chronic stress, which can amplify PTSD risk and co-occurring anxiety or depression.

Financial Struggles

Poverty is a big issue too. About 20% of NYC teens live below the poverty line, according to 2022 Census data. A 2024 study showed that people with low incomes (under $20,000) are over twice as likely to have PTSD compared to those earning $75,000 or more. This likely hits NYC teens in public housing or underserved areas hard. Housing instability and food insecurity have also been shown to exacerbate trauma-related symptoms, with teens in shelters reporting higher rates of hypervigilance and sleep disturbances.

<u>Who's Most at Risk?</u>

- **Girls:** Teen girls in NYC face a higher PTSD risk, with a lifetime prevalence of 10–12% compared to 5–6% for boys. Sexual violence is a big factor—1 in 5 female high schoolers reported experiencing it in 2022, per the NYC Health Department, which can lead to PTSD.

- The NYC Comptroller's December 2025 report emphasized that girls, LGBTQ+ youth, and teens in underserved communities are disproportionately affected by trauma-related mental health crises, with persistent sadness/hopelessness reported by nearly 40% of high school students overall.

- The 2025 indicators (NYC Comptroller report, DOHMH Epi Brief No. 149, NIMH statistics) confirm that poverty, sexual violence, and urban trauma continue to place NYC teen girls and marginalized youth at especially high risk for PTSD. Early trauma-informed care and support are urgently needed.

- **LGBTQ+ Teens:** Transgender and non-binary youth, about 10% of NYC's teens, according to the 2021 Youth Risk Behavior Survey, are especially vulnerable. Discrimination and family rejection drive up their PTSD rates, with 12% of trans youth reporting trauma-related diagnoses in 2021—a trend that's likely still true today, given ongoing stigma.

NYC's unique challenges violence, racism, poverty, and social pressures make it a tough place for some teens, putting them at higher risk for PTSD.

Demographic Vulnerabilities:

- **Girls:** Teen girls in NYC are twice as likely to develop PTSD as boys (10–12% vs. 5–6% over their lifetime). Sexual violence is a big reason—1 in 5 female high schoolers in NYC reported experiencing it in 2022, according to the NYC Health Department, which ramps up their PTSD risk.

- **LGBTQ+ Teens:** About 10% of NYC teens are transgender or non-binary, per the 2021 Youth Risk Behavior Survey. These kids face higher PTSD rates because of discrimination and family rejection. A 2021 study said 12% of trans youth had trauma-related diagnoses, and with stigma still strong, this likely hasn't changed much in 2022–2024.

- **Immigrant and Refugee Teens:** NYC has a huge immigrant population—40% of teens have at least one immigrant parent. Refugee teens from places like Afghanistan, Ukraine, or Central America are especially vulnerable. A 2021 study found up to 30% of refugee teens may have PTSD, and that's relevant for NYC's diverse communities.

- **COVID-19 post-pandemic:** A 2022 study showed a 20% jump in PTSD symptoms worldwide due to isolation, losing loved ones, and messed-up routines. NYC was an early COVID hotspot, with over

30,000 deaths by 2022, and teens faced tough lockdowns and high death rates in BIPOC communities. A 2024 study said 22.2% of U.S. adults had likely PTSD in 2020, dropping to 16.8% by 2022, but teens in NYC are probably still struggling because of ongoing economic and social challenges.

WHAT'S NYC DOING ABOUT IT?

What's NYC Doing About It? (2025 Update)

New York State and NYC have expanded mental health supports in schools and communities in 2025 to address trauma and PTSD:

- **School-Based Mental Health:** The Mental Health Continuum partnership (DOE, NYC Health + Hospitals, DOHMH) continued expanding school-based clinics and services. In March 2025, 16 new clinics opened, bringing the total to serve thousands more students across 50 schools in high-need areas (e.g., South Bronx, Central Brooklyn). These clinics provide therapy, rapid referrals, and trauma-informed care, though funding remains non-baselined and staffing shortages persist.

- **State Investments:** $10 million was allocated early in 2025 for statewide Youth and Teen Mental Health First Aid training rollout, equipping teens and adults to recognize and respond to trauma and PTSD signs. $7.5 million was awarded in September 2025, which funded Youth Safe Spaces (peer-led, non-clinical programs for ages 12–24) to reduce isolation and build resilience.

- **Therapy Options:** Trauma-Focused Cognitive Behavioral Therapy (TF-CBT) remains the gold-standard evidence-based treatment for teen PTSD. Major NYC providers like Bellevue Hospital, Mount Sinai, NewYork-Presbyterian, and NYC Health + Hospitals continue offering TF-CBT, with some expansion through OnTrackNY (for early psychosis, which can overlap with trauma) and school-based programs. However, demand remains high, and wait times for public services can exceed 3 months due to provider shortages, as noted in the Comptroller's 2025 report.

What's NYC Doing About It? (2022–2024)

- **Mental Health in Schools:** New York State put $10 million into school-based mental health programs in 2022–2023, including support for trauma.

- **NYC's ThriveNYC** program is also screening more kids in public schools for mental health issues, but we don't have clear data on PTSD-specific results yet.

- **Therapy Options:** Trauma-Focused Cognitive Behavioral Therapy (TF-CBT) is the go-to treatment for teen PTSD, and places like Bellevue Hospital and Mount Sinai in NYC offer it. But demand spiked after COVID, and wait times for public services can be over 3 months because there aren't enough providers.

- **Community Support:** Groups like the NYC Anti-Violence Project help LGBTQ+ and BIPOC teens with trauma, tackling the unique challenges they face. Still, these programs don't have enough funding or reach, especially in places like Queens or Staten Island.

- **Access to Care:** NYC has top-notch mental health resources, like NYU Langone's psychiatry department, but getting help isn't easy for everyone. About 60% of low-income teens can't get timely care, per 2022 NYC Health Department data.

- Teletherapy has helped since the pandemic, but spotty internet in poorer households makes it tough. A 2024 study said only 25% of teens with PTSD in cities like NYC get proper treatment, showing there's still a big gap.

CHAPTER 4
Be Mindful of Yourself

In the same way, let your light shine before others, so that they may see your good deeds and glorify your Father in heaven.

–Matthew 5:16

LIFE IS WONDERFUL

In this world, you grow through unique experiences. Life is a journey filled with joy, struggle, the bitterness of loss, and the spice of unexpected challenges. Indeed, you grow through all the flavors life would offer, and you are fortunate to have freedoms that many around the world can only dream of. These privileges provide a foundation to pursue your ambitions, learn from your failures, and build a life that reflects your unique spirit. You're incredibly lucky because you were born in this amazing, advanced country, with access to countless resources and opportunities, along with freedoms like worshiping as you choose, speaking freely to express your thoughts, and having equal rights to be protected under the law.

Being a teenager is tough, but staying mindful can help you tackle its challenges and grow into your best self. The teenage years are like a rollercoaster: hormones and emotions are all over the place, and you're caught between fitting in and figuring out who you are. You'll face tons of struggles: school stress from tests, homework, or college preparation; pressure to keep up with friends or match social media's "perfection."

Remember, we are humans and have weaknesses; we will never be perfect. The most important thing is that we can recognize our flaws and work to improve them, and we can become better people. Let's give an example for the very famous statue in the world, "Venus de Milo's broken arms," which, rather than diminishing its value, enhances its global fame by creating mystery, showcasing Hellenistic artistry, and symbolizing resilient beauty. Its flaws make it relatable and iconic, captivating viewers worldwide. If the statue had intact arms, it might not be the famous masterpiece it is today. Sometimes, imperfections are perfect. You don't need to change who you are, just be yourself. In other words, we love the unique you, and that makes this world better!

It took me a while to start this chapter because I often wanted to stop. I experienced a lot of trauma when I was younger, and I didn't want to look back. However, a voice in my heart reminded me to complete this book. This voice always comes at critical moments when I face important choices or stand at the intersection of a decision. I believe this voice is from God. I know his spirit will always be a part of me. It is my honor to have received His grace, and it's my responsibility to give back and help more people find inspiration and live better lives. I hope these stories will inspire you, no matter where you are in life.

Living life is never easy. We all face great and bad moments daily. Many people or teens experience difficulties in their academic and personal lives, but hide these weaknesses and keep them secret. You can do it as well! May you achieve great success in life! Get ready to be a winner, not a loser. Follow the words from the Lord, believe Him that with His grace, you will do the right thing and be responsible. Trust yourself, and you will do great!

A JAR OF LIFE

A few years ago, I watched a short video called "A Valuable Lesson for A Jar of Happier Life." This 5-minute motivational video features a philosophy professor in a classroom setting who imparts timeless life wisdom through interactive demonstrations and simple metaphors.

The video opens with the professor holding up a large glass jar, then he adds large golf balls until they're packed in tightly, prompting the question and asking the class if it's full—yes, it's full. Next, he pours in pebbles, which fill the gaps around the golf balls, and asks once more; the class agrees it's full. Finally, he adds sand, which sifts into the remaining spaces, completely filling the jar.

He explains that the jar represents life: the golf balls symbolize the most important elements—family, school, health, and passions—that must come first. The pebbles are secondary priorities like a job, a home, or a car, while the sand is all the trivial "small stuff."

If you start with the sand, there's no room for what truly matters, so the key is to prioritize the golf balls and set your focus on what's critical to your happiness. A student then asks about a bottle of beer that the professor pours in last, which fits into the cracks; with a wink and applause from the class, the professor quips that no matter how full life seems, there's always room for a couple of beers—emphasizing balance and making space for joy.

What do Golf balls represent in your life?

As a teenager stepping into young adulthood, your life can feel like a puzzle with way too many pieces: the endless homework, friend drama, dealing with puberty, and big questions about what to do next. However, as we mentioned in the "Jar of Life" lesson, you can simplify things using the "Jar of Life" idea. Picture your jar as your everyday routine and the golf balls as the biggest, most important parts that must go in first. These are the must-do priorities just for your teen world, like school, family, and friends, that build a strong base.

**"Be careful how you think; your life is shaped by your thoughts."
Proverbs 4:23 (GNT)**

When you think of this verse from the Bible, what comes to your mind? It says that everything you think will change your life. Because your life is shaped by your thoughts, be careful what you think will shape your life. It also means that what you think impacts what you believe.

I agree with this verse, and it makes me think of when my family and I first started our life in the U.S. Everything in life felt the hardest at the beginning, since we came from a totally different culture—and on top of that, there were language barriers. We had to start with jobs that paid the lowest hourly rates, working at Chinese restaurants, laundromats, and so on. I worked hard for months to support my family. One day, however, one thought came to mind.

"You are very young, only 22 years old. Your career should not come to an end in this way. You need to hold yourself to a higher standard."

I figured my thoughts were probably right, and I needed to pursue my future to a higher level. Even though it's hard, you would never know unless you try it out. In 2012, I started my language study and college journey.

I still remember, fifteen years ago, when our family worked day and night. The lowest pay we received meant working 10 hours a day, seven days a week. We had no choice, living in New York City, where many Chinese immigrants lived, which is why there was so much competition. Many employers kept the pay rates very low because they wanted more profit for their businesses, and they didn't mind if people quit their jobs. They weren't concerned about whether their workers quit, because they could always find people who would work for them. Moreover, we needed income to live, and it was hard to find a decent job unless we had finished our degree or had a strong network. Otherwise, we couldn't survive. However, we had no choice and had to start from somewhere.

Are You Ready to Challenge Yourself?

Remember, He Is Walking With You!

A few months ago, I watched Pastor Rick Warren's sermon, *"The Many Signs in Life That God Is Walking with You."* It's full of simple Bible wisdom to help us spot God's presence during tough times—those "valleys" like hard struggles in life. Pastor Rick explains that valleys are just part of everyday living. You're either coming out of one, stuck in one now, or heading into the next. Don't get caught off guard. Instead, expect them—they're a key part of God's bigger plan.

He breaks down valleys with three clear truths:

1. They're inevitable, woven into life's natural rhythm, so prepare for them with hope instead of shock.

2. They're impartial, striking everyone equally—good folks, believers, or anyone—since our broken world spares no one, though faith doesn't dodge the pain but offers steady strength; and

3. They're unpredictable, crashing in unannounced at the worst moments, like a sudden phone call that turns your world upside down.

Those Bible Verses explain God's purpose:

1) Deuteronomy 11:11 King James Version (KJV): <u>But the land, whither ye go to possess it, is a land of hills and valleys, and drinketh water of the rain of heaven.</u>

Notes the Promised Land includes "hills and valleys"—even in God's will, life has ups and downs.

2) 1 Peter 4:12 (NIV) says: <u>"Dear friends, do not be surprised at the fiery ordeal that has come on you to test you, as though something strange were happening to you."</u>

This verse means not to be surprised by troubles as if something unusual happened.

3) Psalm 34:19 The Living Bible (TLB) says: <u>"The good man does not escape all troubles he has them too. But the Lord helps him in each and every one."</u>

It means: Righteous or "good" people (those living with integrity, faith, or moral uprightness) aren't immune to life's hardships—they face plenty of them, just like anyone else. Troubles aren't a sign of moral failure or divine punishment; they're a universal part of human experience. But the game-changer is God's promise: He actively intervenes, rescues, and supports you through every single one, turning potential defeat into growth and victory.

4) Matthew 5:45 (KJV): <u>"That ye may be the children of your Father which is in heaven: for he maketh his sun to rise on the evil and on the good, and sendeth rain on the just and on the unjust."</u>

This verse is from Jesus' Sermon on the Mount. There, He teaches bold love—like loving your enemies and praying for people who hurt you (verses 43–48). "Rain" and "sun" mean God's everyday blessings: things like weather that help crops grow, keep life going, and balance the world. These come to everyone equally, the good people ("just") with kind hearts, and the mean or selfish ones ("unjust"). It's not about earning it; God's kindness is free and fair for all. In our unfair world, that's why good people still face hard times (nice weather or bad storms hit us all). Struggles don't mean God forgot you—they're part of our broken lives. But for believers, God adds special help: His close care guides you through the storm.

5) Proverbs 27:1 New Living Translation (NLT): "Don't brag about tomorrow, since you don't know what the day will bring."

Don't get too smug or rigid about the future—like saying, "Tomorrow, I'll nail it!" or "Next week is totally planned out." Why not? The future is unpredictable; one day can bring amazing surprises or tough challenges, and you can't see them coming.

The main message is that God is the "God of the valleys." There are also many mountaintops valleys aren't signs of abandonment but opportunities to experience the challenges of His presence.

God also sends three reminders from **Psalm 23:4 (KJV)** for enduring valleys:

6) "Yea, though I walk through the valley of the shadow of death, I will fear no evil: for Thou art with me; Thy rod and Thy staff they comfort me."

It means that even when you go through the darkest and hardest times of life—times of pain, fear, loss, or danger—you are not abandoned.

The phrase "valley of the shadow of death" represents times of deep trouble, grief, or hardship. Moreover, the verse uses the words "walk through" instead of "stay in," reminding us that every valley is temporary and that we will emerge from it with God's help. It also reassures us that God is right beside us—not distant—so we never walk through the valley alone. His presence provides peace, protection, and comfort even when nothing else makes sense. The verse highlights "through" as a sign of hope and temporality, "shadow" as something not real, implying that light is nearby, and "you" as a symbol of personal intimacy with God. Pastor Rick shares his own experiences of loss—such as losing his son, his parents, and brother—to show how enduring life's valleys can deepen one's faith.

You're Not Alone—God Walks with You, notes valleys feel isolating, but God promises companionship; shadows (fears like death or depression) are illusions that can't harm and signal God's light is close—turn to Jesus (the Light) to overcome fear. Valleys feel lonely, but shadows (fears like death) are illusions signaling God's light nearby, and turn to Jesus to conquer them. Signs: Shelter in chaos; rescue when you cry out. God Has a Purpose for Your Valley.

Pain isn't pointless—God shapes it into growth, forging endurance, character, and unshakeable hope, transforming "trouble" into "gateways of hope." Signs: Greater maturity, fresh hope, grit, and transformation.

The Reward Outlasts the Pain—Today's troubles or challenges are tiny and short-lived compared to the endless glory waiting in eternity. Staying faithful through them brings rewards that never end. Someday in heaven, you'll see their true value and regret any whining you did. A key sign? Your outlook shifts, making those burdens feel much lighter to bear.

Does this sound familiar? Yes, that's the story I told you earlier. Everyone has a different background. Don't give up on yourself easily. No matter what, whether you're going through one or multiple valleys, remember—it's God's plan, and He is sending these tests. He wants to see if you can overcome them and become a winner in life. Don't be afraid or feel alone, because His Spirit is always walking with you, and He will make sure you're in good hands.

Remember, there is no easy life in this world—just like Pastor Rick told us in his message 'The Many Signs in Life That God Is Walking with You.' He explained that God teaches us that valleys are simply part of everyday living. You're either coming out of one, stuck in one right now, or heading into the next one. You can't avoid them.

We all face many difficulties in life. You can choose to confront them head-on and learn from them, or you can try to escape them—but if you do, you'll just face the same challenges again and again until you finally overcome them.

I still remember April 2022, during Spring Break, when I had COVID. I had to finish a 10-page graduate thesis essay for my class in order to graduate that week. For several days, I had a very high fever over 100 degrees, along with a bad cough and pain all over my body. I felt like I was in hell. I desperately wanted to lie down and rest, but I didn't have the time—I had to complete the essay, or I would fail the class. At night, I spoke to God and asked for His help. Thankfully, my professor knew about my situation and supported me by emailing guidance multiple times a day. Finally, we finished the essay on the last day of Spring Break, and my sickness started to improve. My professor approved it and allowed me to submit it to the board for graduation review. (Some students don't pass on their first or even second attempt and have to retake the class.)

The good news is that after days of terrible sickness and intense hard work, I passed my essay on the first try! I am so grateful to God and to my professor for standing by my side and supporting me through that tough time.

So, you must have your own 'special time'—a moment like that when you faced something really hard. Can you think of what it is? After reading my story, how do you respond? What do you do? Are you going to solve the problem or let it stay unresolved? Why?

"Forget the former things; do not dwell on the past. See, I am doing a new thing! Now it springs up; do you not perceive it? I am making a way in the wilderness and streams in the wasteland."

(NIV) Isaiah 43:18–19

This passage, spoken by God through the prophet Isaiah to the people of Israel, encourages letting go of past burdens and embracing the new possibilities God is creating. The "former things" refer to past mistakes, hardships, or sins that might weigh heavily on someone's heart. God tells his believers to shift their focus from what was to what is coming—a fresh start, a new path, even in seemingly impossible situations. The imagery of a "way in the wilderness" and "streams in the wasteland" symbolizes hope and provision in places of desolation, suggesting that God can bring life and direction where there seems to be hopelessness. Teenagers often face intense mental health struggles, such as anxiety, depression, or feelings of being overwhelmed by school, relationships, or self-identity. These challenges can feel like a "wilderness" or "wasteland"—barren, isolating, and hopeless.

Your Past Doesn't Define Your Future

I had very poor English skills and very bad memories when I was a teenager living in China. I am the kind of person who grows slowly, but I finally started learning and understanding things when I was 18 years old. So, I was very 'different' and 'special' in a way that I wouldn't want to describe myself. Due to my differences, all my teachers and classmates saw me as weak. They didn't want to get close to me, and they thought I was very dirty. I also experienced a lot of physical bullying, and my teachers knew and were trying to ignore it. They didn't care, and they had abandoned me. In addition, each class group had over 40–50 students. They didn't have time to deal with such matters.

I used to sit in the back or the very last row in the classroom. (Students who sat in the back or last row were seen to have no good future.) I hated the teachers and everything. However, I did have a few girlfriends, and we were great friends. The point was that they could totally understand me. When I felt terrible, they were always on my side to support me and made me think that this world had tiny, beautiful moments.

I am very grateful to my parents, who never gave up on me. No matter how bad my situation was, they always made sure I was in good hands. When I failed my classes (because I was silly), they never blamed me; they just wanted me to be healthy and happy. When I was 20, they decided to send me to the State University of Nebraska to study English because I had very poor English comprehension skills. If it weren't for their hard work and decisions, I wouldn't have the progress and achievements I do today.

I've been in New York City for over 15 years now, and I've finished my bachelor's and my master's degrees, and currently I am learning English and pursuing my second master's degree at the City University of New York.

You're probably jealous of what I've accomplished! But maybe you don't know what I've gone through over those years. So, I'm not a superwoman, I'm just a normal person. I belong to one of you. I've been diagnosed with a major depressive episode with anxiety, and I almost ended my life 10 years ago. Before I started college, I'd made up my mind: I could no longer be the same as before. I needed to be a straight-A student. I was working very hard and juggling jobs. I remember when I'd just started my second semester of college. In that semester, I was taking 6 classes because my major required me to be a full-time student.

Finally, my inner devil was released. I just couldn't focus. I was worried about everything, and I couldn't do anything, and later, I had suicidal thoughts. I felt very warm all over my body, and I was hoping that I could cut somewhere on my body, let my blood out, then it could make me feel better, and I always thought people thought I was stupid; my face and hands were often trembling. I couldn't continue my studies anymore; I had to pause them and get treatment. I had to stop in the middle of the semester; otherwise, the illness would have killed me. I failed 2 classes, and in one class, I got a C that semester. My GPA dropped from a previous 3.9 to 2.0. I took two semesters of leave for absences and concentrated on healing.

I remember when I first started school. I spent most of my time studying at the school's learning center until it closed at 9:00 p.m., and then I'd head home. I also realized that my English listening and speaking skills were very weak. I realized that I have no one with whom I can practice English. I used my spare time at home watching hundreds of dramas and movies, and I used this way to practice my English.

I wish I could be as lucky as you are, having more opportunities and freedom like you all have. I also see that some girls and boys are quitting school and doing the opposite of what students are supposed to do. They sleep in class, smoke weed, and make excuses to reduce their pain and stress from their illnesses. They'll do anything to avoid the school, get their credits, and look for their future. I feel sad because I see some very talented young adults, but they just show up at school and do nothing. I am worried, and I worry about their future.

In the Spring 2025 semester, I never imagined I could earn A+ grades in graduate classes—something that hadn't happened in my 10 years of study. With faith, everything is possible. With God, nothing is impossible: not healing the broken, not protecting the vulnerable, not rebuilding lasting trust. I was expecting an A- or B+ at best, but seeing my grades online left me in disbelief. I'm not trying to brag—I just want others to know that hard work does pay off in the end.

My advice to you is to appreciate what you have right now, go back, and study hard. No matter how hard studying feels right now, pay attention and practice more. Because you are still young, you can learn fast. And remember, practice makes perfect. Please don't wait until you regret it when you get older. By that time, you'll realize the importance of learning. If you waste time, it will never come back. So, don't waste time so easily, and please do something meaningful while you are young. Even though it's long and tedious, remember: your hard work will finally pay off. Don't be like me when I was young, not cherishing time. It was only later that I realized the importance of studying. Trying to make up for what I didn't learn before takes a lot of time and effort, and it's hard. As you grow older, learning and practicing new things requires much more time and energy. So please, treasure your youth. This is the best time of your life.

Life is full of challenges. Indeed, everyone faces difficulties every single day. I choose to be grateful because I live in this world-famous city. I'm thankful that I can walk and enjoy the stunning views of what many consider the most iconic city on Earth. Living so close by, I often stroll along Wall Street, the World Trade Center, and around the East River—places that countless people dream of visiting or living in this major city.

I truly appreciate that God grants me these opportunities: to live here, breathe the fresh air, and pursue dreams I never even imagined before. I'm deeply grateful for my home, my family, and my spiritual parents who love me unconditionally. With God's blessings, I truly have everything I need. Yes, I've endured a great deal of pain from depression, and it's already lasted 10 years. Still, I'm also very grateful that it has become a very close companion in my life. Moreover, I appreciate my sickness because it has strengthened my faith and helped me grow into the best version of myself. Sometimes I find myself wondering: if I'm ever completely healed from this condition one day, would the peace truly last, or would it fade away after a while? Right now, I'm content and happy, yet I know I'd also feel a sense of loss for this "friend" that's woven so deeply into my path.

"Jesus looked at them and said, 'With man this is impossible, but with God all things are possible.'"

Matthew 19:26 (NIV)

THE PAIN OF THE MEMORY

Those voices often show up late at night.

When I close my eyes, it's like smoke dancing everywhere.

They sound angry, threatening, and cruel; I can't help but continue.

I am so terrified of the nights to come.

I feel better when I hurt myself,

because pain makes the voices go away.

Some wounds will heal, but some remain as scars.

Each scar represents a story of my painful memories.

Some of my pals see me differently and laugh at me.

Finally, I realized my serious issues.

I am asking for professional help from experts.

I don't mind what they think, and I am proud of myself.

The doctor told me that "each scar is a battle fought in victory."

Remember,

each scar makes you grow stronger.

You are a smart, talented individual.

When you encounter any difficulties,

Just don't give up right away; please hang in there!

No matter how difficult the questions are,

You will resolve them all.

You will be a powerful, excellent, and successful person—

no different from others!

—The pain of the memory will fade away!

EDUCATION IS THE BEST INVESTMENT IN YOUR LIFE.

Education is a vital foundation for individual growth and broader social progress, especially in the crucial teenage years. Think of the "jar of life," the short lesson: Your life is like a jar packed with goals, obstacles, and everyday pressures. In this setup, education stands out as a major piece: the golf ball that needs to go in right away to leave room for everything else. For young people, these years are a golden window for mental and emotional expansion, going far beyond simple fact-cramming to building lasting abilities that steer your entire future path. Of course, studying can sometimes feel tough, but its impact runs deep.

So, you have to do your own self-determination:

1.   **Do you want to finish high school?**
2.   **Do you find school challenging and want to stop?**

You don't need to give your answer right away, but think wisely—it's critically important for your future. However, you can always change your choices. It feels like you're sailing a boat; it's necessary to maintain normal navigation, so the speed needs to be adjusted regularly, and it can't always stay at the same speed to keep the boat moving.

There is also another example: You probably know Shaquille O'Neal (better known simply as Shaq), the retired American pro basketball legend, who's now a sports analyst on the TV show Inside the NBA and a successful businessman. He appeared on The Ellen DeGeneres Show, talking about how to raise kids. He has six kids. During the interview, he shared one of his most famous rules: "Cheese means money." He has to make sure they can't get his handouts (his legacy or his money) easily, because Shaq is a very famous and rich person in the world. So, to access his cheese (money), they have to present him with two degrees (a bachelor's and a master's).

Nowadays, education matters to everyone, especially if you're living in New York City or another major city. Even if you have, at least, a bachelor's degree, you can barely find a job that can financially support you comfortably. I think this is an understandable and wise decision. If you want to survive in this world, you must show something that you have earned by yourself, something real and substantial that gains recognition from society. It should not be something you rely on from your parents' fame or legacy just because they are well-known. That is not the way. You have to demonstrate your credibility and show the world that you are capable, that you have a degree, and that you can achieve things on your own.

The higher your level of knowledge and education, the more your social circle will improve. You won't only associate with the people you knew before, who may not have had a high level of education. When you complete a higher degree, the social class and the people you interact with will also be of a higher level. Your social network will broaden, giving you the chance to meet people who can help you in your life and career. By knowing them, you may gain better job opportunities.

Furthermore, as you delve deeper into learning and your knowledge grows, your perspective will also broaden, and you will develop your own insights into what you see and hear. By applying the knowledge and vocabulary you've learned, you can understand headline news and share it with your family and friends, and help them translate important documents or letters they might need. Your family and friends will be very proud of you.

I also want to mention more about myself. If I hadn't persisted in completing my studies, I wouldn't have had the chance to find a decent job. More importantly, this job fulfilled one of my dreams: to use the knowledge

I've gained to help those who need it. If I hadn't persisted in finishing my education, I wouldn't have been able to accomplish the things I've always wanted to do. With the knowledge I've acquired, I could write a book—one that I hope will help even more people, offering them a glimmer of hope when they need it most, so they can stand up again.

If I hadn't completed my studies, I couldn't have gone further in life. I wouldn't have had the opportunity to connect with more like-minded friends, nor would I have met the important mentors and spiritual fathers who have shaped my journey. If I hadn't studied hard, I'd still be living (and maybe forever) in someone else's world, letting others define what I can and cannot do.

You are simply you; you will always be the master of your own life. No one else can control you. You have the knowledge; you can use that information to arm yourself when necessary. You are in power, and you are stronger than you think.

Don't Copy from Others—Be Yourself

In today's interconnected world, it is all too easy to feel the weight of expectation. Social media timelines overflow with images of seemingly flawless lives—perfect friends, ideal styles, and effortless successes. What those images rarely show are the failures, insecurities, and quiet struggles happening behind the screen. Comparison becomes dangerous when we forget that we are only seeing highlights, not real life.

As a teenager navigating this landscape, you may find yourself tempted to mimic these ideals, wondering if blending in will bring acceptance or happiness. As teenagers, we all hope to be perfect. However, in this world, nothing and no one can truly be perfect—except the One who created us humans. However, this pursuit often leaves us feeling hollow, like echoes of someone else's story rather than authors of our own. When you constantly copy others, you slowly lose touch with who you are meant to become. Over time, this can lead to confusion, low self-worth, and the feeling that you are never "enough," no matter how hard you try.

Don't Copy from Others, Be Yourself is more than a title; it is a gentle yet firm invitation to reclaim your unique voice. Through real-life stories, reflective exercises, and timeless wisdom, you will learn that true belonging arises not from imitation, but from the courage to stand apart. Imagine a life where your choices reflect your passions, not borrowed trends—where your talents shine brightly because they are yours alone. As you turn these pages, allow yourself to question, to dream, and to grow. Being yourself does not mean being perfect; it means being honest about your strengths, your limits, and your values. That honesty becomes the foundation for a life that feels meaningful rather than performative.

As a teenager, the world of dating can feel like a whirlwind—exciting, confusing, and full of 'what ifs.' At school, girls and boys compare themselves with each other: who has a new girlfriend? Another girl has a super handsome boyfriend and makes other girls and boys jealous. Whether you're swiping on apps, crushing on a classmate, or pondering if it's time to ask someone out, relationships (whether with a girlfriend, boyfriend, or partner) often seem like the ultimate milestone.

Romantic connections can be magical, but they're not always fairy-tale smooth. Whether it's your first hand-hold or navigating deeper feelings, relationships teach us a ton about ourselves and others. Below, I'll break down some positive sides (the heartwarming wins) and downsides (the real-talk challenges) of having a girlfriend, boyfriend, or partner during your teen years. Remember, every experience is unique—what matters is growth, not perfection. But is having a romantic partner a game-changer for the better, or does it come with hidden pitfalls?

The answer depends less on the relationship itself and more on your emotional maturity, self-awareness, and ability to maintain balance in your life.

A good partner can be your biggest cheerleader—celebrating your wins (like acing a test) or lifting you during tough days (like family stress). This creates a safe space to share vulnerabilities, reducing loneliness and building confidence. Shared experiences, from arcade dates to late-night talks, create joyful memories that stick. Your partner might introduce you to cool music, sports, or people, widening your world and making high school less routine. It's like leveling up your social game!

Remember, nothing in life, especially relationships, goes perfectly every time. Bumps and challenges are totally normal, but catching them early can help you bounce back stronger. For starters, a crush gone wrong or a breakup can hurt a lot, especially when you're still figuring out how to protect your heart. It might leave you feeling sad for a bit, doubting yourself, or even feeling zoned out at school or with friends. Plus, there's that pressure to "get over it" super quick, which isn't always fair or realistic. Unprocessed emotional pain can quietly pile up, affecting mental health, academic focus, and self-esteem if it's ignored instead of addressed. Second, all the dates, constant texting, and little arguments can steal time from what matters— like homework, sleep, or chilling with your hobbies. If things feel lopsided (say, you're always the one making plans), it can drag you away from your goals or other friendships. Learning when to set boundaries is just as important as learning how to love. A relationship should support your growth, not replace your identity.

Shaquille O'Neal's 2018 interview on The Ellen DeGeneres Show highlights his old-school, protective style when it comes to dating rules for his children. He openly uses different standards for his sons and daughters, admitting it's not "fair," but everything stems from his strong desire to raise confident, independent people, especially by protecting and empowering his daughters. Shaq's Dating Rules:

- **For his sons:** They can start dating at 18. He encourages them to gain independence quickly, and they typically have to move out of the house around that same age.

- **For his daughters:** They aren't allowed to date (or at least bring boyfriends home or introduce them) until they're 24 (that's the age he specifically mentioned on Ellen, though he's said 25 in some other interviews).

One of his most famous rules, he also said, "Don't bring any boys to my house unless you got a master's [degree]. I don't want to see them at all."

While his rules may sound extreme, they reflect a deeper principle: education, discipline, and self-worth must come before romantic involvement.

Even if a guy shows up looking impressive—like wearing a sharp three-piece suit and holding a master's degree—Shaq says he'd still grill him with questions like "What you trying to do?" to check if he's serious.

Why these rules?

Shaq wants his kids, particularly his daughters, to develop true self-reliance, confidence, and personal success before getting into relationships. He views his girls as "sharper, more thoughtful, and more caring," so he gives them extra time and protection to grow. His main goals are:

- **Putting education first, he's offered to fully pay for their bachelor's, master's, or even a doctorate, telling them to "take your time."**

- **Learning to feel happy and complete on their own, without relying on a man ("You don't need anybody to make you happy").**

- **Building an independent life—perhaps starting their own company or achieving big things—so they grow into strong women who don't depend on anyone else.**

- **Steering clear of early distractions or unreliable guys, he knows "how guys can be" from his own past and wants to shield his daughters from that.**

It's classic protective 'girl dad' energy from Shaq—full of humor and love yet backed by firm boundaries to help his children build the strongest possible future. He stands by these rules because he firmly believes that putting in hard work on yourself will pay off big time in the long run! Moreover, teenage relationships serve as vital stepping stones rather than lifelong commitments; their true value lies in the lessons they impart—fostering emotional resilience, self-awareness, and a clearer vision for future connections. Embrace these experiences as opportunities for growth, prioritizing your personal journey above all, for authenticity in love begins with authenticity in self.

Please consider yourself as doing the right thing: focus on your studies, be responsible now for your future, and don't dwell on the small parts but on the big picture for your life and future.

A few months ago, I learned something from my work that made me think I could share what I've seen and my past experiences with you in the form of poetry. This is a special gift for you, and I hope you can learn something new from it. Sometimes, wisdom is best shared not through rules or lectures, but through stories and art that speak directly to the heart.

KEEP SHINING, BE A UNIQUE YOU

We are all human beings.

No one is smarter or more special than others.

The secret of success depends on your ambition and determination.

Keep in mind that you were born with talents that will surely be useful someday.

We do have the ability to overcome challenges in life.

With every challenge, you are already growing.

Believe in yourself and trust the path you take.

No matter how hard your journey is,

hold onto your beliefs and never give up on your goals.

We do have times when things aren't going our way—experiencing anger, hate, tears, and a loss of confidence.

Remember, no matter how terrible situations are,

do not blame yourself, feel regret, or be afraid.

Stay focused on yourself and keep moving forward.

Everyone is a unique individual.

Please keep being who you are.

You are a unique shining star!

Someday, you will show us your beauty.

You will be proud, and so will we!

Keep shining, be a unique you!

"For I know the plans I have for you," declares the Lord, "plans to prosper you and not to harm you, plans to give you hope and a future."

Jeremiah 29:11 (NIV)

HOPE CREATES MIRACLES

God is real, and He always provides a pathway for me to walk through when I am in danger. He sends His people to protect me. When I feel desperate, He gently reminds me that I am never alone—He is right there with me. Faith does not mean life becomes easy; it means we are never abandoned in the difficult moments. God's presence often shows up quietly, through timing, people, or a sense of peace that cannot be explained.

The same thing happened with my current job. It wasn't that I submitted an application and got hired right away. No, I sent in my application, and it took a few months before they contacted me. Perhaps it was God's perfect timing and will. He fully understood that I had been battling depression, but now I have recovered well, and He has placed me in a teenage mental health facility. Sometimes, unanswered prayers are not refusals, but preparations. God often waits until we are strong enough—not perfect, but healed enough—to step into the work He has prepared for us. I sometimes hear a clear, gentle voice saying:

"Go and help heal those innocent souls. Now you can do it—help them for Me!"

This calling did not come from ambition or personal gain; it came from pain transformed into purpose. What once wounded me has now become the very place where I can bring healing to others.

I don't mind if some people think I'm easy to take advantage of, and if they get lazy, so they could do less work. My true mission is to help these kids. I have higher-priority tasks and a much greater purpose to fulfill. I don't worry about what others think; I don't need to explain myself to anyone. I simply need to do my very best, keep a clear conscience, and bring glory to God. When you know your purpose, other people's opinions lose their power. A clear conscience before God is far more valuable than approval from the world.

Here is another powerful example that shows God is real and actively at work. One day, a teenage boy became extremely agitated and impossible to control. He was yelling, thrashing around, and turning the entire place upside down. The facility staff had no choice but to let him express it until he wore himself out. Moments like these reveal how fragile young hearts can be when they are overwhelmed by pain they don't yet know how to name or release.

When I saw what was happening, my colleague looked over at me and shook his head. Right then, I quietly decided to pray for the boy, pleading from my heart: "Please, God, help him and bring him back to peace…"

A couple of hours later, I heard that he had started to calm down and improve. The very next day, he was successfully discharged from one of our departments. I am so deeply grateful. God gave a miracle, and I thanked God for hearing my prayer and calming the boy down and helping him get better so quickly. Miracles do not always look dramatic; sometimes they look like a calm returning. Safety restored, and a young life given another chance.

I was sitting in class helping the kids with class translation; however, when I overheard a girl talking about the Bible, my heart filled with joy—they were genuinely interested in knowing the Lord! God often opens doors when we are simply being faithful in small, ordinary moments.

I felt deeply honored to join the conversation and talk with those girls about the Ten Commandments from the Bible. A few months later, I was thrilled to hear that their parents had bought them their own Bibles. Even better, they are now attending church services regularly to learn more and grow closer to God. I am so grateful to our Heavenly Father. Thank You, Lord—you are so good! With You by my side, I am not afraid, because You are my Savior. Amen!

"Even though I walk through the darkest valley, I will fear no evil, for you are with me."

—Psalm 23:4 (NIV)

IN THE DARK SIDE

In this dark city, I can't see the light.

I don't know where I am.

Only I can see the dark side.

I can feel the hopelessness and pains from my friend's eyes,

Some guys took my friends to another place, but they never came back.

Perhaps, they brought them to another happy place.

I hope that place will never bring any pain, only joy and happiness.

Where are my mom and dad?

I miss them, and I hope I can give them my kisses and hugs.

I hope I can tell my dearest parents that I love them.

I wish I could listen to their advice. Don't run around.

I know it now, but it is too late.

Where are my mom and dad?

In this dark city, everything looks hopeless and terrifying.

Mom, I am very cold and hungry, and I want to go home.

Can you feel by heart I am calling you?

Please help me get out of here, Mom!

Maybe this is my last time yelling from my heart.

Now it's my turn.

I don't know where these guys are taking me.

Only I can see the dark side, then I fall into sleep.

In the dream, I see my parents and friends.

We are talking, laughing, and singing.

Suddenly, I see a bright light.

I follow the light, walk into it.

I can see beautiful views like heaven,

Everybody who lives here looks happy to stay here.

I realize that I belong to this place now,

The place people always dreamed of.

Fare well, Mom and Dad!

You know I deeply love you guys.

Now I have to separate from you,

Even though it breaks my heart to separate from you all.

I deeply believe that we will have a storm bring the justice back.

By then, we will have a bright future.

Fare well, my dearest parents, please help me to take care of yourself!

Love you guys as always!

BE FAITHFUL, YOU CAN DO THIS!

When teenagers face challenges, depression, or tough times, they often turn to me for guidance and emotional support. I draw from lessons I've learned in school, at work, and through church teachings and sermons. I share short, meaningful stories in an engaging, easy-to-understand way, so they can apply these truths to make their lives a little easier. Teenagers do not need perfect answers; they need presence, patience, and someone who truly listens without judgment.

Pastor Rick Warren reminds us: "Valleys are a part of life. The Bible says in ***Deuteronomy 11:11, 'The land you will soon take over is a land of hills and valleys' (NLT)***." Valleys are inevitable. You may have just come out of one, be in the middle of one right now, or be heading into another. There's no avoiding them in this life—instead, expect them. Valleys happen to everyone. Understanding this truth helps young people stop blaming themselves for their pain and start learning how to walk through it with hope. They're impartial: good things happen to bad people, and bad things happen to good people. We live in a fallen, broken world full of problems. No one is immune or insulated from pain. No one sails through life without difficulties.

I'm truly grateful that I can offer something helpful to support these young people, both in the moment and for the long term. When a teenager isn't feeling well—physically or emotionally—it affects me deeply. In those moments, I gently remind them that no matter how hard things get, God is walking with them. He stays right by their side, supporting them through every valley in life. Sometimes, just knowing that God has not left them gives them the strength to take one more step forward.

It encourages me to see how this truth gives them strength. Knowing God is always with them helps them push through both physical and emotional struggles. They find the courage to keep moving forward because they believe He is right there beside them. So keep the faith, be still…

Trust

Trust—it's such a simple word, and it should be one of the easiest things to give.

Yet these days, it has become incredibly rare and surprisingly difficult to offer. What once felt natural now feels risky, almost dangerous, because trusting the wrong person can cost us emotionally, financially, or even spiritually.

The chaos of our world has made trust so fragile. People break promises. They hide the truth. Some public officials, fully aware that what they're doing is illegal, still choose to commit crimes for personal wealth and power—embezzling taxpayers' money and deeply eroding public confidence in government. When leaders betray trust, the damage spreads far beyond politics; it seeps into families, workplaces, schools, and communities, teaching people to guard their hearts instead of opening them.

As a result, trust between people has been steadily crumbling. We're constantly bombarded with news of crimes that only confirm how fragile—and how rapidly disappearing—human trust has become. Relationships between people are growing more distant, more estranged. Walls are being built where bridges once stood, and self-protection has quietly replaced compassion.

Sometimes I can't help but wonder: how can we possibly restore trust among ourselves as human beings? How do we learn to believe again when disappointment feels safer than hope? There is really only one answer—but most people seem to have already forgotten it.

In this dazzling world of bright lights, luxury, and cutting-edge technology, people are gradually losing themselves, consumed by an endless hunger for wealth and power.

A light in the darkness means there is hope…

And we will always have hope.

Deep in our hearts, we know the truth that holds everything together. The only unbreakable trust comes from God—and from clinging tightly to His perfect plan. We can truly keep trust alive only through our relationship with Him. Because He never lies, never abandons us, and never changes. Human trust may falter, but divine trust remains steady, unmoved by time, circumstance, or failure.

God's plan is the solid ground beneath our feet. He is always working quietly and perfectly, even when we cannot yet see it. Trusting in His timing, His ways, and His loving heart for us makes everything possible.

America was founded on that very same foundation: "In God We Trust."

It is far more than words printed on money or a mere motto—it serves as a powerful reminder that real freedom, true unity, and lasting strength come when we place our trust in something greater than ourselves. It reminds us that a nation, like an individual, cannot stand strong without moral grounding.

We are held in God's grace. I refuse to believe we cannot overcome our challenges. With faith, everything is possible. This is not mere hope—it is the truth: with God, nothing is impossible. Not healing the broken, not protecting the vulnerable, not rebuilding trust that endures. What feels impossible to human effort alone becomes achievable through divine guidance.

"In God We Trust" has left a lasting imprint on American society. It is much more than a slogan on currency—it stands as a profound symbol of trust, resilience, and shared values that have helped shape the nation's identity through times of crisis and division. This motto aligns deeply with America's foundational ideals: individual liberty, moral responsibility, and the conviction that our rights come from a higher source, not merely from human institutions.

Many of the nation's early leaders, influenced by Judeo-Christian principles, viewed faith as essential to virtue and self-governance—echoing George Washington's famous words that religion and morality are "indispensable supports" for political prosperity. They understood that freedom without moral responsibility eventually collapses.

This trust in God has inspired American exceptionalism—not as pride or superiority, but as a humble acknowledgment that true blessings flow when a people rely on divine wisdom. It has fueled perseverance through wars, economic hardships, social struggles, and deep divisions. When Americans turn to prayer, faith, and love—as you so beautifully urged—it fosters lasting unity, healing, and strength. As Scripture declares, "with God all things are possible" (Matthew 19:26), and history proves how faith has sustained movements for justice, freedom, and renewal.

"In God We Trust"—a motto born in tough times. It started during the Civil War in 1861. As the nation faced deep division and hardship, people turned to faith for strength and hope. A minister wrote to the Treasury Secretary, asking to honor God on the nation's coins. That led to the motto appearing for the first time on the two-cent piece—a simple reminder that real strength comes from above. Even then, people understood that survival required more than military power; it required faith.

Fast forward to 1956, during the Cold War. With tensions rising against atheistic communism, President Dwight D. Eisenhower signed it into law as America's official national motto. It was added to all paper money, too. This wasn't just politics—it was a way to say faith builds freedom, unity, and lasting endurance, rooting our trust in something greater than ourselves. Christianity emphasizes forgiveness, helping others, and seeing "light in the darkness," which can build personal resilience.

In our busy, distracting world today, many people—especially young ones—feel lost when it comes to real trust. Social media, pressure from friends, worries about the future, and endless noise make it hard to stay connected to something solid. But here's the good news: we can always go back to the source.

Trust in God, and anything is possible.

Lean on Him through prayer.

Show up with love every day.

He sees every soft, honest part of your heart…

And He's working everything out for good.

I recently watched a YouTube video from Fox News that covered the live hearing/program at Turning Point USA's America Fest. Our current Vice President, JD Vance, made a bold statement during his speech: "Christianity is America's creed—the shared moral language from the Revolution to the Civil War and beyond." He also said:

"The only thing that has truly served as an anchor of the United States of America is that we have been, and by the grace of God, we always will be, a Christian nation." These words stood out to me because they highlight how deeply Christian values and principles have shaped our country's history, moral foundation, and identity. It was inspiring to hear him affirm this so clearly in front of the crowd.

America is a Christian nation—that is a solid fact. No other system, whether socialism or Marxism, can ever replace what we have. Our country was built on biblical principles and values. Other systems will never truly work here. We are protected by God. We love and worship Him. Do you know why America has thousands of patents for creative inventions and the most Nobel Prize winners in the world? It's because we fear God in a healthy, reverent way. God has given us freedom—freedom to think, to speak, to create, and to dream without fear. That freedom unleashes creativity and innovation like nowhere else. No other country can compare with it. America is a great country and I love my country forever!

"America is one Nation under God, indivisible, with liberty and justice for all."

— Dwight D. Eisenhower

MY AMBITION FOR THIS WORLD

I want to mention this Bible verse one more time.

"Be careful how you think; your life is shaped by your thoughts."

Proverbs 4:23 (GNT)

This verse from the Bible speaks deeply to me. It reminds us that our thoughts are powerful—they shape what we believe, how we feel, and ultimately the direction of our entire life. What we allow into our minds matters because it influences everything that follows. Our thoughts eventually become our habits, and our habits shape our destiny.

When I read this verse, it takes me back to my own story. As a young person, I faced painful family betrayal. Some family members thought I was foolish or incapable, even suggesting I needed to go to a special education school. Those negative words and judgments hurt deeply and made me question my worth. At such a young age, I began to understand how words can either wound or strengthen a person. Because of these challenges at home, my parents decided to send me to America for a fresh start.

I arrived in the U.S. feeling uncertain, carrying the weight of those early wounds, language barriers, and a completely different culture. I often felt invisible, misunderstood, and unsure of where I truly belonged.

During those difficult years in America—nearly 16 years now—I've faced countless life challenges: financial struggles, cultural adjustments, moments of loneliness, and times of deep despair. Yet through it all, I know God has always been with me. Even when I didn't fully know how to connect with Him or communicate in prayer, He was there. He sent His servants, kind people, mentors, opportunities—to pull me out of darkness, protect me from evil, and guide me forward.

God has communicated with me in so many ways: through quiet inspirations, through Scripture, through people who encouraged me never to give up, especially in my most desperate periods. He reminded me again and again: "He is always with you." Because of His presence, I never gave up. I've worked many jobs, from small businesses to government agencies, and I've gained valuable experience and knowledge along the way. Each role, no matter how small it seemed at the time, prepared me for the next step.

Today, I'm no longer afraid. That knowledge and those experiences have built me into a working professional, covering and protecting me.

From my own life, I want to share this tip: Never stop learning and always find a job, any job that you are interested in trying—because it would help you, and in the future you could become the most valuable asset to the company.

First, it allows you to earn money for yourself and become independent. Second, you gain real work experience that builds confidence and skills. Third, it helps you understand how hard your parents (and others) work to support a family. My mom used to tell me when I was younger: "Earn money with your own hands. When you spend it, you will feel proud of yourself." She was absolutely right. Working hard, studying diligently, and becoming the best version of yourself brings a deep sense of pride and purpose.

Looking back, I see how Proverbs 4:23 has played out in my life. By choosing to think higher thoughts, believing in my potential, trusting God's plan, and refusing to let past betrayals or hardships define me, I learned to say goodbye to anything from the past. Your past life doesn't define your future. Your future is in your own hands. So my life has been shaped for the better, and God has walked with me every step, turning struggles into strength and doubts into determination. If you're facing your own challenges right now, remember this: Be careful what you think, because your thoughts shape your life. Hold on to positive, faith-filled thoughts. Keep learning, keep working, keep trusting God. He is always by your side, even when you don't see the way forward yet. He will guide you, inspire you, and bring you through every challenge.

I don't know how long my life will last, but I am committed to using my passion to help vulnerable teenagers. I believe this is God's will for me, and I promise Him with all my heart and strength that I will do everything I can to support those kids, give them hope, and help them grow into useful, excellent people in the future.

One day, I heard God speaking to my heart:

"Now is your time to share your experiences with the people who need them—to glorify Me and remind them that I am God, and I am always with you all."

Even though I don't have strong writing skills, I will obey His command and follow our Lord's leading. I pray that this message about mental health will bring healing and support from God, becoming a powerful tool that reaches more and more people across our country. When my final day comes, I want to hold on to Him and say, "Lord, I am ready. I have completed the mission You gave me—to pass on hope and spiritual support to those who need it most." I will be able to say I finished what You asked, and I am proud of that.

This is my heartfelt promise and my deepest desire—to serve God by lifting up the next generation, one story, one encouragement, one act of faith at a time. He has been faithful to me, and now I want to be faithful to Him.

I am so proud to be a Christian!

I feel deeply honored and grateful that the Lord has accepted me into His family. On November 30, 2025, I was baptized at the Brooklyn Tabernacle. My Commitment to the Lord Today, I stand here to make this solemn and joyful commitment to Him:

"I accept Jesus Christ as my Lord and Savior, and I look forward to spending eternity with Him. "Even if there were doubts or questions in my heart before, I believe any uncertainty will vanish the moment I wake up in heaven—that alone will be all the proof I need. I pray that, by His amazing grace alone, I am qualified to enter His presence. I am proud to be a Christian, proud to love and serve my country—the United States of America—and willing to defend it with courage and honor. This moment fills my heart with overwhelming joy and perfect peace.

Thank You, Jesus, for Your endless love, for Your complete forgiveness, and for welcoming me into Your family.

I am forever Yours!

Farewell

Part I

When I was a child,

I never felt alone.

You were my big company,

Told me stories and taught me how to sing songs.

I felt safe and happy when you were around.

When I was young.

I never felt alone.

You were always my best friend.

We were often walking through the park, talking and eating in the same café.

You always taught me life lessons,

encouraged me to be a better person.

I couldn't understand why.

Years later, I went to junior high,

I became a grown-up girl.

I felt alone all the time

You were not around me anymore.

Finally, I understood your advice.

When I look around, you are not here.

Part II

Now, I'm in America.

Pursuing the dream that I always desired.

But you are in another world,

I wasn't there when you were ill,

I was chasing my dream.

I am working hard, and my life is getting better.

I wish I could treat you to a fancy, delicious meal.

Perhaps we could travel somewhere in America,

But you are not in this world anymore,

Only I can see your shadow everywhere.

I heard some theory:

"If you miss somebody very much,

go to the sea, yell his name, he can hear."

I went to the East River, carrying my degree

I yelled, "Grandpa, I miss you,"

and waved the paper in my hand.

Suddenly, the sun shone for a second,

I felt you heard me and tried to give me your response.

Goodbye, Grandpa, I love you very much.

You will always have a big spot in my heart.

I will be the better person that you always expected me to be.

Thank you for always being my best friend.

I miss you and wish you a good life in another world!

Farewell, Grandpa!

Chapter 5
Religion Matters to Our Nation

Every day I sit in class with those wonderful children. Most classes go well, and I learn something new each day. But there's one class I can hardly tolerate for long: social studies. Whenever the teacher discusses literature about nationalism, I get a terrible headache. It's because I keep hearing so much hatred toward America—if they had the opportunity, they'd leave this country or move somewhere else. What troubles me most is not disagreement, but the absence of gratitude for what this nation provides.

I truly don't understand why they feel this way about America. Another possible reason could be that today's mainstream media constantly pushes stories and news that harm our national interests. However, they seem unaware of how many people around the world desperately want to come to this country. Now it's even harder to get in. When people immigrate here, they work incredibly hard—they escape difficulties in their own countries to pursue life, liberty, and the pursuit of happiness. Maybe someday they will understand the American Dream and realize they can achieve it. Perhaps because of their age, if they get older, they will come to understand. Freedom is often most appreciated by those who have lived without it.

But one thing that truly comforts and encourages me is that all the children still have a deep reverence for God—they genuinely want to draw closer to Him. Perhaps this is exactly what God means: with Him, nothing is impossible, even changing hearts or opening eyes to the truth one day.

I want to remind us all of how important the Bible's impact on American values is. Because nowadays, there have been so many changes. However, I'm proud to be American, and I'm a Christian. I believe that America needs to come back to its origins. Also, America's identity as a land of opportunity, resilience, and moral purpose is a fusion of Christianity, with its emphasis on human dignity, redemption, and community, and American values like liberty, democracy, individualism, and the rule of law. This isn't a mere coincidence; it's the philosophical and historical engine that propelled the U.S. from 13 colonies to a global superpower. Furthermore, the Bible isn't just a sacred text for Christians—it's the moral, cultural, and philosophical cornerstone of American life, shaping everything from the nation's founding documents to everyday language and values. When a nation loses its moral compass, progress without purpose becomes dangerous.

Not only was the Bible America's first 'best-seller,' by 1690, but a third of all books printed in the colonies were Bibles or related works. American Founders like John Adams also declared, 'Our Constitution was made only for moral and religious people… it is wholly inadequate to the government of any other.' They drew directly from Scripture for concepts like equality and justice. Without these biblical guidelines, America's experiment in self-rule might have faltered. Early education, for example, (like the McGuffey Readers in 1836), used the Bible to teach virtue, ensuring citizens could govern responsibly. In 2025, as democracy faces global tests, this heritage reminds us: Biblical principles of covenant and accountability underpin the rule of law.

Do you know?

It's a controversial theory that America is a Christian nation. However, the interesting fact is that the Bible was the ***Most Cited Source of the American Founding Era.*** In 1776, the United States originated with 13 foundational states, stemming from the original 13 British colonies that proclaimed their independence. Those colonies were:

1. New Hampshire,

2. Massachusetts,

3. Rhode Island,

4. Connecticut,

5. New York,

6. New Jersey,

7. Pennsylvania,

8. Delaware,

9. Maryland,

10. Virginia,

11. North Carolina,

12. South Carolina, and

13. Georgia.

The constitutions of these early states, including Pennsylvania's, stipulated that public officeholders must affirm their faith in God and the divine inspiration of the Scriptures, with many explicitly requiring the profession of the Lord Jesus Christ as Lord and Savior. Furthermore, 55 of the 56 signers of the Declaration of Independence were Bible-believing, church-attending Christians.

<u>The first Puritan immigrants in Massachusetts and Connecticut believed that the Bible was God's divinely inspired written Word, and this sacred book was the foundation of the Puritans' morality and colonial societies.</u>

<u>**Who were Puritans? Why did they come to America?**</u>

The Puritans, led by John Winthrop, came to America in 1630 in search of prosperity and for religious and political freedom. Their religious faith and views were very influential in their goals for coming to America and in the forming of their new colonies.

Winthrop noted many of the Puritans' reasons for migration in his statement from 1629, "Reasons to be considered for justifying the undertakers of the intended plantation in New England." The Puritans, he explains, tried to escape economic hardship and what they saw as worldly and evil corruption of churches and schools in England and Europe. They saw America as a place where they could live out their beliefs, purify and fully reform the church, and advance the Christian Gospel.

The Puritans came to America with a big dream: to build a fair and God-loving community where they could practice their religion without fear, spread the teachings of Jesus, and follow fair, ethical rules based on their deep beliefs.

They focused on upholding Bible-based principles in their new communities, building colonies where Scripture (the Bible) was a role model that could shape their ideal daily life. Most importantly, they aimed to set a remarkable example—a "city on a hill"—that would motivate people everywhere to live better lives. In Winthrop's well-known 1630 sermon, A Model of Christian Charity, he described this plan in detail, urging the group to form a God-centered community held together by Christian love, harmony, and sacred commitments.

Drawing from Jesus' words in Matthew 5:14—"You are the light of the world. A city that is set on a hill cannot be hidden"—Winthrop reminded them, "For we must be as a city upon a hill, with the eyes of all people upon us," calling on them to serve as a guiding light for Europe and the rest of the world.

The Puritans in early Massachusetts and Connecticut viewed the Bible as God's inspired Word. It served as the bedrock of their ethics and their settlements. The Bible lays out God's moral law through:

- **The Ten Commandments,**

- **The Two Great Commandments, and**

- **The teachings of Moses, the prophets, Jesus, and the apostles.**

Ancient Israel followed additional ceremonial rules, but the Puritans saw these as specific to the Jewish nation and not part of the universal moral law. In Exodus 20:1–17, God gives the Ten Commandments to Moses and the Israelites:

1. Worship no other gods.

2. Make no idols.

3. Do not misuse God's name.

4. Keep the Sabbath holy.

5. Honor your parents.

6. Do not murder.

7. Do not commit adultery.

8. Do not steal.

9. Do not lie about your neighbor.

10. Do not covet what belongs to your neighbor.

These commands reflect a deeper principle—the Law of Love, captured in the Two Great Commandments:

- Love God with all your heart, soul, and mind (Deuteronomy 6:5; Matthew 22:37).

- Love your neighbor as yourself (Leviticus 19:18; Matthew 22:39).

When a religious leader asked Jesus what the greatest commandment was, He answered:

"Love the Lord your God with all your heart, with all your soul, and with all your mind." This is the first and the greatest. The second is like it: "Love your neighbor as yourself." All the Law and the Prophets hang on these two commandments (Matthew 22:37–40).

THE PURITANS IN AMERICA CREATED THE FIRST WRITTEN CONSTITUTION OF LAW

In 1639, Connecticut's Puritans created a new set of written rules called the Fundamental Orders of Connecticut. All members of the community accepted and followed them. Therefore, it became the world's first fully written constitution and the first real system for people to govern themselves. This marked a major shift in political history because most governments at the time relied on monarchies, inherited power, or unwritten customs rather than formal agreements created by the people themselves. It all started with a talk by Puritan preacher Thomas Hooker to the colony's leaders. He said the people should have power and that the government needs everyone's help. Hooker's message introduced the revolutionary idea that legitimate authority comes from the consent of the governed rather than from royal appointment or social status. Because of his ideas, the Puritans set up a fair system where people ran things themselves. Their constitution included important rules like:

- The Rule of Law

- Elected representatives

- Voting by secret ballot

- Due process of law

- Trial by jury

- No taxation without representation

- Prohibitions against cruel and unusual punishment

Many of these provisions echoed the 1636 laws of the Plymouth Pilgrims. Together, these early colonial frameworks helped establish patterns of civic participation that later shaped American democratic expectations, teaching citizens that government required accountability and public involvement.

Connecticut: The First American Colony and the Constitution State

Connecticut is the "Constitution State" because it was the first American colony to create a full written constitution for running its own government. The Fundamental Orders became an example that other colonies followed. For instance, it inspired people in Massachusetts to write their own detailed set of laws in 1641, called the Massachusetts Body of Liberties. This influence demonstrated how ideas could spread between colonies, creating a shared political culture rooted in written rights and legal protections long before the United States formally existed.

The Puritans modeled their written constitutions after the ancient Israelites' tradition of recording laws. For instance, the Ten Commandments were carved into stone. In the same way, the Puritans put every civil agreement and legal framework in writing, placing great value on the written word. This habit later ensured that America's core documents—The Declaration of Independence, the United States Constitution, and the Bill of Rights—were all formally established.

The "Rule of Law" in the Constitution

The Rule of Law is the principle that every person, including the people in power, such as the President of the U.S., a king, or a boss, must obey the law. No one is above it. The law is impartial and applies equally to everyone, with no favoritism. It is based on the belief that all people are equal before God and deserve fair treatment under the law. This idea of fairness and equality comes from natural rights, God's creation, and the Bible. The Rule of Law also creates stability within society by ensuring that justice does not depend on wealth, influence, or personal connections, but instead rests on consistent and predictable legal standards.

In 1536, John Calvin wrote in his book that the Bible teaches two key truths:

1. **Every person is made in God's image.**

2. **Every person is also imperfect because of sin.**

Because of this, he said human laws should be just and equal, just like God's laws for the Israelites. Calvin believed that because humans are imperfect, systems of government must include safeguards, checks, and clear rules to prevent abuse of authority. In 1638, Puritan leader Thomas Hooker, in America, agreed. He pointed to Deuteronomy 17:10–11, where God tells His people: "Decide cases by the law I gave you—not by your own opinions."

In other words, the Rule of Law means: Apply the same fair rules to everyone, no matter who they are, because true justice comes from God's standard.

BIBLICAL PRACTICES IN AMERICAN CONSTITUTIONS

The Rule of Law was first practiced by early Americans and later made a core part of the U.S. Constitution by the Founding Fathers. The idea started with England's Magna Carta in 1215, but it wasn't fully put into action. In the 1600s, important British thinkers like Sir Edward Coke, Samuel Rutherford, and John Locke strongly supported the idea that everyone should be equal under the law.

In 1832, French writer Alexis de Tocqueville visited America and wrote in his book Democracy in America: "Christianity teaches that all people are equal before God, so it makes sense that the law treats every citizen the same." Tocqueville also observed that American democracy succeeded partly because religious beliefs encouraged moral responsibility among citizens, strengthening community trust and civic cooperation. In the end, America turned the Rule of Law into reality fair, equal justice for everyone.

The Origin of American Education

The Puritans Promoted Bible Teaching

The Puritans strongly believed that people should read the Bible. They made laws requiring larger towns to open schools and teach children how to read and write.

In 1647, the Puritans passed the Old Deluder Satan Act, which ordered every community to start and pay for a grammar school and hire a teacher. The law's goal was to stop Satan—the "Old Deluder"—from tricking people who couldn't read and keeping them from God's Word. This Puritan law became the foundation for America's public school system.

<u>**Why Puritans Pushed Bible Reading in Schools?**</u>

The Puritans got their ideas from the Protestant Reformation—a big church shake-up in Europe. They believed every Christian, not just priests or the pope, should read and understand the Bible for themselves. This belief challenged centuries of centralized religious authority and reshaped how ordinary people viewed knowledge, faith, and personal responsibility. This came from two key ideas by Martin Luther:

1. **Priesthood of all believers – Every follower of Jesus is like a "priest" who can talk to God directly.**

2. **Sola scriptura ("Bible only") – The Bible is the #1 authority on faith and life. Nothing else tops it.**

They pointed to 2 Timothy 3:16: "All Scripture is God-breathed and useful for teaching, correcting, and training in righteousness."

This also means that church leaders could twist the truth if people could not read the Bible themselves. The Puritans remembered how the Catholic Church before the Reformation kept the Bible in Latin—most people couldn't read it and got misled. That's why they said:

Everyone needs to read the Bible!

If you don't, false teachers can trick you.

Literacy, therefore, became a spiritual safeguard as well as a social responsibility, ensuring that faith was rooted in understanding rather than blind obedience.

Moreover, they established top colleges like Harvard, Yale, and Dartmouth, all to train leaders who knew God and the Bible.

In addition, Harvard's rules said: "Every student must know that the real point of life and learning is to know God and Jesus Christ—that's eternal life (John 17:3). Put Christ at the center of all knowledge."

These schools shaped America's early leaders, including the Founding Fathers. Bible-based education wasn't just a class—it was the foundation of learning. The Puritans' strong focus on education shaped America's public schools, boosted widespread reading skills, and established the value of a knowledgeable public.

The Founder of Common Law

William Blackstone's Commentaries on the Laws of England, authored by a faithful Christian scholar from England, serves as a foundational legal treatise that systematizes the principles of common law, also termed judge-made or case law, as an outgrowth of the Scriptures. Blackstone did not see law as a human invention alone, but as a moral system reflecting divine justice. It relies primarily on judicial precedents from prior court decisions, rather than a codified body of statutes, to guide future rulings. This expansive tradition profoundly shaped jurisprudence in the United Kingdom, the United States, and other common law jurisdictions, with core tenets like the <u>presumption of innocence,</u> <u>due process</u>, and <u>trial by jury</u> of one's peers, all deriving from biblical sources. These principles protected individuals from arbitrary power and reinforced the belief that justice must be transparent and accountable.

These ideas are all rooted in biblical teachings, especially the command not to twist justice by favoring the rich or the poor. This rule appears in Leviticus 19, right before the famous line, "Love your neighbor as yourself." The verse just before it says: Don't show favoritism based on wealth or poverty. That's the foundation of "blind justice" in Western tradition—treating everyone the same.

The New Testament echoes this with the idea that in Christ, there is no slave or free, no Jew or Gentile—everyone is equal. This is where the core belief in human equality comes from.

These principles are deeply rooted in the Bible. Common law—the legal system built on court decisions and past cases rather than just written statutes—is the foundation of America's justice system, inherited directly from England during colonial times. It matters because it keeps the law consistent, reliable, and fair; judges follow earlier rulings from higher courts to decide new cases, avoiding random decisions and allowing the law to grow naturally with society.

In the U.S., common law governs key areas like injuries, contracts, and property rights when no specific law exists. It strongly shaped the Founding Fathers when they wrote the Constitution and Bill of Rights, especially ideas like fair trials and jury rights. This continuity ensured that liberty was protected not by personalities, but by enduring principles.

The Ten Commandments and Their Impact on Our Lives

The Ten Commandments, found in the Old Testament of the Bible (Exodus 20:1–17 and Deuteronomy 5:4–21), are a precious gift from our Heavenly Father, offering fundamental principles for living a life of purpose and peace. It offers moral and spiritual guidelines that hold remarkable value for people of all ages. Those commandments are a vital guide for teenagers navigating the challenges of personal development, identity formation, and decision-making, providing a foundational framework for ethical living, personal responsibility, and spiritual grounding. Especially in today's world, teens face unique pressures from social media comparisons to academic stress. These commandments—rooted in biblical values that helped shape America's foundation—foster resilience and mental health by guiding them toward worship of God and emotional well-being.

The Ten Commandments:

1. "Thou shalt have no other gods before me."

Exodus 20:3

The first commandment, translated in modern English as "You shall have no other gods before me," calls us to worship only the one true God. It is wrong to worship any god other than the one true God, as all other gods are considered false in the Christian faith. Christians believe that only one God, revealed through Jesus Christ, should be worshiped.

It means avoiding anything that could take God's rightful place at the center of our lives, whether wealth, fame, influencers, personal ambitions, or the pursuit of fleeting happiness that ultimately leaves us empty. Instead, we are called to trust in God's love and guidance and to prioritize Him in our hearts, minds, and daily actions. When we keep God first, we find true fulfillment rather than chasing promises that cannot satisfy.

For teenagers especially, this commandment is vital in a world full of constant pressures, such as seeking peer approval or chasing social media validation. These things can quietly become modern "gods" that distract from what truly matters. Staying rooted in faith through this commandment provides stability, purpose, and resilience. It helps teens shape a strong identity in Christ and make wise decisions as they navigate the challenges of adolescence.

2. "Thou shalt not make unto thee any graven image."

Exodus 20:4

The second commandment, translated in modern English as "You shall not make idols," calls people to worship God alone without creating or bowing to any images, idols, or representations.

It provides a God-given path to discover purpose and peace in a world filled with distractions and pressures. By keeping God at the center of their lives and avoiding idols such as material things, social media popularity, or personal ambitions, teens protect their mental well-being and strengthen their faith. This sacred gift equips them to navigate adolescence with thankfulness and resilience, steering clear of the anxiety and emptiness that come from chasing fleeting trends. It reminds them that God values their well-being and invites them to find joy in His eternal love.

"You shall not make for yourself an image in the form of anything in heaven above or on the earth beneath or in the waters below. You shall not bow down to them or worship them; for I, the Lord your God, am a jealous God, punishing the children for the sin of the parents to the third and fourth generation of those who hate me, but showing love to a thousand generations of those who love me and keep my commandments." (Exodus 20:4–6)

3 "Thou shalt not take the name of the Lord thy God in vain."

Exodus 20:7

The third commandment, translated in modern English as "You shall not take the name of the Lord your God in vain" (Exodus 20:7), means that we should treat God's name with reverence and care. We are called to use it thoughtfully in worship and prayer rather than carelessly or disrespectfully.

For young adults navigating a world of casual language, social media, and peer influences, this commandment provides a God-given path to integrity and peace. By speaking and acting authentically, teens protect their mental well-being, foster trusting relationships, and strengthen their faith. It's a reminder that God cares deeply about their well-being and invites them to find joy in honoring Him through mindful communication.

This commandment teaches teens to honor God's authority through reverent speech, promoting integrity and kindness in relationships. This aligns with the biblical values that influenced America's foundation, fostering a culture of faith and trust. By honoring God's name, teens help build a community rooted in love and mutual respect.

4 "Remember the Sabbath day, to keep it holy."

Exodus 20:8–10

The fourth commandment, translated in modern English as "Remember the Sabbath day, to keep it holy," calls us to dedicate one day a week to worship, prayer, and connecting with God. For Christians, this day is typically Sunday, while for Jews it is Saturday.

This practice offers teens a vital way to find peace, purpose, and balance in a busy, fast-paced world. By setting aside time to rest and focus on God, they can step away from constant activity and pressure. It helps protect their mental health, build stronger relationships, and grow spiritually while avoiding the exhaustion and burnout that often come from nonstop schedules.

It serves as a beautiful reminder that God deeply values their well-being and invites them to find true joy and refreshment in His presence. Observing the Sabbath allows teens to recharge physically, emotionally, and spiritually, creating space for what truly matters.

5 "Honour thy father and thy mother."

Exodus 20:12

The fifth commandment, translated in modern English as "Honor your father and your mother" (Exodus 20:12 and Deuteronomy 5:16), is especially important for teenagers. It offers a God-given way to build strong family relationships and emotional stability in a challenging world.

By showing respect, gratitude, and love to their parents, teens protect their mental health, foster supportive connections, and grow in faith. This simple act of honor helps them find balance and resilience, while avoiding the stress, conflict, and isolation that often come from strained family dynamics.

It serves as a powerful reminder that God deeply values their well-being and invites them to find strength, peace, and purpose in honoring their family. When teenagers embrace this commandment, they lay a foundation for healthy relationships that can last a lifetime.

6. "Thou shalt not kill."

Exodus 20:13

The sixth commandment, translated in modern English as "Do not murder," means we should value all life as sacred. It calls us to choose kindness and peace over harm—not only in our physical actions but also in our words and attitudes toward others.

It matters deeply for teens because it fosters compassion, reduces conflict, and builds trusting relationships, all while protecting mental health and deepening faith. This God-given gift empowers them to navigate adolescence with empathy and resilience, helping them find true joy in honoring God's love for every person.

7. "Thou shalt not commit adultery."

Exodus 20:14

The seventh commandment, translated in modern English as "Do not commit adultery," means to honor the sacredness of relationships and maintain purity in actions and thoughts.

For teens navigating a world filled with romantic pressures, media influences, and evolving identities, this commandment offers a God-given way to build healthy relationships and emotional stability. By valuing respect, boundaries, and commitment, teens protect their mental health, foster meaningful connections, and grow in faith.

It's a reminder that God values their well-being and invites them to find joy in honoring the family and Him through pure and respectful relationships.

8. "Thou shalt not steal."

Exodus 20:15

The eighth commandment, translated in modern English as "Do not steal," encourages teenagers to embrace honesty and integrity by respecting others' property and rights.

In today's world, full of peer pressure, social media influences, and temptations to take shortcuts, this commandment provides a God-given path to build trust and emotional peace. By choosing truthfulness over stealing, whether it involves physical items, digital content, or intellectual work, teens safeguard their mental health, nurture meaningful relationships, and strengthen their faith. This divine gift empowers them to navigate adolescence with authenticity and resilience, avoiding the guilt and anxiety that come from dishonest behavior. It serves as a reminder that God cares for their well-being and calls them to find joy in living with honesty.

9. "Thou shalt not bear false witness against thy neighbor."

Exodus 20:16

The ninth commandment, translated into modern English as "Do not give false witness against your neighbor," urges teenagers to speak truthfully and avoid lying or spreading false information about others.

For young adults navigating a world of social media, gossip, and peer dynamics, this commandment offers a God-given way to build trust and emotional stability. By choosing honesty and kindness in their words, teens protect their mental health, foster strong relationships, and grow in faith.

This divine gift helps them navigate adolescence with integrity and resilience, avoiding the stress and guilt of deceitful actions. It is a reminder that God values their well-being and invites them to find joy in living truthfully and compassionately.

10. "Thou shalt not covet."

Exodus 20:17

The tenth commandment, "Thou shalt not covet thy neighbor's goods" (Exodus 20:17 and Deuteronomy 5:21), is translated in modern English as "Do not covet." This means: You shall not covet your neighbor's house; you shall not covet your neighbor's wife, nor his male servant, nor his female servant, nor his ox, nor his donkey, nor anything that is your neighbor's.

These commandments remind teenagers to avoid envying what others have and to cultivate contentment with their own blessings. For teens navigating a world of social media, peer comparisons, and materialistic pressures, this commandment offers a God-given way to find peace and gratitude. It protects teens' mental health, builds stronger relationships, and helps them navigate adolescence with contentment and resilience, avoiding the stress and dissatisfaction of constant comparison.

It's a reminder that God values their well-being and invites them to find joy in His love and sufficiency.

Commandments Matter for Teenagers in Life

The Ten Commandments are vital because they reflect God's design for a fulfilling life, rooted in worship and love. For teenagers, these principles counter negative cultural influences, such as materialism and peer pressure, which can harm their mental health. We need to follow the Ten Commandments; by following them, teens develop self-discipline, build supportive relationships, and find spiritual peace, all of which protect against anxiety, depression, and loneliness. America's foundation is influenced by biblical values.

These commandments are especially critical for all of us.

The First Commandment: "Thou shalt have no other gods before me." Exodus 20:3 Modern English Translation**: You shall have no other gods before Me.**

This commandment calls teens to keep God as the center of their lives, trusting His love and guidance over distractions like social media, popularity, or material things. It means rooting their identity in faith, not external validation.

The fourth commandment: "Remember the Sabbath day, to keep it holy." Exodus 20:8–10

This commandment urges teens to dedicate one day a week (e.g., Sunday for Christians) to rest, worship, and connection with God and family, setting it apart as sacred. It's about pausing from schoolwork, screens, and busyness to recharge. You need to go to Church to worship God yourself and feel God's love, and get ready for the new week to start school or work.

The Fifth Commandment: "Honour thy father and thy mother." Exodus 20:12

<u>Modern English Translation</u>: **Respecting parents helps build mutual trust. Families should encourage open communication with each other and reinforce family unity, which can be a source of emotional support.**

The Ninth Commandment: "Thou shalt not bear false witness against thy neighbor." Exodus 20:16

<u>Modern English Translation</u>: **Do not give false witness against your neighbor.**

The commandment: "Do not give false witness against your neighbor." Bearing false witness refers to lying or sharing false information about someone, particularly in ways that could cause them harm or bad consequences. This might happen in serious situations, like a courtroom, or in casual moments, such as spreading gossip or rumors. Here, "neighbor" doesn't just mean the person next door—it includes anyone, like friends, classmates, family, or even strangers. For teenagers, this commandment teaches honesty and fairness in how we talk about or treat others. It's about steering clear of lies, half-truths that could damage someone's reputation, emotions, or relationships, while also taking accountability for the impact of your words.

The tenth commandment: "Thou shalt not covet." Exodus 20:17

The tenth commandment, "Thou shalt not covet thy neighbor's goods" (Exodus 20:17 and Deuteronomy 5:21), translated in modern English as "Do not covet," meaning you shall not covet your neighbor's house.

Teenagers often face situations where coveting comes up naturally—through social media, peer groups, or societal expectations.

Teenagers often encounter situations where coveting arises naturally, driven by social media, peer influences, or societal pressures. Here's why this commandment is relevant for them:

1. **Social Media and Comparison:** Apps like Instagram, TikTok, or Snapchat frequently highlight others' seemingly perfect lives—stylish outfits, exotic trips, or social status. Coveting these can leave teens feeling dissatisfied with their own circumstances. By learning to recognize these comparisons as often curated and unrealistic, teens can develop discernment and focus on authentic self-worth rather than digital appearances.

2. **Mental Health and Contentment:** Constantly desiring what others have can cause stress, lower self-worth, or a feeling of never measuring up. By resisting coveting, teens can cultivate gratitude, which promotes happiness and supports mental health. Moreover, practicing contentment helps teens manage anxiety, reduces feelings of inadequacy, and builds emotional resilience against external pressures.

3. **Stronger Relationships:** Envy can damage friendships. For instance, jealousy over a friend's new gadget, academic success, or popularity might breed resentment or competitive behavior. This commandment urges teens to support their friends' achievements rather than feeling envious. It also encourages empathy, teaching teens to celebrate others' successes and maintain positive social connections rather than fostering rivalry or isolation.

4. **Preventing Poor Choices**: Coveting can lead teens to make harmful decisions, such as lying, cheating, or stealing to obtain what someone else has. This commandment acts as a guide, cautioning against letting jealousy

drive actions. By internalizing this principle, teens are more likely to develop self-discipline and moral decision-making skills that carry into adulthood.

5. **Developing Character**: Embracing contentment fosters maturity and integrity. It teaches teens to pursue their own goals honestly, focusing on personal growth rather than fixating on others' possessions or successes. Additionally, this mindset nurtures a long-term vision for life, encouraging teens to value persistence, effort, and character over immediate gratification or superficial comparisons.

Not only so, but we also glory in our sufferings, because we know that suffering produces perseverance; perseverance, character; and character, hope. And hope does not put us to shame, because God's love has been poured out into our hearts through the <u>Holy Spirit</u>, who has been given to us."

Romans 5:3–5 (NIV)

Romans 5:3–5 shows us that the challenges have a purpose. Paul says that tough times can build perseverance, which shapes your character, and character leads to hope. For teens, this is very important! You might deal with stress from school, family pressures, or feelings like anxiety or depression. These struggles don't mean you're weak—they're like steps God uses to help you grow stronger and more hopeful. But in many cultures, talking about mental health can feel wrong.

People might say, "Don't talk about your feelings," or "Keep family issues private." This can make teens feel ashamed, like they're supposed to be perfect or always strong. Paul says hope doesn't bring shame because God's love is already in you. So, it's okay to ask for help, share your struggles, or seek support.

CHAPTER 6
Breaking the Stigma: Mental Health and Recovery Across Cultures

We know mental health challenges can be tough, but they do not define your future. As a staff member at a teen mental health facility, I see your amazing potential and the bright path waiting for you. Many teens like you have received medical and counseling support. They're getting back to their everyday lives—returning to school, starting college, and chasing their dreams. You can do this too!

As the saying goes, 'When God closes a door, He opens a window.' This means that when you're struggling with mental health challenges, God is aware and may open another 'door'—a new gift or talent—as you work toward recovery. He may even bless you with multiple talents. However, you must actively engage in the process to overcome these challenges and have the courage and belief that you can accomplish the task, that you can finish this mission, and that you have a bright future. Be patient and keep your faith strong!

Recently, I learned that in many countries, due to cultural norms, mental health challenges are often viewed as shameful, carrying the stigma of "loss of face" that can affect a family's reputation. This may lead individuals to keep their struggles private, sharing them only with close family to avoid judgment, discrimination, or isolation. For example, in China, parents often hide a child's depression and other mental health issues to avoid gossip. Some families discourage therapy, instead urging children to 'study harder' or 'be stronger,' believing effort alone can resolve the issue.

In India, a girl with anxiety may be encouraged to remain silent to protect her marriage prospects, and many families prefer consulting religious healers before seeking psychiatric help. In certain Middle Eastern cultures, mental health challenges are sometimes viewed as personal weaknesses or spiritual issues rather than medical conditions, making it difficult for young adults to seek support.

In some African and Latin American communities, teens with depression or trauma often face social exclusion, and mental health issues may be expressed through physical ailments instead of verbal communication. This adds another layer of difficulty in identifying and addressing the problem.

Peer pressure also plays a significant role in teen mental health across cultures. Teens may fear judgment or bullying from friends if they openly discuss therapy or their struggles, which reinforces stigma. Programs that encourage peer-led support groups have shown to reduce isolation and promote early intervention.

Technology is another factor that has both positive and negative effects. Social media can heighten anxiety and feelings of inadequacy, but digital platforms also provide access to counseling apps, online therapy sessions, and virtual support networks, making mental health resources more accessible than ever. Learning to navigate technology wisely is an important skill for modern teens.

In recent years, public awareness of mental health has continued to grow, with more and more people recognizing that mental health is as vital as physical health. In developed countries, such as the United States, Canada, and European nations, individuals can access professional help and treatment in environments that uphold equal rights. For example, U.S. laws and policies protect your right to receive treatment without discrimination, providing meaningful opportunities to recover or effectively manage your condition. We understand that you are here and may face a challenging journey ahead.

Taking Steps to Break the Stigma

No matter where you're from, you can help break the mental health stigma. Start by talking openly about your feelings with someone you trust, like a friend, family member, or counselor. Sharing your story can make others feel less alone and show that it's okay to seek help. For example, if you're in a culture where mental health is kept quiet, you could talk to a trusted adult or join a support group to find understanding. Every small conversation helps change how people view mental health.

You can also use creative outlets to share your experiences safely—writing in a journal, creating art, or recording music or videos. These activities not only help you process emotions but can also inspire others who are struggling to open up. Even online communities and moderated forums can provide safe spaces for teens to speak freely about mental health without fear of judgment.

Another way to break stigma is through education. Learning about mental health conditions, understanding symptoms, and knowing treatment options can help teens challenge myths and misconceptions. The more knowledge you share with your peers, the more empowered your community becomes. Schools can play a role too, by organizing mental health awareness events or peer-led workshops.

Your Unique Mental Health Journey

Everyone's mental health journey is unique, just like your personality. Some teens recover quickly, others need more time—and that's okay! Mental health challenges are treatable, and recovery is a chance to discover your strength and potential. Whether you're from a culture that hides mental health struggles or one that encourages open talk, you have the power to take control. Keep taking small steps, stay hopeful, and believe in yourself—amazing things can happen!

The teens I've worked with show this every day: some return to school, others start jobs, and many find new passions. Even if you face setbacks, like pausing treatment, you can always start again. It's important to remember that progress isn't always linear. Some days will feel harder than others, and that's normal. Celebrate small victories—like attending a session, speaking up about your feelings, or trying a new coping strategy. Each effort is part of building resilience.

Your future is bright, and every step brings you closer to it. You've got this!

When you are in middle or high school, teachers often ask, "What do you want to do in the future?"

Students might say, "I want to be an engineer, a businessman, or a doctor." These are excellent ideas. Sharing them shows you're thinking about your future, and that's called brainstorming—a way to come up with ideas and plan your path.

Brainstorming is essential

Brainstorming is a crucial concept. It isn't just for school; it's a skill for life. In high school or college, you'll write essays for your classes. Teachers give specific rules for each essay, like how to organize it or what to include. To do well, you need to brainstorm ideas, use clear sentences, and check your grammar to meet those rules. This helps you earn good grades.

Brainstorming also strengthens critical thinking. When you brainstorm, you explore multiple solutions, weigh pros and cons, and decide what works best. These are the same skills employers value when solving problems, creating projects, or planning events. Brainstorming prepares you to approach challenges creatively and thoughtfully rather than reacting impulsively.

But it's not just about grades—learning to plan and meet deadlines teaches you skills you'll need later, like in a job you might do in the future. For example, if you work at a company, your boss might give you a project with a deadline. Finishing it on time shows you're responsible and helps you keep your job.

Deadlines and Responsibility: Why They're Important

Many teachers or professors require their students to submit assignments on time. If students miss the due date, they may lose points or receive no grade for the assignment. Many students find this unacceptable, but it is a basic rule they must follow. This rule applies not only in school but also to future careers. For example, if you work at a company and your employer asks you to complete a project within a specific timeframe, you must finish it on time or earlier to earn your paycheck.

As an employee, you must follow your employer's instructions to meet deadlines. Failure to meet deadlines can have serious consequences in both school and the workplace. Just as teachers deduct points for late assignments, employers may view missed deadlines as a lack of responsibility. Professionalism is important because failing to show these qualities could damage your reputation and limit future opportunities, even beyond your current job. Good habits like punctuality and reliability are transferable skills—qualities that colleges and future employers actively look for.

Developing good habits early, such as managing time effectively and prioritizing tasks, is essential for success. In school, students can practice these skills by planning their assignments, breaking them into smaller tasks, and setting personal deadlines ahead of the due date.

Time management also helps protect your mental health. When you plan ahead, you reduce last-minute stress and avoid feeling overwhelmed. Teens who learn to balance school, work, and personal life develop a sense of control and resilience that benefits them long-term.

Over the past two years, I've worked with young adults in teen mental health facilities. I'm so proud of their hard work. Many have joined programs like the Summer Youth Employment Program (SYEP), where they gain job skills and earn money for college. I see pride in their eyes as they realize their efforts pay off. Some teens leave our facilities after making great progress, which is exciting but also bittersweet. Others have to pause treatment because of family or personal challenges, which can be tough. But there's always hope. When you're ready to make a change, you can start again and build a brighter future.

Teenagers often face intense mental health struggles, such as anxiety, depression, or feelings of being overwhelmed by school, relationships, or self-identity. These challenges can feel like a "wilderness" or "wasteland"—barren, isolating, and hopeless. The verse offers encouragement in the following ways:

Say Goodbye to the Past

We always carry guilt, shame, or trauma from past experiences, like bullying, failure, or family issues. These experiences can weigh heavily, making it feel impossible to move forward. Teenagers often feel trapped by what has happened, thinking they must carry it forever. This is hard for teenagers to do. It also calls on them to "forget the former things" and reminds them that they don't have to be defined by their past. This isn't about ignoring what happened—it's about acknowledging it, learning from it, and then choosing not to let it control your future.

They can release those burdens, perhaps through journaling, talking to a trusted friend or counselor, or prayer, to make space for healing.

Tell yourself, "Tomorrow will be a new beginning."

For young adults struggling with mental health, this can be a reminder that their current pain isn't the end of the story. Life is full of opportunities to reset and redefine yourself. New opportunities—like making new friends, participating in therapy sessions, or personal growth—can emerge, even when things feel hopeless. Setting small, achievable goals for the next day helps teens feel a sense of control and purpose, reducing feelings of helplessness. Tell yourself, "I have a terrible life, and I need to get over it right away and restart everything in life tomorrow."

Finding a Path Forward

Encouragement to Perceive Hope: The question "Do you not perceive it?" advises and encourages young adults to actively look for signs of hope and progress in their lives. This could be as simple as recognizing a good day, a kind word from someone, or a step toward feeling better. It encourages a mindset shift from despair to hope.

Focus on Now!

Focus on what you can do today. Overthinking what might happen can make you feel discouraged and want to give up. Instead, take small steps toward healing. Follow your doctor's advice, take your medications as prescribed, and show up to therapy sessions on time. Adding daily self-check-ins, like journaling your mood or achievements, helps track progress and reinforces a sense of agency.

Trust the process; it takes time, but you're stronger than you think. Every step you take builds your confidence and helps you grow. Remember: healing is not linear. Some days will feel harder than others, and that's okay. Persistence, patience, and self-compassion are key. Celebrate each small step, and remind yourself that each moment is a chance to move forward.

Step by Step and Keep Moving Forward

No matter where you are in your journey, you have the power to shape your future. Your past experiences do not dictate your destiny—they are lessons, not labels. Your past does not mean the future will remain unchanged; worrying about what will happen in the future won't help.

Focus on small, manageable steps today—like catching up with your schoolwork, attending therapy, reading a book, or trying something new. Even taking a short walk, practicing a hobby, or journaling your thoughts counts as progress. Small steps build confidence and momentum. Have a fun time with your peers. Social support is crucial—positive relationships can help you stay motivated and remind you that you're not alone in this journey. Every effort counts, and each step brings you closer to your goals. You've got this!

We are very proud to see that at the end of every summer and winter semester, many of our young patients leave our mental health facilities. We're incredibly proud of their progress, but it's hard to say goodbye to them. These teens are kind, bright, and full of potential.

However, there are some who have to pause their treatment because of family challenges or personal issues, and somehow they discontinue their program. It's important to understand that stepping back doesn't equal failure—life circumstances can be unpredictable. Pausing can be a chance to regroup and return stronger. However, we still feel very sorry to hear that, and we hope someday they will be able to recognize how mental health matters in their life. We hope they'll return to treatment when things get better or when they see how important mental health is. There's always hope! When you choose to make a change, it can be the start of a bright new chapter.

"My prayer is not for them alone. I pray also for those who will believe in me through their message, 21 that all of them may be one, Father, just as you are in me and I am in you. May they also be in us so that the world may believe that you have sent me. 22 I have given them the glory that you gave me, that they may be one as we are one— 23 I in them and you in me—so that they may be brought to complete unity. Then the world will know that you sent me and have loved them even as you have loved me."

(NIV) John 17:20–23

When we look at John 17:20–23, we see Jesus praying for His followers to be united, just like He is with the Father. Unity isn't just about being in the same place—it's about truly understanding each other, sharing the same values, and talking openly. It's a unity that goes beyond appearances; it's about hearts and intentions being aligned. In the same way, families are meant to show this kind of harmony by listening well, showing respect, and loving one another.

Communication is a bridge that helps to connect parents and teenagers, and school teachers. Teens during puberty might feel like no one understands them, and their parents might think their kids aren't listening. Both feelings are real, but unity happens when everyone tries to really hear each other. This means setting aside distractions, like phones or TVs, and giving full attention to conversations. Listening carefully, speaking kindly, and being clear help families build trust, solve problems, and grow closer. Even small daily actions, like checking in about their day or asking genuine questions, can strengthen bonds. This idea doesn't just apply to families—it works in schools, workplaces, and communities as well. Wherever people come together, good communication builds unity, but careless words can tear it apart. Words carry weight; a gentle correction or supportive comment can make a huge difference in someone's confidence and well-being. Kind and thoughtful words bring people closer.

That's why Jesus' prayer for unity is so meaningful—true unity depends on communication filled with love. For teens, learning to talk openly and respectfully with their family is a skill they'll use forever. It also teaches empathy: understanding someone else's feelings before responding helps reduce arguments and builds stronger relationships. It strengthens their family and helps them succeed in school, friendships, and future jobs. When we communicate clearly, honestly, and with care, we don't just fix issues— we show the kind of unity Jesus prayed for, a unity that shares God's love with the world.

Just as Jesus prayed in John 17:20–23 for believers to be one—so the world may know God's love—our families, schools, and communities can reflect that same divine unity when we choose loving, clear communication. Even in conflict, patience and humility can restore understanding, showing that unity is a practice, not a one-time achievement. It's not always easy, but with practice and God's help, it becomes a testimony of His love working through us. By intentionally practicing listening, affirming, and understanding, teens can be agents of peace and harmony in their families and communities.

Communication is the Key to Creating Unity

In my own experience during graduate school, I discovered how poor communication could quickly derail group projects, create unnecessary stress, and hinder progress. But when I began practicing active listening, offering clear and respectful feedback, and making sure everyone felt heard, our team didn't just get the work done—we developed real trust and stronger collaboration. I also realized that taking a moment to clarify misunderstandings early prevented conflicts from escalating later, a principle that applies equally in family life.

The same truth applies at home: when teenagers and parents communicate with empathy, patience, and honesty, what could have been misunderstandings often become powerful opportunities for growth and deeper connection. Just as consistent effort and perseverance in challenging seasons have led to meaningful breakthroughs in my own life, the same steady commitment to loving, open communication can bring lasting unity and love within a family. Even small daily habits, like checking in with a simple "How was your day?" or sharing your feelings without judgment, can strengthen trust over time.

Effective Communication Matters

Effective communication is not only critical in business but also impacts the safety and security of various aspects of life, such as schools (teachers, students) and families (parents, relatives). Effective communication enables others to understand information more quickly and accurately. In contrast, ineffective communication can damage personal, academic, and professional relationships. For example, misinterpreting a teacher's instructions or a parent's guidance can lead to frustration, stress, and unnecessary conflict. Recognizing the importance of clear expression can prevent these issues.

As teenagers grow, they often seek greater independence, and parents have the responsibility to guide them and set boundaries to ensure their safety. When both sides learn to listen and speak with respect, family communication can become significantly stronger. It helps teens feel valued and heard, while parents feel respected and understood—creating a balance that fosters trust and cooperation.

Good communication between teenagers and their families is not always easy, but it is one of the most important parts of building trust and understanding at home. It requires patience, consistency, and willingness to forgive mistakes. Conflict is normal, but handling it respectfully sets an example for healthy relationships throughout life. As teenagers grow, they often want more independence, and their parents still feel responsible for guiding and protecting them. This difference can sometimes cause arguments or misunderstandings. However, if both sides learn how to listen and speak with respect, family communication can become much stronger.

Listening is just as important as speaking. Many teenagers feel that parents do not understand them, but sometimes parents feel the same way. When a teenager takes the time to listen carefully and shows respect, it encourages parents to listen in return. This creates a two-way conversation rather than a one-sided argument.

Tips for Better Communication at Home and School

Be honest and respectful

Families appreciate honesty, but they respond much better when you use a calm, gentle voice instead of yelling.

- Stay respectful and choose your words carefully to reduce conflict and build understanding. Use language that shows respect and empathy—this helps others feel heard instead of defensive.

- For parents: Start by validating your teen's feelings (e.g., "I can see why that frustrates you") before offering advice. This simple step opens the door to real, two-way conversation.

- For teachers: Ask open-ended questions like "How are you feeling about this assignment?" to show you care about more than just grades.

For example, instead of saying, "You always mess this up," try: "I've noticed this has been challenging lately—let's work together to find a solution." This keeps the conversation collaborative, helps everyone stay engaged, and makes people feel valued. Remember: your tone matters just as much as your words. A gentle, patient delivery can turn a tough discussion into a moment of real connection and growth.

Listen carefully

Pay attention to what your parents or teachers are saying before responding. This shows respect and helps avoid misunderstandings.

Positive example: Your teacher is explaining how to do a math problem. Instead of interrupting to ask a question, you wait until they finish, then raise your hand to clarify. This shows you respect their explanation and helps you understand better.

Negative example: Your parents are explaining why you need to finish your chores before watching TV. Instead of listening, you interrupt and say, "But I want to watch TV now!", without letting them finish. This shows disrespect and causes confusion because you didn't understand their full explanation.

Your Tone and Body Language

Positive example: One of your parents is explaining why you need to clean your room before going to a friend's house. You stay quiet, nod to show you're listening, and then say, "Got it, I'll tidy up my room first." This shows respect and helps you understand their reasoning clearly.

Negative example: Your teacher asks why you're late to class. Instead of responding politely, you roll your eyes, cross your arms, and say in a grumpy tone, "I don't know, it's not a big deal." This makes your response seem rude and unapproachable, which can lead to misunderstandings.

Communication isn't just about speaking words—it's also about how you present yourself. Your body language, facial expressions, and posture communicate just as much as your words. For example, standing or sitting with arms crossed can seem defensive, while an open posture signals you are approachable and ready to listen. A gentle voice, calm expression, and welcoming posture make your words easier to receive and help prevent misunderstandings. Even when discussing a disagreement, maintaining composure shows respect and helps the other person stay open to your perspective. Your tone reflects your emotions, so always speak with care, even when addressing problems.

Language is like an art form, similar to music. Every conversation is like performing in a concert. Before addressing concerns, you must practice the entire piece of music and read the notes carefully. Just as musicians rehearse to ensure harmony, practicing how to express your thoughts clearly prevents confusion and builds confidence in communication. If the music contains errors or inconsistencies, it feels off. The same applies to language: when you practice speaking, pay attention to English grammar and punctuation, and keep learning, you will become a great communicator. This will help you connect with your family and peers. Communication is the key to creating unity.

Listening is just as important as talking. Pay close attention to what your parents or teachers are saying with real interest. Don't interrupt, and let them finish sharing their thoughts. Active listening also involves noticing emotions, tone, and context, not just the words. This helps you understand the full message and respond thoughtfully. To make sure you understand, repeat back what you heard in your own words.

Positive example: Your teacher is explaining why your recent essay needs improvement. You sit quietly, make eye contact, and wait until they're done. Then you say, "So, you're saying my essay needs more examples to support my points, right?" This shows you listened carefully, respected their input, and checked your understanding to avoid confusion.

Negative example: Your teacher is explaining why your essay needs improvement, but you interrupt halfway through and say, "I don't get why this is a big deal!" You don't let them finish, miss key details, and seem disrespectful, which leads to miscommunication.

Additional Tip: Effective communication is a two-way street. Always combine speaking, listening, and observing non-verbal cues. By doing so, you build understanding, reduce arguments, and strengthen your relationships at home, school, and beyond.

Show your Appreciation

Saying "thank you" when someone helps you strengthens your bond with them. It shows you value their time and effort, encouraging them to help again in the future. Expressing gratitude also improves your own well-being—studies show that people who regularly practice thankfulness feel happier, more confident, and less stressed. A simple "Thanks for the help!" can build trust and create a warm, friendly atmosphere.

Positive example: A classmate shares their notes with you because you missed class. If you grab the notes and walk off without a word, they might not feel great about helping you again. But if you smile and say, "Thanks so much for sharing your notes! That's a huge help." They'll feel valued. Your gratitude makes them way more likely to help you out next time.

Negative example: Your friend carries a heavy box for you. Instead of saying "thank you," you just take the box and start opening it without even looking at them. This way, your friend might feel ignored, like their effort didn't matter. Next time, they might think twice before helping you again.

Additional Tip: Appreciation doesn't have to be verbal—it can be a note, a small gesture, or returning the favor later. Recognizing others' efforts consistently makes you someone people enjoy working or spending time with, and builds a positive, supportive community around you.

Final Note

Free Online Self-Screening Tools for Checking Your Mental Health—Suitable for Teens and Adults!

Remember: Your mental health matters!

Here are some reputable, free, and confidential online resources where you can take preliminary self-screening tests (also called self-assessments or quizzes) for common mental health concerns like depression, anxiety, ADHD, bipolar disorder, PTSD, OCD, addiction, and more. Important reminder: These are not official diagnoses—they are screening tools based on validated questions (such as the PHQ-9 for depression or GAD-7 for anxiety) that are widely used in the U.S. and North America. They can help signal whether your symptoms might warrant talking to a doctor, therapist, or psychiatrist. Always consult a qualified professional for a proper assessment and support.

Top Recommended Websites

1. **Mental Health America (MHA) Screening**

   https://screening.mhanational.org/screening-tools

   One of the most trusted and widely recommended free platforms. It provides quick, anonymous screenings for depression, anxiety, ADHD, bipolar disorder, PTSD, OCD, psychosis/schizophrenia, addiction (including gambling), eating disorders, social anxiety, postpartum depression, and more. It also includes a dedicated Youth Mental Health Test (for teens/youth) and a Parent Test for assessing a child's mental health. All are free, confidential, and require no sign-up.

2. **Psychology Today Mental Health & Personality Tests**

   https://www.psychologytoday.com/us/tests

   Offers a broad selection of quick, free, anonymous assessments (most take about 3 minutes). Includes the general "Your Mental Health Today Test" for overall coping and well-being, plus targeted tests for depression, bipolar disorder, generalized anxiety, social anxiety, addiction (alcohol, cannabis, gambling), PTSD, OCD, ADHD, eating disorders, and many others. User-friendly and provided by a well-established psychology resource.

3. **Talkspace Free Mental Health Screenings**

   https://www.talkspace.com/assessments

   Provides short, free online tests primarily focused on depression, anxiety (including generalized anxiety disorder), and general mental health. No sign-up required, quick to complete, and designed to help you decide if professional support might be beneficial.

4. **American Psychiatric Association (APA) DSM-5-TR Assessment Measures**

   https://www.psychiatry.org/psychiatrists/practice/dsm/ed ucational-resources/assessment-measures

   Offers official downloadable PDF screening tools (free to use online or print). These include cross-cutting symptom measures (Levels 1 and 2) for broad symptoms like depression, anxiety, anger/ irritability, mania, sleep issues, substance use, and more—with versions for adults, children (ages 6–17 via parents), and youth (ages 11–17 self-report). Also features disorder-specific severity scales such as the PHQ-9 for depression. These are clinically oriented tools primarily for professionals to support evaluations and monitoring, but are publicly accessible.

5. **Child Mind Institute Symptom Checker (especially helpful for teen/young person concerns)**
https://childmind.org/symptomchecker/

   A free, anonymous tool for parents/caregivers to check potential mental health or learning issues in children and teens (ages 1–18+). It covers symptoms like sadness/moodiness, worries/fears, attention problems, impulsivity, and more (including depression-related signs). Quiz-style format with severity sliders; generates **possible** associated conditions and encourages professional follow-up. Great for teen depression screening.

Additional Great Websites:

- **Here to Help (Canada-based but open to everyone)**
  https://www.heretohelp.bc.ca/screening/online

  Anonymous and free screenings for depression, anxiety (with age-specific versions), mood disorders, well-being, body image/eating attitudes, and substance use (including teen-appropriate options). Straightforward and no restrictions by location.

- **Connected Mind (multi-condition screener)**
  https://connectedmind.me/screening

  Free, anonymous, no-sign-up tool that screens for multiple conditions at once: depression, anxiety, ADHD, bipolar disorder, substance use disorder, and somatic symptom disorder. Instant results provided.

- **Mind Diagnostics** → https://www.mind-diagnostics.org/

  Variety of free, quick tests (2–5 minutes) for depression, anxiety, adult ADHD, PTSD, borderline personality disorder, eating disorders, gambling addiction, mania, and more. Immediate confidential feedback with risk-level indicators; no account needed.

- **NIMH (National Institute of Mental Health)** → https://www.nimh.nih.gov/

  Does not offer direct interactive self-screening quizzes, but it's an excellent source for reliable, evidence-based information on mental health conditions, treatments, and research—plus clear links to crisis resources. Ideal for learning more before or after using other screenings.

If you're in crisis or need immediate help (especially if feeling suicidal or unsafe), please skip the screenings and reach out right away:

- In the US: Call or text 988 (Suicide & Crisis Lifeline—available 24/7)

- Or text HOME to 741741 (Crisis Text Line)

References

Bible Quote

- The Holy Bible, New International Version. (2011). Isaiah 40:29–31. Biblica.
  https://www.bible.com/bible/111/ISA.40.29–31.NIV

Mental Health Month

- Brown University Health Blog Team. (2024, April 26). The importance of Mental Health Awareness Month. Brown University Health. https://www.brownhealth.org/be-well/importance-mental-health-awareness-month
- Mental Health America. (n.d.). Mental Health Month. https://mhanational.org/mental-health-month
- Mental Health America. (n.d.). Our history. https://mhanational.org/our-history
- National Alliance on Mental Illness. (n.d.). Mental Health Awareness Month. https://www.nami.org/get-involved/awareness-events/mental-health-awareness-month
- National Alliance on Mental Illness. (n.d.). Mental health by the numbers. https://www.nami.org/about-mental-illness/mental-health-by-the-numbers
- Substance Abuse and Mental Health Services Administration. (n.d.). Mental Health Awareness Month. https://www.samhsa.gov/about/digital-toolkits/mental-health-awareness-month

Chapter 1: Your mental health matters!

- National Center for Complementary and Integrative Health. (n.d.). Stress. U.S. Department of Health and Human Services, National Institutes of Health. https://www.nccih.nih.gov/health/stress
- National Center for Complementary and Integrative Health. (n.d.). Relaxation techniques: What you need to know. U.S. Department of Health and Human Services, National Institutes of Health. https://www.nccih.nih.gov/health/relaxation-techniques-what-you-need-to-know
- National Center for Complementary and Integrative Health. (n.d.). Wellness and well-being. U.S. Department of Health and Human Services, National Institutes of Health. https://www.nccih.nih.gov/health/wellness-and-well-being
- World Health Organization. (2022). Mental health: Strengthening our response. https://www.who.int/news-room/fact-sheets/detail/mental-health-strengthening-our-response
- Centers for Disease Control and Prevention. (2024). About mental health. https://www.cdc.gov/mental-health/about/index.html
- Donatelle, R. J., & Ketcham, P. (2018). Access to health (15th ed.). Pearson Education.
- Mentally Fit Pro. (2024, May). Guide to mental health for teens & young adults. https://mentallyfitpro.com/
- Centers for Disease Control and Prevention. (2024). Youth Risk Behavior Survey data summary & trends report: 2013–2023. https://www.cdc.gov/yrbs/dstr/index.html
- Maternal and Child Health Bureau. (2024). Adolescent mental and behavioral health, 2023 (National Survey of Children's Health Data Brief). Health Resources and Services Administration. https://mchb.hrsa.gov/sites/default/files/mchb/data-research/nsch-data-brief-adolescent-mental-behavioral-health-2023.pdf

- World Health Organization. (2024, September 25). Teens, screens and mental health. WHO Regional Office for Europe. https://www.who.int/europe/news/item/25-09-2024-teens--screens-and-mental-health

Emotional wellness (health). Psychologically healthy people possess several core characteristics

- Donatelle, R. J., & Ketcham, P. (2018). Access to health (15th ed.). Pearson Education.
- National Center for Complementary and Integrative Health. (n.d.). Stress. U.S. Department of Health and Human Services, National Institutes of Health. https://www.nccih.nih.gov/health/stress
- National Center for Complementary and Integrative Health. (n.d.). Relaxation techniques: What you need to know. U.S. Department of Health and Human Services, National Institutes of Health. https://www.nccih.nih.gov/health/relaxation-techniques-what-you-need-to-know
- World Health Organization. (2022, October). Mental health: Strengthening our response. https://www.who.int/news-room/fact-sheets/detail/mental-health-strengthening-our-response
- Centers for Disease Control and Prevention. (2024). About mental health. https://www.cdc.gov/mental-health/about/index.html
- Substance Abuse and Mental Health Services Administration. (2023). Creating a healthier life: A whole-person approach to wellness. https://www.samhsa.gov/wellness
- American Psychological Association. (n.d.). Emotional health. https://www.apa.org/topics/emotional-health
- World Health Organization. (2003). Creating an environment for emotional and social well-being: An important responsibility of a health-promoting and child-friendly school. https://apps.who.int/iris/handle/10665/42819

Spiritual Health—Dysfunctional families

- Substance Abuse and Mental Health Services Administration. (2016). Creating a healthier life: A step-by-step guide to wellness. https://www.samhsa.gov/wellness
- Substance Abuse and Mental Health Services Administration. (n.d.). Eight dimensions of wellness. https://www.samhsa.gov/wellness-initiative/eight-dimensions-wellness
- World Health Organization. (2021). Mental health of adolescents. https://www.who.int/news-room/fact-sheets/detail/adolescent-mental-health
- National Institute of Mental Health. (2024). Child and adolescent mental health. https://www.nimh.nih.gov/health/topics/child-and-adolescent-mental-health
- World Health Organization. (2022). Mental health: Strengthening our response. https://www.who.int/news-room/fact-sheets/detail/mental-health-strengthening-our-response
- Centers for Disease Control and Prevention. (2024). About mental health. https://www.cdc.gov/mental-health/about/index.html
- World Health Organization & UNICEF. (2020). Helping adolescents thrive toolkit. https://www.who.int/publications/i/item/9789240013148

Common Questions About Teens' Mental Health

- Centers for Disease Control and Prevention. (2024). Youth Risk Behavior Survey data summary & trends report: 2013–2023. https://www.cdc.gov/yrbs/dstr/index.html
- Maternal and Child Health Bureau. (2024). Adolescent mental and behavioral health, 2023 (National Survey of Children's Health Data Brief). Health Resources and Services Administration. https://mchb.hrsa.gov/sites/default/files/mchb/data-research/nsch-data-brief-adolescent-mental-behavioral-health-2023.pdf
- World Health Organization. (2024, September 25). Teens, screens and mental health. WHO Regional Office for Europe. https://www.who.int/europe/news/item/25-09-2024-teens--screens-and-mental-health

How Do I Know If I Need Help for My Mental Health?

- Maternal and Child Health Bureau. (2024). Adolescent mental and behavioral health, 2023 (National Survey of Children's Health Data Brief). Health Resources and Services Administration. https://mchb.hrsa.gov/sites/default/files/mchb/data-research/nsch-data-brief-adolescent-mental-behavioral-health-2023.pdf
- Mentally Fit Pro. (2024, May). Guide to mental health for teens & young adults. https://mentallyfitpro.com/
- National Institute of Mental Health. (n.d.). Child and adolescent mental health. U.S. Department of Health and Human Services, National Institutes of Health. Retrieved December 15, 2025, from https://www.nimh.nih.gov/health/topics/child-and-adolescent-mental-health

How Do I Know If I Need Help for My Mental Health?

- Maternal and Child Health Bureau. (2024). Adolescent mental and behavioral health, 2023 (National Survey of Children's Health Data Brief). Health Resources and Services Administration. https://mchb.hrsa.gov/sites/default/files/mchb/data-research/nsch-data-brief-adolescent-mental-behavioral-health-2023.pdf
- Mentally Fit Pro. (2024, May). Guide to mental health for teens & young adults. https://mentallyfitpro.com/
- National Institute of Mental Health. (n.d.). Child and adolescent mental health. U.S. Department of Health and Human Services, National Institutes of Health. Retrieved December 15, 2025, from https://www.nimh.nih.gov/health/topics/child-and-adolescent-mental-health

1) Actor: Johnson: Page 15

- Johnson, D. [@TheRock]. (2023, May 12). Appreciate chopping up depression with my guys on @thepivot[Post]. X. https://x.com/TheRock/status/1657069953491533853
- Johnson, D. [@TheRock]. (2024, October 10). Mental Health Check In [Post]. X. https://x.com/TheRock/status/1844448237450883438
- Lapook, J. (2023, May 15). Dwayne 'The Rock' Johnson shares struggles with depression. ABC News. https://abcnews.go.com/GMA/Culture/dwayne-rock-johnson-shares-struggles-depression/story?id=99320228
- O'Neil, S. (2023, May 12). Dwayne Johnson shares what he learned from his battles with depression: 'It can't be fixed if you keep that pain inside'. People. https://people.com/health/dwayne-johnson-shares-his-saving-grace-after-3-separate-battles-with-depression-youre-never-alone/

- Siegel, T. (2023, May 12). Dwayne Johnson talks about depression, mental health struggles. The Hollywood Reporter. https://www.hollywoodreporter.com/lifestyle/lifestyle-news/dwayne-johnson-bouts-of-depression-mental-health-struggles-1235486866/

2) Musician: Lady Gaga

- Born This Way Foundation. (n.d.). Home. https://bornthisway.foundation/
- Born This Way Foundation. (2016, December). Head stuck in a cycle, I look off and I stare: A personal letter from Gaga. https://bornthisway.foundation/personal-letter-gaga/
- Kreisler, L. (2018, November 9). Lady Gaga opens up about mental health struggles. Variety. https://variety.com/2018/scene/news/lady-gaga-mental-health-struggles-1203023093/
- Patel, J. (2020, January 6). Lady Gaga reveals she has PTSD: 'I suffer from a mental illness'. Billboard. https://www.billboard.com/music/pop/lady-gaga-interview-oprah-2020-vision-tour-8547328/
- Ryzik, M. (2020, May 21). Lady Gaga talks mental health, mentoring Ariana Grande and making 'Chromatica' in Zane Lowe interview. Variety. https://variety.com/2020/music/news/lady-gaga-mental-health-mentorship-making-chromatica-interview-zane-lowe-1234612226/

3) Business Leader: Elon Musk,

- Faber, D. (2023, May 16). Elon Musk says sacrificing sleep for productivity gave him 'brain pain' [Interview transcript]. CNBC. https://www.cnbc.com/2023/05/18/elon-musk-sacrificing-sleep-for-productivity-gave-me-brain-pain.html

- Lemon, D. (Host). (2024, March 18). Elon Musk details his prescription ketamine use [Video interview]. CNN. https://www.cnn.com/2024/03/18/tech/elon-musk-ketamine-use-don-lemon-interview

- Musk, E. [@elonmusk]. (2017, July 31). The reality is great highs, terrible lows and unrelenting stress [Post]. X (formerly Twitter). (As cited in multiple reports, e.g., https://www.independent.co.uk/life-style/health-and-families/elon-musk-ketamine-depression-microdose-b2365648.html)

- Swisher, K. (2018, November). Elon Musk on working 120-hour weeks [Interview]. Recode. (Referenced in) https://www.cnbc.com/2018/11/05/elon-musk-on-working-120-hours-a-week-youll-go-bonkers.html

4. About Michael Phelps

- Boys & Girls Clubs of America. (2021, November). Michael Phelps' top 5 mental health tips for teens. https://www.bgca.org/news-stories/2021/November/michael-phelps-top-5-mental-health-tips-for-teens/

- Cable News Network. (2018, January 19). Michael Phelps: "I am extremely thankful that I did not take my life." https://www.cnn.com/2018/01/19/health/michael-phelps-depression/index.html

- Drehs, W. (2020, May 18). Michael Phelps: 'This is the most overwhelmed I've ever felt'. ESPN. https://www.espn.com/olympics/story/_/id/29186389/michael-phelps-most-overwhelmed-ever-felt

- Pfeffer, S. E. (2022, May 3). Michael Phelps says therapy 'saved' him during his darkest moment: 'I didn't want to be alive'. People. https://people.com/health/michael-phelps-says-therapy-saved-him-in-darkest-moment/

5) Writer: J.K. Rowling

- Amini, A. (2008, March 23). JK Rowling contemplated suicide. The Telegraph. https://www.telegraph.co.uk/news/uknews/1582552/JK-Rowling-contemplated-suicide.html

- Brown, M. (2012, September 22). JK Rowling: 'The worst that can happen is that everyone says, That's shockingly bad' The Guardian. https://www.theguardian.com/books/2012/sep/22/jk-rowling-book-casual-vacancy

- CNN. (2008, March 23). Harry Potter author: I considered suicide. http://edition.cnn.com/2008/SHOWBIZ/03/23/rowling.depressed/index.html

- Lumos Foundation. (n.d.). Our founder & life president. https://www.wearelumos.org/who-we-are/jkrowling/

- Treneman, A. (2000, June 30). J.K. Rowling, the interview. The Times (UK). https://www.accio-quote.org/articles/2000/0600-times-treneman.html

How to take care of your mental health?

- Centers for Disease Control and Prevention. (2025, January 31). Sadness & depression. https://www.cdc.gov/emotional-well-being/managing-difficult-emotions/sadness-depression.html

- Centers for Disease Control and Prevention. (2025, August 1). Mental health conditions and care. https://www.cdc.gov/mental-health/about-data/conditions-care.html

- Mental Health America. (2025, December 12). Get professional help if you need it. https://mhanational.org/resources/get-professional-help-if-you-need-it/

- National Institute of Mental Health. (2024a). Caring for your mental health. U.S. Department of Health and Human Services, National Institutes of Health.

https://www.nimh.nih.gov/health/topics/caring-for-your-mental-health

- National Institute of Mental Health. (2024b). Depression. U.S. Department of Health and Human Services, National Institutes of Health. https://www.nimh.nih.gov/health/topics/depression

- World Health Organization. (2025, August 29). Depressive disorder (depression). https://www.who.int/news-room/fact sheets/detail/depression

Seeking Mental Health Support

- Centers for Disease Control and Prevention. (2024, December 3). Promoting mental health and well-being in schools: An action guide. https://www.cdc.gov/mental-health-action-guide/about/index.html

- National Institute of Mental Health. (2024, December). Caring for your mental health. U.S. Department of Health and Human Services, National Institutes of Health https://www.nimh.nih.gov/health/topics/caring-for-your-mental-health

- National Institute of Mental Health. (2024, February). Psychotherapies. U.S. Department of Health and Human Services, National Institutes of Health. https://www.nimh.nih.gov/health/topics/psychotherapies

- Nemours KidsHealth. (n.d.). Going to a therapist (for teens). https://kidshealth.org/en/teens/therapist.html

- Substance Abuse and Mental Health Services Administration. (n.d.). Wellness Recovery Action Plan (WRAP). https://www.wellnessrecoveryactionplan.com/

- Alternative SAMHSA wellness resources: https://www.samhsa.gov/wellness.)

- World Health Organization. (2022). World mental health report: Transforming mental health for all. https://www.who.int/publications/i/item/9789240049338

Major Categories of Mental Disorders

- American Psychiatric Association. (2025, July). What is mental illness? https://www.psychiatry.org/patients-families/what-is-mental-illness

- World Health Organization. (2025, September 30). Mental disorders. https://www.who.int/news-room/fact-sheets/detail/mental-disorders

- National Institute of Mental Health. (2024, September). Mental illness. https://www.nimh.nih.gov/health/statistics/mental-illness

- Mayo Clinic. (2022, August 12). Teen depression - Symptoms and causes.https://www.mayoclinic.org/diseases-conditions/teen-depression/symptoms-causes/syc-20350985

- National Institute of Mental Health. (2022). Teen depression. https://www.nimh.nih.gov/health/publications/teen-depression

- WebMD. (2024, September 2). Recognizing schizophrenia in teens. https://www.webmd.com/schizophrenia/recognizing-schizophrenia-in-teens

- Medical News Today. (2023, June 20). Schizophrenia in teens: Signs, treatment, and more. https://www.medicalnewstoday.com/articles/schizophrenia-in-teens

- Healthline. (2024, June 14). The importance of mental fitness. https://www.healthline.com/health/depression/mental-fitness

- Positive Psychology. (2020, July 8). Journaling for mindfulness: 44 prompts, examples & exercises.

  https://positivepsychology.com/journaling-for-mindfulness/

- Mayo Clinic. (2023, December 23). Resilience: Build skills to endure hardship.
  https://www.mayoclinic.org/tests-procedures/resilience-training/in-depth/resilience/art-20046311

- National Institute of Mental Health. (2024, February). Help for mental illnesses. https://www.nimh.nih.gov/health/find-help

- National Institute of Mental Health. (2024, February). Psychotherapies.
  https://www.nimh.nih.gov/health/topics/psychotherapies

Mental Fitness = Physical Fitness

- American Psychiatric Association. (n.d.). Lifestyle to support mental health.
  https://www.psychiatry.org/patients-families/lifestyle-to-support-mental-health

- Better Health Channel. (n.d.). Exercise and mental health. Victorian Government.

  https://www.betterhealth.vic.gov.au/health/healthyliving/exercise-and-mental-health

- Callaghan, P. (2004). Exercise: A neglected intervention in mental health care? Journal of Psychiatric and Mental Health Nursing, 11(4), 476–483.

  https://doi.org/10.1111/j.1365-2850.2004.00751.x

- Chekroud, S. R., Gueorguieva, R., Zheutlin, A. B., Paulus, M., Krumholz, H. M., Krystal, J. H., & Chekroud, A. M. (2018). Association between physical exercise and mental health in 1·2 million individuals in the USA between 2011 and 2015: A cross-sectional study. The Lancet Psychiatry, 5(9), 739–746. https://doi.org/10.1016/S2215-0366(18)30227-X

- Kandola, A., Ashdown-Franks, G., Hendrikse, J., Sabiston, C. M., & Stubbs, B. (2019). Physical activity and depression: Towards understanding the antidepressant mechanisms of physical activity. Neuroscience & Biobehavioral Reviews, 107, 525–539. https://doi.org/10.1016/j.neubiorev.2019.09.040

- Mahindru, A., Patil, P., & Agrawal, V. (2023). Role of physical activity on mental health and well-being: A review. Cureus, 15(1), Article e33475. https://doi.org/10.7759/cureus.33475

- Mandolesi, L., Polverino, A., Montuori, S., Foti, F., Ferraioli, G., Sorrentino, P., & Sorrentino, G. (2018). Effects of physical exercise on cognitive functioning and wellbeing: Biological and psychological benefits. Frontiers in Psychology, 9, Article 509. https://doi.org/10.3389/fpsyg.2018.00509

- Mental Health Foundation. (n.d.). Physical activity and mental health.

- https://www.mentalhealth.org.uk/explore-mental-health/a-z-topics/physical-activity-and-mental-health.

- Paluska, S. A., & Schwenk, T. L. (2000). Physical activity and mental health: Current concepts. Sports Medicine, 29(3), 167–180. https://doi.org/10.2165/00007256-200029030–00003

- Stanton, R., & Reaburn, P. (2014). Exercise and the treatment of depression: A review of the exercise program variables. Journal of Science and Medicine in Sport, 17(2), 177–182. https://doi.org/10.1016/j.jsams.2013.03.010

Categories of Mental Health Disorders

- American Psychiatric Association. (2022). Diagnostic and statistical manual of mental disorders (5th ed., text rev.). https://doi.org/10.1176/appi.books.9780890425787

- Centers for Disease Control and Prevention. (2025, June 10). Data and statistics on children's mental health. https://www.cdc.gov/children-mental-health/data-research/index.html

- Cleveland Clinic. (2025, September 17). Mental health disorders: What are the types? https://my.clevelandclinic.org/health/diseases/22295-mental-health-disorders

- National Institute of Mental Health. (n.d.). Child and adolescent mental health. https://www.nimh.nih.gov/health/topics/child-and-adolescent-mental-health

- National Institute of Mental Health. (n.d.). Mental illness. https://www.nimh.nih.gov/health/statistics/mental-illness

- World Health Organization. (2025, September 1). Mental health of adolescents.https://www.who.int/news-room/fact-sheets/detail/adolescent-mental-health

- World Health Organization. (2025, September 30). Mental disorders.https://www.who.int/news-room/fact-sheets/detail/mental-disorders

Depression

- Brody D.J., Hughes J.P. Depression Prevalence in Adolescents and Adults: United States, August 2021–August 2023. NCHS Data Brief, No. 527. Hyattsville, MD: National Center for Health Statistics; 2025.
  https://www.cdc.gov/nchs/products/databriefs/db527.htm

- National Center for Health Statistics. National Health and Nutrition Examination Survey (NHANES) Data. Centers for Disease Control and Prevention, 2021–2023.
  https://www.cdc.gov/nchs/nhanes/index.htm

- National Institute of Mental Health. Major Depression. NIMH Statistics; updated 2023.
  https://www.nimh.nih.gov/health/statistics/major-depression

- National Institute of Mental Health. Teen Depression: More Than Just Moodiness. NIMH Brochure; updated 2023
  https://www.nimh.nih.gov/health/publications/teen-depression

- Mayo Clinic Staff. Teen Depression - Symptoms and Causes. Mayo Clinic; updated 2022
  https://www.mayoclinic.org/diseases-conditions/teen-depression/symptoms-causes/syc-20350985

- 988 Suicide & Crisis Lifeline. Official Website. Substance Abuse and Mental Health Services Administration (SAMHSA); ongoing.
  https://988lifeline.org/

- Substance Abuse and Mental Health Services Administration. 988 Suicide & Crisis Lifeline. SAMHSA; updated 2025.
  https://www.samhsa.gov/mental-health/988

Anxiety Disorder

- Maternal and Child Health Bureau. Adolescent Mental and Behavioral Health, 2023. Health Resources and Services Administration (HRSA) Data Brief; October 2024. https://mchb.hrsa.gov/sites/default/files/mchb/data-research/nsch-data-brief-adolescent-mental-behavioral-health-2023.pdf
- National Institute of Mental Health. Any Anxiety Disorder. NIMH Statistics; updated 2023. https://www.nimh.nih.gov/health/statistics/any-anxiety-disorder
- World Health Organization. Mental Health of Adolescents. WHO Fact Sheet; updated September 2025. https://www.who.int/news-room/fact-sheets/detail/adolescent-mental-health
- National Institute of Mental Health. Anxiety Disorders. NIMH Health Topics; updated 2023. https://www.nimh.nih.gov/health/topics/anxiety-disorders
- Centers for Disease Control and Prevention. Data and Statistics on Children's Mental Health. CDC; updated June 2025. https://www.cdc.gov/children-mental-health/data-research/index.html
- Substance Abuse and Mental Health Services Administration. 988 Suicide & Crisis Lifeline. SAMHSA; ongoing. https://988lifeline.org/
- American Academy of Child and Adolescent Psychiatry. Your Adolescent - Anxiety and Avoidant Disorders. AACAP Resource Center. https://www.aacap.org/aacap/Families_and_Youth/Resource_Centers/Anxiety_Disorder_Resource_Center/Your_Adolescent_Anxiety_and_Avoidant_Disorders.aspx

Bipolar Disorder

- National Institute of Mental Health. Bipolar Disorder. NIMH Health Topics; updated 2023–2025. https://www.nimh.nih.gov/health/topics/bipolar-disorder

- National Institute of Mental Health. Bipolar Disorder in Children and Teens. NIMH Brochure; updated 2023. https://www.nimh.nih.gov/health/publications/bipolar-disorder-in-children-and-teens

- National Institute of Mental Health. Bipolar Disorder Statistics. NIMH; accessed 2025. https://www.nimh.nih.gov/health/statistics/bipolar-disorder

- World Health Organization. Bipolar Disorder. WHO Fact Sheet; updated September 2025. https://www.who.int/news-room/fact-sheets/detail/bipolar-disorder

- Mayo Clinic Staff. Bipolar Disorder - Symptoms and Causes. Mayo Clinic; updated 2024. https://www.mayoclinic.org/diseases-conditions/bipolar-disorder/symptoms-causes/syc-20355955

- American Academy of Child and Adolescent Psychiatry. Bipolar Disorder Resource Center. AACAP; ongoing. https://www.aacap.org/aacap/Families_and_Youth/Resource_Centers/Bipolar_Disorder_Resource_Center/Home.aspx

- Substance Abuse and Mental Health Services Administration. 988 Suicide & Crisis Lifeline. SAMHSA; ongoing. https://988lifeline.org/

Attention-Deficit/Hyperactivity Disorder (ADHD)

- Centers for Disease Control and Prevention (CDC). (2024). Data and Statistics on ADHD. https://www.cdc.gov/adhd/data/index.html

- Centers for Disease Control and Prevention (CDC). (2024). Symptoms of ADHD. https://www.cdc.gov/adhd/signs-symptoms/index.html

- National Institute of Mental Health (NIMH). (2024). Attention-Deficit/Hyperactivity Disorder (ADHD). https://www.nimh.nih.gov/health/topics/attention-deficit-hyperactivity-disorder-adhd

- National Institute of Mental Health (NIMH). (2024). Attention-Deficit/Hyperactivity Disorder: What You Need to Know. https://www.nimh.nih.gov/health/publications/attention-deficit-hyperactivity-disorder-what-you-need-to-know

- Children and Adults with Attention-Deficit/Hyperactivity Disorder (CHADD). (2024). General Prevalence of ADHD. https://chadd.org/about-adhd/general-prevalence/

- American Academy of Child and Adolescent Psychiatry (AACAP). (2023). ADHD Resource Center. https://www.aacap.org/aacap/Families_and_Youth/Resource_Centers/ADHD_Resource_Center/Home.aspx

- Danielson, M. L., et al. (2024). "ADHD Prevalence Among U.S. Children and Adolescents in 2022." Journal of Clinical Child & Adolescent Psychology.

Eating Disorders

- National Institute of Mental Health (NIMH). (2024). Eating Disorders. https://www.nimh.nih.gov/health/topics/eating-disorders

- National Institute of Mental Health (NIMH). (2024). Eating Disorders: About More Than Food. https://www.nimh.nih.gov/health/publications/eating-disorders

- National Eating Disorders Association (NEDA). (2024). Statistics & Research on Eating Disorders. https://www.nationaleatingdisorders.org/statistics/

- National Eating Disorders Association (NEDA). (2024). Learn: Types & Symptoms of Eating Disorders. https://www.nationaleatingdisorders.org/learn/by-eating-disorder

- Mayo Clinic. (2024). Eating Disorders. https://www.mayoclinic.org/diseases-conditions/eating-disorders/symptoms-causes/syc-20353603

- American Psychiatric Association. (2024). What are Eating Disorders? https://www.psychiatry.org/patients-families/eating-disorders/what-are-eating-disorders

- Galmiche, M., et al. (2019). "Prevalence of eating disorders over the 2000–2018 period: a systematic literature review." American Journal of Clinical Nutrition. (Summarized via NEDA and NIMH resources). https://academic.oup.com/ajcn/article/109/5/1402/5475038

- Arcelus, J., et al. (2011). "Mortality rates in patients with anorexia nervosa and other eating disorders: a meta-analysis." JAMA Psychiatry. https://jamanetwork.com/journals/jamapsychiatry/fullarticle/1107207

Schizophrenia

- World Health Organization (WHO). (2025). Schizophrenia Fact Sheet. https://www.who.int/news-room/fact-sheets/detail/schizophrenia
- National Institute of Mental Health (NIMH). (2024). Schizophrenia. https://www.nimh.nih.gov/health/topics/schizophrenia
- National Institute of Mental Health (NIMH). (2024). Schizophrenia Statistics. https://www.nimh.nih.gov/health/statistics/schizophrenia
- American Psychiatric Association (APA). (2024). What is Schizophrenia? https://www.psychiatry.org/patients-families/schizophrenia/what-is-schizophrenia
- National Alliance on Mental Illness (NAMI). (2024). Schizophrenia. https://www.nami.org/about-mental-illness/mental-health-conditions/schizophrenia/
- Mayo Clinic. (2024). Schizophrenia: Symptoms & Causes. https://www.mayoclinic.org/diseases-conditions/schizophrenia/symptoms-causes/syc-20354443
- Palmer, B. A., et al. (2005). "The Lifetime Risk of Suicide in Schizophrenia: A Reexamination." Archives of General Psychiatry. https://jamanetwork.com/journals/jamapsychiatry/fullarticle/208396
- McGrath, J., et al. (2008). "Schizophrenia: A Concise Overview of Incidence, Prevalence, and Mortality." Epidemiologic Reviews.

Post-Traumatic Stress Disorder (PTSD)

- National Institute of Mental Health (NIMH). (2024). Post-Traumatic Stress Disorder. https://www.nimh.nih.gov/health/topics/post-traumatic-stress-disorder-ptsd

- National Institute of Mental Health (NIMH). (2024). Statistics: Post-Traumatic Stress Disorder (PTSD). https://www.nimh.nih.gov/health/statistics/post-traumatic-stress-disorder-ptsd

- World Health Organization (WHO). (2024). Post-Traumatic Stress Disorder Fact Sheet. https://www.who.int/news-room/fact-sheets/detail/post-traumatic-stress-disorder

- American Psychiatric Association (APA). (2024). What is Posttraumatic Stress Disorder (PTSD)? https://www.psychiatry.org/patients-families/ptsd/what-is-ptsd

- PTSD: National Center for PTSD (U.S. Department of Veterans Affairs). (2024). PTSD in Children and Teens. https://www.ptsd.va.gov/professional/treat/specific/ptsd_child_teens.asp

- Mayo Clinic. (2024). Post-Traumatic Stress Disorder (PTSD): Symptoms & Causes. https://www.mayoclinic.org/diseases-conditions/post-traumatic-stress-disorder/symptoms-causes/syc-20355967

- Merikangas, K. R., et al. (2010). "Lifetime Prevalence of Mental Disorders in U.S. Adolescents: Results from the National Comorbidity Survey Replication–Adolescent Supplement (NCS-A)." Journal of the American Academy of Child & Adolescent Psychiatry.

- Kessler, R. C., et al. (2012). "Prevalence, Persistence, and Sociodemographic Correlates of DSM-IV Disorders in the National Comorbidity Survey Replication Adolescent Sample." Archives of General Psychiatry.

Pages 1–2

- **Brody, D. J., & Pratt, L. A. (2025). Depression prevalence in adolescents** and adults: United States, August 2021–August 2023 (NCHS Data Brief No. 527). National Center for Health Statistics, Centers for Disease Control and Prevention. https://www.cdc.gov/nchs/products/databriefs/db527.htm

- Centers for Disease Control and Prevention. (2024). Youth Risk Behavior Survey data summary & trends report: 2013–2023. https://www.cdc.gov/yrbs/dstr/pdf/YRBS-2023-Data-Summary-Trend-Report.pdf

- Centers for Disease Control and Prevention. (2025). Data and Statistics on Children's Mental Health. https://www.cdc.gov/children-mental-health/data-research/index.html

- National Institute of Mental Health. (n.d.). Mental illness. https://www.nimh.nih.gov/health/statistics/mental-illness

- Substance Abuse and Mental Health Services Administration. (2025). Key substance use and mental health indicators in the United States: Results from the 2024 National Survey on Drug Use and Health. https://www.samhsa.gov/data/sites/default/files/reports/rpt56287/2024-nsduh-annual-national-report.pdf

- Sappenfield, O., Alberto, C., Minnaert, J., & National Survey of Children's Health. (2024). Adolescent mental and behavioral health, 2023. Health Resources and Services Administration,

Maternal and Child Health Bureau.
https://www.ncbi.nlm.nih.gov/books/NBK603531/

Pages 2–5

- Mental Health America. (2025). The state of mental health in America 2025. https://mhanational.org/the-state-of-mental-health-in-america

- Reinert, M., Nguyen, T., & Fritze, D. (2025). The state of mental health in America 2025. Mental Health America. https://mhanational.org/wp-content/uploads/2025/09/State-of-Mental-Health-2025.pdf

- Substance Abuse and Mental Health Services Administration. (2025). Key substance use and mental health indicators in the United States: Results from the 2024 National Survey on Drug Use and Health (HHS Publication No. PEP25-07-001). https://www.samhsa.gov/data/sites/default/files/reports/rpt56287/2024-nsduh-annual-national-report.pdf

- Substance Abuse and Mental Health Services Administration. (2025). 2022–2024 NSDUH: Major depressive episode or serious thoughts of suicide in the past year among adolescents. https://www.samhsa.gov/data/report/nsduh-22-24-pst-yr-mde-or-serious-thoughts-suicide-amg-adolescents

Pages 5–10

- Mental Health America. (2025). The state of mental health in America 2025. https://mhanational.org/the-state-of-mental-health-in-america

- Mental Health America. (2025). The state of mental health in America 2025 [PDF report]. https://mhanational.org/wp-content/uploads/2025/09/State-of-Mental-Health-2025.pdf

- Substance Abuse and Mental Health Services Administration. (2025). Key substance use and mental health indicators in the United States: Results from the 2024 National Survey on Drug Use and Health (HHS Publication No. PEP25-07-001). https://www.samhsa.gov/data/sites/default/files/reports/rpt56287/2024-nsduh-annual-national-report.pdf
- Substance Abuse and Mental Health Services Administration. (2025). 2022–2024 NSDUH substate region estimates by age group [or related detailed tables for pooled youth estimates, including MDE treatment/no treatment by state]. https://www.samhsa.gov/data/report/2022-2024-nsduh-substate-region-estimates
- Johnston, L. D., Miech, R. A., Patrick, M. E., Schulenberg, J. E., & Couper, M. P. (2025). Monitoring the Future national survey results on drug use, 1975–2024: Overview, key findings on adolescent drug use. Institute for Social Research, University of Michigan. https://monitoringthefuture.org/results/annual-reports/

Pages 10–14

- Mental Health America. (2024). The state of mental health in America 2024. https://mhanational.org/the-state-of-mental-health-in-america
- Mental Health America. (2024). The state of mental health in America 2024 [PDF report]. https://mhanational.org/sites/default/files/2024%20State%20of%20Mental%20Health%20in%20America%20Report.pdf
- Substance Abuse and Mental Health Services Administration. (2023). Key substance use and mental health indicators in the United States: Results from the 2022 National Survey on Drug Use and Health (HHS Publication No. PEP23-07-001).

https://www.samhsa.gov/data/sites/default/files/reports/rpt427
31/2022-nsduh-nnr.pdf

- Substance Abuse and Mental Health Services Administration.
  (2024). 2021–2023 NSDUH: Guide to state tables and summary of
  small area estimation methodology.
  https://www.samhsa.gov/data/report/2021-2023-nsduh-guide-
  state-tables

Pages 14–17

- Centers for Disease Control and Prevention. (2023). Youth Risk
  Behavior Survey data summary & trends report: 2011–2021.
  https://www.cdc.gov/yrbs/dstr/pdf/YRBS_Data-Summary-
  Trends_Report2023_508.pdf
- Mental Health America. (2024). The state of mental health in
  America 2024. https://mhanational.org/the-state-of-mental-
  health-in-america
- Mental Health America. (2024). The state of mental health in
  America 2024 [PDF report]. https://mhanational.org/wp-
  content/uploads/2024/12/2024-State-of-Mental-Health-in-
  America-Report.pdf
- Reinert, M., Fritze, D., & Nguyen, T. (2024). The state of mental
  health in America 2024. Mental Health America.
- Stone, D. M., Holland, K. M., Bartholow, B., Crosby, A. E., Davis,
  S., & Wilkins, N. (2023). Recent changes in suicide rates, by race
  and ethnicity and age group—United States, 2018–2021. Morbidity
  and Mortality Weekly Report, 72(6), 160–162.
  https://www.cdc.gov/mmwr/volumes/72/wr/mm7206a4.htm
- Substance Abuse and Mental Health Services Administration.
  (2023). Key substance use and mental health indicators in the
  United States: Results from the 2022 National Survey on Drug Use
  and Health (HH S Publication No. PEP23-07-001).

https://www.samhsa.gov/data/sites/default/files/reports/rpt427
31/2022-nsduh-nnr.pdf

Pages 17–19

- Centers for Disease Control and Prevention. (2022). Adolescent Behaviors and Experiences Survey—United States, January–June 2021. https://www.cdc.gov/mmwr/volumes/71/su/su7103a5.htm
- Krause, K. H., Verlenden, J. V., Szucs, L. E., Rasberry, C. N., Moore, S., Yeargin-Allsopp, M., Claussen, A. H., Lebrun-Harris, L., Alexander, S., Underwood, J. M., & Ethier, K. A. (2022). Disruptions to school and home life among high school students during the COVID-19 pandemic—Adolescent Behaviors and Experiences Survey, United States, January–June 2021. Morbidity and Mortality Weekly Report, 71(Suppl. 3), 17–24. https://www.cdc.gov/mmwr/volumes/71/su/pdfs/su7103a5-H.pdf
- Mental Health America. (2022). The state of mental health in America 2023. https://mhanational.org/issues/state-mental-health-america
- Mental Health America. (2022). The state of mental health in America 2023 [PDF report]. https://mhanational.org/wp-content/uploads/2025/03/2023-SoMH.pdf
- Reinert, M., Fritze, D., & Nguyen, T. (2022). The state of mental health in America 2023. Mental Health America.
- Substance Abuse and Mental Health Services Administration. (2023). 2021–2022 NSDUH: Model-based estimated prevalence for states and substate regions [or related state tables for youth MDE]. https://www.samhsa.gov/data/report/2021-2022-nsduh-state-prevalence-estimates

Pages 19–24

- Mental Health America. (2022). The state of mental health in America 2023. https://mhanational.org/issues/state-mental-health-america

- Mental Health America. (2022). The state of mental health in America 2023 [PDF report]. https://mhanational.org/wp-content/uploads/2025/03/2023-SoMH.pdf

- Reinert, M., Fritze, D., & Nguyen, T. (2022). The state of mental health in America 2023. Mental Health America.

- Substance Abuse and Mental Health Services Administration. (2023). Key substance use and mental health indicators in the United States: Results from the 2022 National Survey on Drug Use and Health (HHS Publication No. PEP23-07-001). https://www.samhsa.gov/data/sites/default/files/reports/rpt42731/2022-nsduh-nnr.pdf

- Substance Abuse and Mental Health Services Administration. (2024). 2021–2022 NSDUH: Model-based estimated prevalence for states. https://www.samhsa.gov/data/report/2021-2022-nsduh-state-prevalence-estimates

Pages 24–29

- Centers for Disease Control and Prevention. (2023). Youth Risk Behavior Survey data summary & trends report: 2011–2021. https://www.cdc.gov/yrbs/dstr/pdf/YRBS_Data-Summary-Trends_Report2023_508.pdf

- Mental Health America. (2025). The state of mental health in America 2025. https://mhanational.org/the-state-of-mental-health-in-america

- Mental Health America. (2025). The state of mental health in America 2025 [PDF report]. https://mhanational.org/wp-content/uploads/2025/09/State-of-Mental-Health-2025.pdf

- New York City Department of Health and Mental Hygiene. (2024). The state of mental health of New Yorkers. https://www.nyc.gov/assets/doh/downloads/pdf/mh/state-of-mental-health-new-yorkers.pdf
- New York City Department of Health and Mental Hygiene. (2024). Special report on social media and mental health. https://www.nyc.gov/assets/doh/downloads/pdf/mh/social-media-mental-health-report-2024.pdf
- New York City Mayor's Office. (2023, November 15). Mayor Adams, DOHMH Commissioner Dr. Vasan launch 'NYC Teenspace,' tele-mental health service for NYC teens [Press release]. https://www.nyc.gov/office-of-the-mayor/news/869-23/mayor-adams-dohmh-commissioner-dr-vasan-launch-teenspace-tele-mental-health-service-nyc
- New York City Mayor's Office. (2024, May 23). Mayor Adams celebrates early success of 'NYC Teenspace,' free tele-mental health service for NYC teenagers [Press release]. https://www.nyc.gov/mayors-office/news/2024/05/mayor-adams-celebrates-early-success-nyc-teenspace-free-tele-mental-health-service-nyc
- New York State Attorney General. (2023). Inaccurate and inadequate: Health plan's mental health provider network directories. https://ag.ny.gov/sites/default/files/reports/mental-health-report_0.pdf
- New York State Governor's Office. (2025, May 7). Governor Hochul announces $4.5 million awarded to fund services for children and youth living with mental illness [Press release]. https://www.governor.ny.gov/news/governor-hochul-announces-45-million-awarded-fund-services-children-and-youth-living-mental

- New York State Office of Mental Health. (2023). Youth mental
  health listening tour 2023 report
  https://omh.ny.gov/omhweb/statistics/youth-mh-listening-tour-
  report.pdf
- New York State Office of Mental Health. (2024). 2024 report on
  suicide prevention activities.
  https://omh.ny.gov/omhweb/statistics/2024-omh-suicide-
  prevention-report.pdf

Pages 29–34

- New York City Department of Health and Mental Hygiene. (n.d.).
  NYC Teenspace. https://www.nyc.gov/site/doh/health/health-
  topics/teenspace.page
- New York City Department of Health and Mental Hygiene.
  (2024). The state of mental health of New Yorkers.
  https://www.nyc.gov/assets/doh/downloads/pdf/mh/state-of-
  mental-health-new-yorkers.pdf
- New York City Department of Health and Mental Hygiene.
  (2025). Suicide-related behaviors among New York City public
  high school and middle school students (Epi Data Brief No. 149).
  https://www.nyc.gov/assets/doh/downloads/pdf/epi/databrief1
  49-youth-suicide-behaviors-2025.pdf
- Adams, E. (Mayor of New York City). (2023, March 2). Care,
  community, action: A mental health plan for New York City.
  Mayor's Office. https://www.nyc.gov/assets/doh/care-
  community-action-mental-health-plan/index.html
- New York City Comptroller. (2025, December). Classrooms,
  counselors, clinics: Building a mental health care continuum in
  New York City public schools. https://comptroller.nyc.gov/wp-
  content/uploads/2025/12/Mental-Health-Services-in-NYC-
  Public-Schools.pdf

- Mayor's Office of Community Mental Health. (n.d.). B-HEARD: Behavioral Health Emergency Assistance Response Division. https://mentalhealth.cityofnewyork.us/b-heard

New York State Resources and Initiatives

- Hochul, K. (Governor of New York). (2025, December 26). Governor Hochul signs legislation to require warning labels on social media platforms [Press release]. https://www.governor.ny.gov/news/governor-hochul-signs-legislation-require-warning-labels-social-media-platforms
- Hochul, K. (Governor of New York). (2026, January 13). Governor Hochul unveils proposals building on her nation-leading commitment to protect the well-being of New York's youth [Press release]. https://www.governor.ny.gov/news/governor-hochul-unveils-proposals-building-her-nation-leading-commitment-protect-wellbeing-new
- New York State Office of Mental Health. (n.d.). Transforming New York State's continuum of mental health care (Governor Hochul's $1 billion plan). https://www.governor.ny.gov/programs/transforming-new-york-states-continuum-mental-health-care
- New York State Office of Mental Health. (2024). 2024 report on suicide prevention activities. https://omh.ny.gov/omhweb/statistics/2024-omh-suicide-prevention-report.pdf

Pages 34–40

- Mayor's Office of Community Mental Health. (2025a, February 14). 2025 OCMH annual report. https://mentalhealth.cityofnewyork.us/wp-content/uploads/2025/02/2025-OCMH-Annual-Report.pdf

- Mayor's Office of Community Mental Health. (2025b, January 3). Bridging the Gap: Challenges and solutions for a thriving behavioral health workforce [White paper]. https://mentalhealth.cityofnewyork.us/wp-content/uploads/2025/01/2025-OCMH-Bridging-the-Gap-White-Paper.pdf
- Lander, B. (New York City Comptroller). (2025, December). Classrooms, counselors, clinics: Building a mental health care continuum in New York City public schools. https://comptroller.nyc.gov/wp-content/uploads/2025/12/Mental-Health-Services-in-NYC-Public-Schools.pdf
- New York City Department of Health and Mental Hygiene. (2024, May 31). The state of mental health of New Yorkers. https://www.nyc.gov/assets/doh/downloads/pdf/mh/state-of-mental-health-new-yorkers.pdf

New York State Resources and Initiatives

- Hochul, K. (Governor of New York). (2025, December 26). Governor Hochul signs legislation to require warning labels on social media platforms [Press release]. https://www.governor.ny.gov/news/governor-hochul-signs-legislation-require-warning-labels-social-media-platforms
- New York State Office of Mental Health. (n.d.). OMH reports (including youth-focused updates on expansions like Youth Safe Spaces, Youth Mental Health First Aid, Youth ACT teams, 988 Lifeline, and bed additions). https://omh.ny.gov/omhweb/statistics
- New York State Office of Mental Health. (2025, Winter). OMH news (State of the State updates on youth mental health investments, Teen Mental Health First Aid, safe spaces, and crisis services).

https://omh.ny.gov/omhweb/resources/newsltr/docs/omhnews winter2025.pdf

- **National and Related Reports Influencing NYS/NYC Data**

- Mental Health America. (2025). The state of mental health in America 2025. https://mhanational.org/the-state-of-mental-health-in-america
- New York Health Foundation. (2024, October 2). Bouncing back: New Yorkers' mental health progress and remaining challenges [Data brief]. https://nyhealthfoundation.org/resource/bouncing-back-new-yorkers-mental-health-progress-and-remaining-challenges

Pages 40–45

- Mental Health America. (2025). The state of mental health in America 2025. https://mhanational.org/the-state-of-mental-health-in-america
- Reinert, M., Nguyen, T., & Fritze, D. (2025). The state of mental health in America 2025. Mental Health America. https://mhanational.org/wp-content/uploads/2025/09/State-of-Mental-Health-2025.pdf
- Substance Abuse and Mental Health Services Administration. (2025). 2024 National Survey on Drug Use and Health: Detailed tables and reports (including major depressive episode and treatment among adolescents aged 12–17). https://www.samhsa.gov/data/data-we-collect/nsduh-national-survey-drug-use-and-health/national-releases/2024
- Centers for Disease Control and Prevention. (2024). Youth Risk Behavior Survey: 2023 results. https://www.cdc.gov/yrbs/results/2023-yrbs-results.html

- Sappenfield, O., Alberto, C., Minnaert, J., Donney, J., Lebrun-Harris, L., & Ghandour, R. (2024). National Survey of Children's Health: Adolescent mental and behavioral health, 2023 [Data brief]. Maternal and Child Health Bureau, Health Resources and Services Administration. https://mchb.hrsa.gov/sites/default/files/mchb/data-research/nsch-data-brief-adolescent-mental-behavioral-health-2023.pdf
- Kaiser Family Foundation. (2024, February 6). Recent trends in mental health and substance use concerns among adolescents. https://www.kff.org/mental-health/recent-trends-in-mental-health-and-substance-use-concerns-among-adolescents

New York City and New York State Resources

- New York City Department of Health and Mental Hygiene. (2024, May 31). The state of mental health of New Yorkers. https://www.nyc.gov/assets/doh/downloads/pdf/mh/state-of-mental-health-new-yorkers.pdf
- New York Health Foundation. (2024, October 2). Bouncing Back: New Yorkers' mental health progress and remaining challenges. https://nyhealthfoundation.org/resource/bouncing-back-new-yorkers-mental-health-progress-and-remaining-challenges

National U.S. Resources and Reports (Anxiety, Bipolar, ADHD)

- Centers for Disease Control and Prevention. (2025). Data and statistics on children's mental health. https://www.cdc.gov/children-mental-health/data-research/index.html
- Danielson, M. L., Claussen, A. H., Bitsko, R. H., Holbrook, J. R., Kogan, M. D., Blumberg, S. J., Visser, S. N., Perou, R., & Ghandour, R. M. (2024). ADHD prevalence among U.S. children and adolescents in 2022: Diagnosis, severity, co-occurring

disorders, and treatment. Journal of Clinical Child & Adolescent Psychology. Advance online publication. https://doi.org/10.1080/15374416.2024.2335625 (also available via PMC: https://pmc.ncbi.nlm.nih.gov/articles/PMC11334226/

- Kaiser Family Foundation. (2024, February 6). Recent trends in mental health and substance use concerns among adolescents. https://www.kff.org/mental-health/issue-brief/recent-trends-in-mental-health-and-substance-use-concerns-among-adolescents/

- Merikangas, K. R., He, J. P., Burstein, M., Swanson, S. A., Avenevoli, S., Cui, L., Benjet, C., Georgiades, K., & Swendsen, J. (2010). Lifetime prevalence of mental disorders in U.S. adolescents: Results from the National Comorbidity Survey Replication–Adolescent Supplement (NCS-A). Journal of the American Academy of Child & Adolescent Psychiatry, 49(10), 980–989. https://doi.org/10.1016/j.jaac.2010.05.017

- National Institute of Mental Health. (n.d.). Bipolar Disorder (Statistics Section Based on NCS-A). https://www.nimh.nih.gov/health/statistics/bipolar-disorder

- Substance Abuse and Mental Health Services Administration & Health Resources and Services Administration. (2024). National Survey of Children's Health (NSCH) 2022 data. Maternal and Child Health Bureau. https://mchb.hrsa.gov/data-research/national-survey-childrens-health

New York City and New York State Resources

- New York City Department of Health and Mental Hygiene. (2024, May 31). The state of mental health of New Yorkers. https://www.nyc.gov/assets/doh/downloads/pdf/mh/state-of-mental-health-new-yorkers.pdf

- New York Health Foundation. (2024, October 2). Bouncing back: New Yorkers' mental health progress and remaining challenges. https://nyhealthfoundation.org/resource/bouncing-back-new-yorkers-mental-health-progress-and-remaining-challenges

- New York State Department of Health. (2024). New York State profile of children and youth with special health care needs, 2022–2023. https://www.health.ny.gov/community/special_needs/docs/cshcn_profile_2022-2023.pdf

Other Key Reports

- Trilliant Health. (2023). Trends shaping the health economy: Behavioral health. https://www.trillianthealth.com/market-research/reports/behavioral-health-trends-shaping-the-health-economy
- Mental Health America. (2025). The State of Mental Health in America 2025. https://mhanational.org/the-state-of-mental-health-in-america

Pages 52–54

- National Institute of Mental Health. (n.d.). Schizophrenia. https://www.nimh.nih.gov/health/statistics/schizophrenia
- National Institute of Mental Health. (n.d.). Schizophrenia. https://www.nimh.nih.gov/health/topics/schizophrenia
- Centers for Disease Control and Prevention. (2024). Youth Risk Behavior Survey: 2023 results. https://www.cdc.gov/yrbs/results/2023-yrbs-results.html
- Sappenfield, O., Alberto, C., Minnaert, J., Donney, J., Lebrun-Harris, L., & Ghandour, R. (2024). Adolescent mental and behavioral health, 2023 [Data brief]. Maternal and Child Health Bureau, Health Resources and Services Administration, U.S. Department of Health and Human Services. https://mchb.hrsa.gov/sites/default/files/mchb/data-research/nsch-data-brief-adolescent-mental-behavioral-health-2023.pdf

- World Health Organization. (2025, October 6). Schizophrenia [Fact sheet]. https://www.who.int/news-room/fact-sheets/detail/schizophrenia

New York City Resources and Reports

- Lander, B. (New York City Comptroller). (2025, December). Classrooms, counselors, clinics: Building a mental health care continuum in New York City public schools. https://comptroller.nyc.gov/wp-content/uploads/2025/12/Mental-Health-Services-in-NYC-Public-Schools.pdf
- New York City Department of Health and Mental Hygiene. (2024, May 31). The state of mental health of New Yorkers. https://www.nyc.gov/assets/doh/downloads/pdf/mh/state-of-mental-health-new-yorkers.pdf
- New York City Department of Health and Mental Hygiene. (2025, September). Suicide-related behaviors among New York City public high school and middle school students (Epi Data Brief No. 149). https://www.nyc.gov/assets/doh/downloads/pdf/epi/databrief149-youth-suicide-behaviors-2025.pdf

New York State Resources and Reports

- New York State Office of the State Comptroller. (2024, March). Mental health inpatient service capacity in New York State. https://www.osc.ny.gov/files/reports/pdf/mental-health-inpatient-service-capacity.pdf
- New York State Office of Mental Health. (n.d.). OnTrackNY: Coordinated specialty care for first-episode psychosis. https://ontrackny.org/

National and Related Resources

- Recovery.com. (2025–2026). Best schizophrenia treatment centers in New York. https://recovery.com/new-york/schizophrenia
- Substance Abuse and Mental Health Services Administration. (2025). Key substance use and mental health indicators in the United States: Results from the 2024 National Survey on Drug Use and Health. https://www.samhsa.gov/data/sites/default/files/reports/rpt562 87/2024-nsduh-annual-national-report.pdf

New York City Resources and Reports

- Lander, B. (New York City Comptroller). (2025, December). Classrooms, counselors, clinics: Building a mental health care continuum in New York City public schools. https://comptroller.nyc.gov/wp-content/uploads/2025/12/Mental-Health-Services-in-NYC-Public-Schools.pdf

- New York City Department of Health and Mental Hygiene. (2025, September). Suicide-related behaviors among New York City public high school and middle school students (Epi Data Brief No. 149). https://www.nyc.gov/assets/doh/downloads/pdf/epi/databrief1 49-youth-suicide-behaviors-2025.pdf

- New York City Department of Health and Mental Hygiene. (2024, May 31). The state of mental health of New Yorkers. https://www.nyc.gov/assets/doh/downloads/pdf/mh/state-of-mental-health-new-yorkers.pdf

- New York City Department of Health and Mental Hygiene. (2025, September). Recent trends in cannabis use and associated morbidity in New York City, 2015 to 2023 (Epi Data Brief No. 148). https://www.nyc.gov/assets/doh/downloads/pdf/epi/databrief1 48-cannabis-2025.pdf

New York State Resources and Initiatives

- Hochul, K. (Governor of New York). (2025, December 26). Governor Hochul signs legislation to require warning labels on social media platforms [Press release]. https://www.governor.ny.gov/news/governor-hochul-signs-legislation-require-warning-labels-social-media-platforms

National/U.S. Eating Disorders Resources and Studies

- Toulany, A., Kurdyak, P., Guttmann, A., et al. (2025). Long-term trends in new and pre-existing eating disorder acute presentations among adolescents and young adults during and after the COVID-19 pandemic: A population-based cohort study. Journal of Adolescent Health, 77(4), 756–765. https://doi.org/10.1016/j.jadohealth.2025.06.012

- National Eating Disorders Association. (n.d.). Eating disorders statistics. https://www.nationaleatingdisorders.org/statistics

- National Association of Anorexia Nervosa and Associated Disorders. (n.d.). Eating disorders statistics. https://anad.org/eating-disorder-statistic

- Westwater, M. L., et al. (2023). Biological factors modulate eating disorder risk in early adolescents. Nature Mental Health. https://news.yale.edu/2023/08/02/biological-factors-modulate-eating-disorder-risk-early-adolescents

New York City and New York State Resources and Initiatives

- Lander, B. (New York City Comptroller). (2025, December). Classrooms, counselors, clinics: Building a mental health care continuum in New York City public schools. https://comptroller.nyc.gov/wp-content/uploads/2025/12/Mental-Health-Services-in-NYC-Public-Schools.pdf

- New York City Department of Health and Mental Hygiene. (2025, September). Suicide-related behaviors among New York City public high school and middle school students (Epi Data Brief No. 149).
https://www.nyc.gov/assets/doh/downloads/pdf/epi/databrief149-youth-suicide-behaviors-2025.pdf

- Hochul, K. (Governor of New York). (2025, September 2). Governor Hochul announces $7.5 million awarded to establish Youth Safe Spaces [Press release].
https://www.governor.ny.gov/news/governor-hochul-announces-75-million-awarded-establish-youth-safe-spaces

- Hochul, K. (Governor of New York). (2025, January 23). Governor Hochul announces $10 million available to support Youth and Teen Mental Health First Aid [Press release].
https://www.governor.ny.gov/news/governor-hochul-announces-10-million-available-support-youth-and-teen-mental-health-first-aid

- New York State Senate. (2023–2024). Senate Bill S5225: Requires health certificates for students entering schools to include an assessment for eating disorders.
https://www.nysenate.gov/legislation/bills/2023/S5225

National/U.S. Resources and Studies

- Levin, R. Y., & Liu, R. T. (2024). Post-traumatic stress disorder in a national sample of preadolescent children 9 to 10 years old: Prevalence, correlates, clinical sequelae, and treatment utilization. Translational Psychiatry, 14(1), Article 138.
https://doi.org/10.1038/s41398-024-02868-1

- Hamblen, J., & Barnett, E. (n.d.). PTSD in children and adolescents. National Center for PTSD, U.S. Department of

Veterans Affairs.
https://www.ptsd.va.gov/professional/treat/specific/ptsd_child_teens.asp

- National Center for PTSD. (2025). How common is PTSD in children and teens? U.S. Department of Veterans Affairs. https://www.ptsd.va.gov/understand/common/common_children_teens.asp

- Trilliant Health. (2023). Trends shaping the health economy: Behavioral health. https://www.trillianthealth.com/market-research/reports/behavioral-health-trends-shaping-the-health-economy

New York City and New York State Resources

- Lander, B. (New York City Comptroller). (2025, December). Classrooms, counselors, clinics: Building a mental health care continuum in New York City public schools. https://comptroller.nyc.gov/wp-content/uploads/2025/12/Mental-Health-Services-in-NYC-Public-Schools.pdf

- New York City Department of Health and Mental Hygiene. (2025, September). Suicide-related behaviors among New York City public high school and middle school students (Epi Data Brief No. 149). https://www.nyc.gov/assets/doh/downloads/pdf/epi/databrief149-youth-suicide-behaviors-2025.pdf

- Hochul, K. (Governor of New York). (2025, September 2). Governor Hochul announces $7.5 million awarded to establish Youth Safe Spaces [Press release]. https://www.governor.ny.gov/news/governor-hochul-announces-75-million-awarded-establish-youth-safe-spaces

- Hochul, K. (Governor of New York). (2025, January 23). Governor Hochul announces $10 million available to support

Youth and Teen Mental Health First Aid [Press release]. https://www.governor.ny.gov/news/governor-hochul-announces-10-million-available-support-youth-and-teen-mental-health-first-aid

Pages 1–2

- English Standard Version Bible. (2001). Crossway. (Original work published ca. 100 CE)
- Musée du Louvre. (n.d.). Vénus de Milo. Collections du Louvre. https://collections.louvre.fr/en/ark:/53355/cl010277627
- Musée du Louvre. (n.d.). Ideal Greek beauty - Venus de Milo and the Galerie des Antiques. https://www.louvre.fr/en/explore/the-palace/ideal-greek-beauty

Pages 3–4

- Good News Translation Bible. (1979). American Bible Society. (Original work published ca. 950–200 BCE)
- Bible Gateway. (n.d.). Proverbs 4:23 (GNT). https://www.biblegateway.com/passage?search=Proverbs+4%3A23&version=GNT
- Bible.com (YouVersion). (n.d.). Proverbs 4:23 (GNT). https://www.bible.com/bible/68/PRO.4.23.GNT
- Kay, M. (Producer). (2016, May 4). A valuable lesson for a happier life [Video]. YouTube. https://www.youtube.com/watch?v=SqGRnlXplx0
- Next Steps NH. (2020, October 7). A valuable lesson for a happier life [Video]. https://nextsteps-nh.org/video/a-valuable-lesson-for-a-happier-life
- Woodburn, W. (2020, May 23). Life lesson inside a glass jar. Woody Woodburn. https://woodywoodburn.com/life-lesson-inside-a-glass-jar

Pages 5–7

- American Bible Society. (1979). Good News Translation Bible (GNT). (Original work published ca. 950–200 BCE)

- Biblica. (2011). New International Version Bible (NIV). (Original work published ca. 1400 BCE–100 CE)
- Crosscards.com. (2019, March 20). Three things to remember about the valleys [Daily devotional]. Daily Hope with Rick Warren. https://www.crosscards.com/devotionals/daily-hope-with-rick-warren/three-things-to-remember-about-the-valleys-daily-hope-with-rick-warren-march-20-2019.htm
- Crosswalk.com. (2023, January 19). Valleys are a part of life [Daily devotional]. Daily Hope with Rick Warren. https://www.crosswalk.com/devotionals/daily-hope-with-rick-warren/daily-hope-with-rick-warren-january-19-2023.html
- King James Version Bible. (1611). (Original work published ca. 1400 BCE–100 CE)
- Living Bible. (1971). Tyndale House Publishers. (Original work published ca. 1400 BCE–100 CE)
- New Living Translation Bible. (2015). Tyndale House Publishers. (Original work published ca. 1400 BCE–100 CE)
- Warren, R. (n.d.). The God of my valleys (Downloadable MP3). Pastor Rick Store. https://store.pastorrick.com/products/the-god-of-my-valleys-downloadable-mp3

Pages 7–10

- American Bible Society. (1979). Good News Translation Bible (GNT). (Original work published ca. 950–200 BCE)
- Biblica. (2011). New International Version Bible (NIV). (Original work published ca. 1400 BCE–100 CE)
- Crosscards.com. (2019, March 20). Three things to remember about the valleys [Daily devotional]. Daily Hope with Rick Warren. https://www.crosscards.com/devotionals/daily-hope-with-rick-warren/three-things-to-remember-about-the-valleys-daily-hope-with-rick-warren-march-20-2019.html
- Crosswalk.com. (2023, January 19). Valleys are a part of life [Daily devotional]. Daily Hope with Rick Warren. https://www.crosswalk.com/devotionals/daily-hope-with-rick-warren/daily-hope-with-rick-warren-january-19-2023.html
- King James Version Bible. (1611). (Original work published ca. 1400 BCE–100 CE)

- New Living Bible. (1971). Tyndale House Publishers. (Original work published ca. 1400 BCE–100 CE)
- New Living Translation Bible. (2015). Tyndale House Publishers. (Original work published ca. 1400 BCE–100 CE)
- Saddleback Church. (n.d.). Living in the goodness of God: The God of my valleys [Video]. https://saddleback.com/watch/living-in-the-goodness-of-god/the-god-of-my-valleys?autoplay=true
- Sermons-Online.org. (2025, June 22). The many signs in life that God is walking with you - Rick Warren. https://sermons-online.org/rick-warren/the-many-signs-in-life-that-god-is-walking-with-you
- Warren, R. (n.d.). The God of my valleys (Downloadable MP3). Pastor Rick Store. https://store.pastorrick.com/products/the-god-of-my-valleys-downloadable-mp3

Reference for the new Bible verse

- Bible Gateway. (n.d.). Matthew 19:26 (New International Version). https://www.biblegateway.com/passage/?search=Matthew+19%3A26&version=NIV (Original work published ca. 50–100 CE)

Pages 7.5–16.5

- American Bible Society. (1979). Good News Translation Bible (GNT). (Original work published ca. 950–200 BCE)
- Biblica. (2011). New International Version Bible (NIV). (Original work published ca. 1400 BCE–100 CE)
- Crosscards.com. (2019, March 20). Three things to remember about the valleys [Daily devotional]. Daily Hope with Rick Warren. https://www.crosscards.com/devotionals/daily-hope-with-rick-warren/three-things-to-remember-about-the-valleys-daily-hope-with-rick-warren-march-20-2019.html
- Crosswalk.com. (2023, January 19). Valleys are a part of life [Daily devotional]. Daily Hope with Rick Warren. https://www.crosswalk.com/devotionals/daily-hope-with-rick-warren/daily-hope-with-rick-warren-january-19-2023.html

- DeGeneres, E. (Host). (2018, April). The Ellen DeGeneres Show: Shaquille O'Neal [Television broadcast episode]. Warner Bros. Television.
- King James Version Bible. (1611). (Original work published ca. 1400 BCE–100 CE)
- Living Bible. (1971). Tyndale House Publishers. (Original work published ca. 1400 BCE–100 CE)
- New Living Translation Bible. (2015). Tyndale House Publishers. (Original work published ca. 1400 BCE–100 CE)
- Saddleback Church. (n.d.). Living in the goodness of God: The God of my valleys [Video]. https://saddleback.com/watch/living-in-the-goodness-of-god/the-god-of-my-valleys?autoplay=true
- Sermons-Online.org. (2025, June 22). The many signs in life that God is walking with you - Rick Warren. https://sermons-online.org/rick-warren/the-many-signs-in-life-that-god-is-walking-with-you
- Wang, H. (n.d.). Keep shining, be a unique you [Original poem]. (Personal communication/shared work; no published source identified.)
- Warren, R. (n.d.). The God of my valleys (Downloadable MP3). Pastor Rick Store. https://store.pastorrick.com/products/the-god-of-my-valleys-downloadable-mp3

Additional reference for the Shaq interview details

- SPORTbible. (2024, November 8). Shaquille O'Neal has non-negotiable rules his sons and daughters must follow in their dating lives. https://www.sportbible.com/nba/shaquille-oneal-nba-children-son-daughter-dating-rules-318472-20241108

Pages 16.5–18

- American Bible Society. (n.d.). Psalms 23:4 (NIV). Bible.com. https://www.bible.com/bible/111/PSA.23.4.NIV
- Bible Study Tools. (n.d.). Psalm 23:4. https://www.biblestudytools.com/psalms/23-4.html

- Warren, R. (2023, January 19). Valleys are a part of life. Daily Hope with Rick Warren. LightSource.com. https://www.lightsource.com/devotionals/daily-hope-with-rick-warren/valleys-are-a-part-of-life-daily-hope-with-rick-warren-january-19-2023-11870866.html
- Warren, R. (2019, March 20). Three things to remember about the valleys. Daily Hope with Rick Warren. Crosscards.com. https://www.crosscards.com/devotionals/daily-hope-with-rick-warren/three-things-to-remember-about-the-valleys-daily-hope-with-rick-warren-march-20-2019.html

Pages 19–21.5

- Avalon Project, Yale Law School. (n.d.). George Washington's Farewell Address, 1796. https://avalon.law.yale.edu/18th_century/washing.asp
- Bible Gateway. (n.d.). Matthew 19:26 (NIV). https://www.biblegateway.com/passage?search=Matthew+19%3A26&version=NIV
- Britannica. (n.d.). In God we trust. https://www.britannica.com/topic/In-God-we-trust
- Congress.gov. (2011). H. Rept. 112-47 - Reaffirming "In God We Trust" as the official motto of the United States. https://www.congress.gov/committee-report/112th-congress/house-report/47/1
- Fox News. (2025). JD Vance: "Christianity is the Creed of the United States" [Video]. YouTube. https://www.youtube.com/watch?v=CBEpOZXIgi4
- History.com Editors. (2009, November 16; updated 2025). President Eisenhower signs "In God We Trust" into law. HISTORY. https://www.history.com/this-day-in-history/july-30/president-eisenhower-signs-in-god-we-trust-into-law
- Pew Research Center. (2007, September 12). A half century after it first appeared on the dollar bill, "In God We Trust" still stirs opposition. https://www.pewresearch.org/religion/2007/09/12/a-half-century-after-it-first-appeared-on-the-dollar-bill-in-god-we-trust-still-stirs-opposition

- U.S. House of Representatives: History, Art & Archives. (n.d.). The legislation placing "In God We Trust" on national currency. https://history.house.gov/Historical-Highlights/1951-2000/The-legislation-placing-In-God-We-Trust-on-national-currency
- U.S. Department of the Treasury. (n.d.). In God We Trust. https://www.treasury.gov/about/education/Pages/in-god-we-trust.aspx

Pages 22–25

- American Bible Society. (n.d.). Proverbs 4:23 (GNT). YouVersion Bible App. https://www.bible.com/bible/68/PRO.4.23.GNT
- Bible Gateway. (n.d.). Proverbs 4:23 (GNT). https://www.biblegateway.com/passage?search=Proverbs+4%3A23&version=GNT
- The Brooklyn Tabernacle. (n.d.). Next steps with Jesus: Water baptism. https://www.brooklyntabernacle.org/next-steps-2
- The Brooklyn Tabernacle. (2025, November 30). Sunday service – 12 p.m. November 30, 2025 [Video]. YouTube. https://www.youtube.com/watch?v=reXV5lAY3yM
- The Brooklyn Tabernacle. (2025, November 30). 2025.11.30. "Going Down, Going Up," Jim Cymbala [Video sermon]. YouTube. https://www.youtube.com/watch?v=pFi80x2Y2v0

Religion Matters to Our Nation

- **28.5** – The Puritans… First Written Constitution of Law
- American Heritage Education Foundation. (2017, June 22). A city on a hill: Why John Winthrop and the Puritans came to America. https://americanheritage.org/a-city-on-a-hill-why-john-winthrop-and-the-puritans-came-to-america
- American Heritage Education Foundation. (2018, May 11). The Bible was the most cited source of the American founding era. https://americanheritage.org/the-influence-of-the-bible-on-americas-founding-era-the-most-cited-source
- Center for the Study of the American Constitution, University of Wisconsin-Madison. (n.d.). Religious tests and oaths in state constitutions, 1776–1784. https://csac.history.wisc.edu/religion-

and-the-ratification/religious-test-clause/religious-tests-and-oaths-in-state-constitutions-1776-1784

- Digital History, University of Houston. (n.d.). Reasons for Puritan migration. https://www.digitalhistory.uh.edu/disp_textbook.cfm?psid=68&smtID=3F
- Founders Online, National Archives. (n.d.). From John Adams to Massachusetts Militia, 11 October 1798. https://founders.archives.gov/documents/Adams/99-02-02-3102
- Hanover College History Department. (n.d.). John Winthrop, "A Modell of Christian Charity" (1630). https://history.hanover.edu/courses/excerpts/111winthrop.html
- Ohio University. (n.d.). McGuffey Readers. https://www.ohio.edu/cas/ping-institute/humanities-park/mcguffey-readers
- The First Amendment Encyclopedia, Middle Tennessee State University. (2009, January 1). Religious oaths. https://firstamendment.mtsu.edu/article/religious-oaths
- WallBuilders. (2023, August 23). FAQ: America's Founders as Christians. https://wallbuilders.com/resource/americas-founders-as-christians

"The Puritans in America Created the First Written Constitution of Law (Before the founder of common law)

- Avalon Project, Yale Law School. (n.d.). Fundamental Orders of Connecticut (1639). https://avalon.law.yale.edu/17th_century/order.asp
- Connecticut History | a CTHumanities Project. (n.d.). The Fundamental Orders of Connecticut. https://connecticuthistory.org/the-fundamental-orders-of-connecticut
- Connecticut History | a CTHumanities Project. (n.d.). The free consent of the people: Thomas Hooker and the Fundamental Orders. https://connecticuthistory.org/the-free-consent-of-the-people-thomas-hooker-and-the-fundamental-orders

- First Amendment Encyclopedia, Middle Tennessee State University. (2009, January 1). Old Deluder Satan Act of 1647. https://firstamendment.mtsu.edu/article/old-deluder-satan-act-of-1647

- Heritage Foundation. (n.d.). Tocqueville on Christianity and American democracy. https://www.heritage.org/civil-society/report/tocqueville-christianity-and-american-democracy

- Online Library of Liberty. (n.d.). 1639: Fundamental Orders of Connecticut. https://oll.libertyfund.org/pages/1639-fundamental-orders-of-connecticut

- Paul Revere House. (2020, May 15). That Old Deluder Satan: Puritan emphasis on compulsory education. https://www.paulreverehouse.org/that-old-deluder-satan-puritan-emphasis-on-compulsory-education

- Teaching American History. (n.d.). The Fundamental Orders of Connecticut. https://teachingamericanhistory.org/document/the-fundamental-orders-of-connecticut

Commandments Matter for Teenagers in Life

- Connecticut History | a CTHumanities Project. (n.d.). The Fundamental Orders of Connecticut.

  https://connecticuthistory.org/the-fundamental-orders-of-connecticut

- Connecticut History | a CTHumanities Project. (n.d.). The free consent of the people: Thomas Hooker and the Fundamental Orders. https://connecticuthistory.org/the-free-consent-of-the-people-thomas-hooker-and-the-fundamental-orders

- First Amendment Encyclopedia, Middle Tennessee State University. (2009, January 1). Old Deluder Satan Act of 1647. https://firstamendment.mtsu.edu/article/old-deluder-satan-act-of-1647

- Heritage Foundation. (n.d.). Tocqueville on Christianity and American democracy.

  https://www.heritage.org/civil-society/report/tocqueville-christianity-and-american-democracy

- Online Library of Liberty. (n.d.). 1639: Fundamental Orders of Connecticut.

  https://oll.libertyfund.org/pages/1639-fundamental-orders-of-connecticut

- Paul Revere House. (2020, May 15). That Old Deluder Satan: Puritan emphasis on compulsory education.

  https://www.paulreverehouse.org/that-old-deluder-satan-puritan-emphasis-on-compulsory-education

- Teaching American History. (n.d.). The Fundamental Orders of Connecticut. https://teachingamericanhistory.org/document/the-fundamental-orders-of-connecticut

Before Breaking the Stigma: Mental Health and Recovery Across Cultures

- Bible Gateway. (n.d.). Exodus 20 (New International Version). https://www.biblegateway.com/passage/?search=Exodus+20&version=NIV

- (Primary source for the Ten Commandments in NIV, including verses 3, 8–11, 12, 16, and 17.)

- Bible Gateway. (n.d.). New International Version Bible. https://www.biblegateway.com/versions/New-International-Version-NIV-Bible/

- Bible Gateway. (n.d.). Romans 5:3-5 (New International Version). https://www.biblegateway.com/passage/?search=Romans+5%3A3-5&version=NIV

- New International Version Bible. (2011). Zondervan. (Original work published 1978)

  https://www.biblegateway.com/passage/?search=Exodus+20%3A4-6&version=NIV

- YouVersion. (n.d.). Romans 5:3-5 (New International Version). https://www.bible.com/bible/111/ROM.5.3-5.NIV

Breaking the Stigma

- Bible Gateway. (n.d.). Isaiah 43:18-19 (New International Version). https://www.biblegateway.com/passage/?search=Isaiah+43%3A18-19&version=NIV

- YouVersion (Bible.com). (n.d.). Isaiah 43:18-19 (New International Version). https://www.bible.com/bible/111/ISA.43.18-19.NIV

- Bible Gateway. (n.d.). New International Version Bible. https://www.biblegateway.com/versions/New-International-Version-NIV-Bible/

- The Gospel Coalition. (2020, August 17). When God closes a door, does he open a window? https://www.thegospelcoalition.org/article/closes-door-open-window

For cultural mental health stigma examples (representative sources matching the described patterns):

- Behavioral Health News. (2025, March 12). Mental health and matchmaking: How stigma affects South Asian marriage prospects. https://behavioralhealthnews.org/mental-health-and-

matchmaking-how-stigma-affects-south-asian-marriage-prospects
(Discusses stigma in India/South Asia, including impacts on marriage prospects and preference for silence or non-psychiatric approaches.)

- Frontiers in Psychiatry. (2022). Disease information disclosure among patients with mental illness and their family members in China.
https://www.frontiersin.org/journals/psychiatry/articles/10.3389/fpsyt.2022.1036568/full
(Addresses low disclosure rates in China due to stigma, loss of face, and family reputation concerns.)

- New York City Department of Youth & Community Development. (n.d.). Summer Youth Employment Program (SYEP).

- https://www.nyc.gov/site/dycd/services/jobs-internships/summer-youth-employment-program-syep.page
(Official page for SYEP, highlighting youth skill-building, paid work, and positive development outcomes relevant to recovery and future planning.)

- Ng, C. H., et al. (various studies cited in reviews). (2020). Overview of stigma against psychiatric illnesses and advancements of anti-stigma activities in six Asian societies. International Journal of Environmental Research and Public Health, 17(1), 280.

https://www.mdpi.com/1660-4601/17/1/280

(Covers stigma in Asian contexts, including China's "loss of face," family shame, and cultural factors.)

- Bible Gateway. (n.d.). John 17:20-23 (New International Version). https://www.biblegateway.com/passage/?search=John+17%3A20-23&version=NIV

- YouVersion (Bible.com). (n.d.). John 17 (New International Version). https://www.bible.com/bible/111/JHN.17.NIV

- Bible Gateway. (n.d.). New International Version Bible. https://www.biblegateway.com/versions/New-International-Version-NIV-Bible/

- More resources about John 17 Bible Study Tools. (n.d.). John 17:20–23 (NIV). https://www.biblestudytools.com/john/17.html

- Sabbath School Net. (2019, May 16). Friday: Further thought - Keys to family unity https://ssnet.org/blog/friday-further-thought-keys-to-family-unity

- Tomorrow's World. (2012, May-June). Face time. https://www.tomorrowsworld.org/magazines/2012/may-june/face-time

- American Psychiatric Association. (n.d.). DSM-5-TR online assessment measures. https://www.psychiatry.org/psychiatrists/practice/dsm/educational-resources/assessment-measures

- Child Mind Institute. (n.d.). Symptom checker. https://childmind.org/symptomchecker/

- Connected Mind. (n.d.). Free anonymous mental health screening. https://connectedmind.me/screening

- Crisis Text Line. (n.d.). Home. https://www.crisistextline.org/

- Mental Health America. (n.d.). Take a mental health test. https://screening.mhanational.org/screening-tools

- Mind Diagnostics. (n.d.). Mental health tests - Free results online. https://www.mind-diagnostics.org/

- National Institute of Mental Health. (n.d.). Home. https://www.nimh.nih.gov/

- Psychology Today. (n.d.). Mental health and personality tests. https://www.psychologytoday.com/us/tests

- Talkspace. (n.d.). Mental health tests: Free screening online. https://www.talkspace.com/assessments

- Here to Help. (n.d.). Online screenings for depression, anxiety, mood disorders… https://www.heretohelp.bc.ca/screening/online

- 988 Suicide & Crisis Lifeline. (n.d.). Home. https://988lifeline.org/